Contemporary
Feminist Thought

Hester Eisenstein

G. K. Hall & Co., Boston

Contemporary Feminist Thought
Hester Eisenstein

A Publication in Women's Studies
Barbara Haber, Series Editor

Copyright © 1983 by Hester Eisenstein
All Rights Reserved
Published by G. K. Hall & Co.
70 Lincoln Street
Boston, Massachusetts 02111

Book Design by Barbara Anderson
Book Production by Elizabeth Holthaus

Library of Congress Cataloging in Publication Data

Eisenstein, Hester.
Contemporary feminist thought.

Bibliography
Includes index.
1. Feminism—United States—History.   2. Feminism—
United States.   I. Title.
HQ1426.E39   1983   305.4'2'0973   83-11867
ISBN 0-8161-9042-9
ISBN 0-8161-9048-8 (Pbk.)
First Paperback Edition, March 1984

Printed on permanent/durable acid-
free paper and bound in the United
States of America

[H]istory is more than a
narration—it is a political
stake. . . . [H]istory is . . . *a place
of struggle in itself.*

> Christine Delphy,
> "Women's Liberation in
> France: The Tenth Year"

Not a word of all that I have . . .
said, . . . or tried to indicate, came
out of alien, cool, objective
knowledge; it is all within me, I have
been through it all.

> Thomas Mann, "Germany and the
> Germans"

Contents

III Beyond the Impasse of Difference

Preface and Acknowledgments

This book grew out of a course that I taught at Barnard College in New York from 1975 to 1980. It is addressed to (at least) two audiences. For the reader new to feminism, it is intended as an introduction and a guide to further reading. I hope that the book will be of use in Women's Studies courses, and in courses on political and social theory, literary criticism, psychology, sociology, and other topics requiring a grounding in feminist concepts. It should also be of interest to the general reader concerned with issues of gender, politics, and society. For the reader already fully conversant with feminist concepts, it is a critical history and analysis of their development in the United States, offered as a contribution to the ongoing debate over the future of feminist theory and the women's movement.

The book was conceived in New York, but gestated and delivered in Sydney. I thus have obligations on two continents. Despite some profound political disagreements, I want to acknowledge my intellectual debt to the members of the Yale University History Department, with whom I studied and worked from 1961 to 1970. I thank the members of the Barnard College and Columbia University community, with whom a dialogue about the issues raised here was sustained for a decade. I am grateful to Jane S. Gould, Elizabeth Janeway, Janie Kritzman, Nancy K. Miller, Susan Riemer Sacks, and Catharine R. Stimpson (Douglass College, Rutgers University); to the other participants in the Scholar and the Feminist conference series planning committees, and the members of the Columbia University Seminar on Women and Society, and to my students.

For their advice and support, I thank my parents, Ruth and Myron Eisenstein, my late parents-in-law, Hannah and Albert Kessler, and Clive S. Kessler, my husband and friend. I am grateful, as well, to Karen Machover, my mentor; to Elisabeth Page Purcell, Elizabeth W. K. Silk, Ellen B. Sweet, and the other members of my New York women's group;

ix

Frances Goldin, my agent; and Caroline L. Birdsall and John Iremonger, my editors in Boston and Sydney.

I particularly want to thank my sisters in the Sydney feminist community for their welcome and help in many forms. My thanks to Pam Benton, Joan Bielski, Betinna Cass, Colleen Chesterman, Eva Cox, Liz Fell, Jan Larbalastier, Valerie Levy, Frances Lovejoy, Lesley Lynch, Jill Matthews, Helen Mills, Rosemary Pringle, Juliet Richter, Chris Ronalds, Jozefa Sobski, Sue Tiffin, Chris Westwood, Donelle Wheeler, and Allison Ziller. I also thank the other members of the *Refractory Girl* collective. My experience convinces me that there is indeed such a thing as the international women's movement.

For their useful comments on the manuscript, my thanks to Caroline Birdsall, Frances Goldin, Barbara Haber, John Iremonger, Lesley Lynch, Catharine R. Stimpson, and Sue Tiffin. Any remaining errors in fact or interpretation are of course my responsibility alone.

Hester Eisenstein

Note: parts of chapters 1 and 11 were published (in slightly different form) in *Thesis Eleven,* 5/6 (1982).

Introduction

This book is a history and critique of contemporary feminist thought, principally in the United States, from 1970 to the present. The focus is chiefly although not exclusively on the ideas of radical feminism, as expressed in the work of Kate Millett and Shulamith Firestone, and on the elaboration of these ideas in the writings of Adrienne Rich, Nancy Chodorow, and Mary Daly, among others. The book is organized into three parts. Part I considers those writers who, building on the foundations laid down by Simone de Beauvoir and Betty Friedan, established the framework for the renewed discussion of feminism in the 1970s. In this phase of the debate, the socially constructed differences between the sexes were judged to be the chief source of female oppression. In the main, feminist theory concentrated on establishing the distinction between sex and gender, and developed an analysis of sex roles as a mode of social control. Arguing for the reduction of the polarization between masculinity and femininity, it pointed, explicitly or implicitly, to the replacement of gender polarization with some form of androgyny.

Part II of the book traces the development of a second phase of contemporary feminist theory, namely, the rejection of androgyny and the adoption of a woman-centered perspective. The sex-roles analysis of the early 1970s was taken up and given wide circulation in the media and the academy, and had evoked a widespread but selective response in many quarters. As a result, women were being encouraged to overcome the defects of their feminine conditioning, and to seek to enter those areas of public life previously closed to them. The concomitant element of the radical feminist analysis, namely, the nature of the patriarchal structure that oppressed women, went virtually unmentioned. Women were to adapt themselves to the structure, rather than the other way around.

In part as a reaction to these developments, beginning in the mid-1970s the view of female differences from men began to change. Instead of being considered the source of women's oppression, these differences were now judged to contain the seeds of women's liberation. As outlined by the historian Gerda Lerner, the poet Adrienne Rich, and others, the woman-centered perspective located specific virtues in the historical and psychological experience of women. Instead of seeking to minimize the polarization between masculine and feminine, it sought to isolate and to define those aspects of female experience that were potential sources of strength and power for women, and, more broadly, of a new blueprint for social change.

Part III of the book argues that, in some recent feminist theory, the woman-centered analysis has brought radical feminism to a theoretical and practical impasse. By shifting from a focus on sex roles and androgyny to a woman-centered perspective, Rich, Chodorow, and others were able to extend and to deepen the analysis of the social construction of gender initiated by Millett and Firestone. But in the subsequent development of this line of argument in the work of Mary Daly, Susan Griffin, and others, some of these original insights have been lost. Instead, a potentially reactionary concept has begun to emerge, that of the intrinsic moral superiority of women. As advanced by these writers, the concept is triply problematic: in its implicit attribution of female superiority to physiological causes; in its renunciation of rationality and clarity as fundamentally male and therefore flawed; and in its pessimistic depiction of women as the innocent, passive, and powerless victims of male violence. The penultimate chapter of this section reviews some of the continuities and points of similarity in the work of these writers with that of their predecessors in the decade since 1970, and suggests some elements of weakness that may have contributed to the current impasse: a divorce from Marxism and the political left; a consistent emphasis on psychology at the expense of economic factors; and a false universalism that addresses itself to all women, with insufficient regard for differences of race, class, and culture. The final chapter points to some possible new directions for feminist theory in the 1980s, in the face of renewed antifeminism and right-wing resurgence throughout the Western world.

Before turning to the analysis, I want to discuss some of the assumptions that I bring to it, and to make some general remarks about the body of theory examined here.

Body of work under consideration: its unprecedented character

In the useful definition supplied by the historian Linda Gordon, feminism is "an analysis of women's subordination for the purpose of figuring out how to change it."[1] The second wave of the women's movement produced a body of writing that is of particular significance in the history of feminist thought, and, indeed, in the history of social theory generally. In writing an account of very recent feminist writing, I do not wish to contribute, either explicitly or by implication, to the mistaken notion that feminist ideas sprang full-blown from, say, the heads of the editors of *Ms.* magazine, with no precedent in the past. One of the important rediscoveries of the second wave is the continuous history of feminist thought, traceable at least to the fifteenth century, and, some would argue, all the way back to the time of Sappho.[2] But, as Iris Young has written, "these new-wave feminists, who called themselves radical feminists, began developing questions, categories, and analyses which broke wholly new ground and irrevocably altered the perceptions of most progressive people."[3] The ideas expressed on lesbianism, heterosexism, rape, and gender identity, to mention only a few topics, went, in their depth and implications, beyond the groundbreaking work of Charlotte Perkins Gilman and Simone de Beauvoir.

This body of writing, then, represents a distinctive and original contribution. Some of its elements have entered public consciousness and policy at a number of different points. It is time, therefore, to begin a critical assessment of this contribution. Where does it leave us, and what hints does it give us as to the future directions of the women's movement?[4]

Utopian quality of feminist thought:
it is about social change

Another point about the work under consideration here concerns what I take to be its utopian quality. In Thomas More's coinage, utopia means "nowhere." It is a picture of a society so unlike our present reality as to be nearly unimaginable. In some versions of this tradition, a utopia is a dream, a kind of game about how we might see ourselves, or perhaps, a literary inversion of habits and roles that, like the ritual of role-reversal for one day of the year, reinforces the status quo for the rest of the calendar. But I mean utopian in a different sense. I refer to the intention, in creating a picture of an alternative society, actually to change the current reality, by means of creating a model, or pieces of a model, of a society organized along different lines.[5]

That feminist theory is utopian grows directly out of the fact that what is at issue is woman's place. However one defines it, woman's place is integrally embedded in social life. To shift or disrupt it, as has begun to happen in recent years, is potentially to shift and disrupt much else, from personal identity and sexual mores, to family arrangements, childrearing customs, and educational patterns, and from religious ideology to political and economic structures. In thus characterizing the significance of woman's place, I implicitly reject the view that to remove all of the obstacles to the full participation of women in public life, and, in reciprocal fashion, to men in domestic life, would be simply a change of faces. The argument is often made in defense of the extension of women's rights, as a way of convincing those who hesitate to hire women in positions of influence, that women should be allowed their share of the pie, because nothing else will change. In conceding a few powerful positions to a small number of exceptional women, present arrangements of access to power, privilege, and decision making will remain overwhelmingly in the hands of those who now rule.[6]

Others take the view that the insertion of women into places formerly held by men will change society for the better. This view depends upon the conviction, held by some contemporary feminists and by some of their foremothers in the nineteenth-century American women's movement, that access by women to the public sphere will improve society by means of women's inherent virtue, that is, their intrinsic moral superiority to men. I do not share this view. With Nancy Chodorow, I believe that women, like men, are socially produced beings, and can change. And with Jane Addams, I believe that women are perfectly capable of being corrupted by power, but up to the present historical moment simply have not been given the opportunity.[7]

Both of these arguments depend upon a model in which women occupy places previously closed to them, but in which the structures of power have otherwise remained unaltered. But the feminist utopia presents a very different picture, of a society perhaps unrecognizable from where we now stand, but which could emerge, over the very long haul, out of the many changes now being sought by members of the women's movement around the world. In my understanding of the term "feminist," then, I see an element of visionary, futurist thought. This encompasses a concept of social transformation that, as part of the eventual liberation of women, will change all human relationships for the better. Although centrally about women, their experience, condition, or "estate," in Juliet Mitchell's formulation, feminism is therefore also fundamentally about men, and about social change.[8]

Feminism grows out of liberalism: it is a political theory (but not only that)

It is important to examine the connections between late twentieth-century feminist thought, and Western social and political theory gener-

ally. In undertaking to connect feminist theory with this tradition, I do not
mean to imply that it can be either equated with or reduced to it. But I
believe that it is useful to evoke such a historical context, at least in broad
terms. Zillah R. Eisenstein has argued convincingly that feminist theory
grows out of liberalism, and it seeks to explode and transcend it, much in
the manner claimed by Marx for communism.[9] I think that this point can be
extended: I would argue that feminism draws upon at least three streams
of thought.

The first is that of the "rights of man," the ideas of the seventeenth- and
eighteenth-century philosophers and political theorists, Locke, Rousseau,
and others, whose writings formed the basis of the explicit goals of the
French and American revolutions. Liberal theory contested the divine
right of monarchs and aristocrats to political rule, and legitimized political
participation for members of the propertied classes, provided that they
were men. Not surprisingly, these arguments gave rise at the same time to
equivalent claims for the rights of women, claims that are at this writing still
to be fully met. Essentially the rights of liberalism were the rights of the
citizen: participation in public life, including most crucially the vote, and the
right to hold political office. They also included the basis of that participation, namely, the right to hold property in one's own name.[10]

The second stream is the tradition of socialist theory. "Utopian" and
"scientific" or Marxist socialist theory both grew from the realization that
political liberalism was hollow without the economic means to realize it. As
Anatole France pointed out in a famous remark, "the law in its majestic
equality forbids the rich as well as the poor to sleep under bridges, to beg in
the streets, and to steal bread." Socialist theory of the nineteenth century
added economic rights, specifically, the right to economic justice, to
political ones. Both theoretically, and in the revolutionary battles of mid-
century, a struggle began for the democratization not only of political, but
of property rights. The ultimate extension of this effort was, as Marx
proposed, the ownership of the means of production by the proletariat.
Equality of legal rights, without other social changes, meant the perpetuation of inequalities of status. True social justice meant economic equality.[11]

The third stream is that of the late nineteenth- and early twentieth-
century examination of sexuality and sexual behavior in its social and
political context. In the first instance, this tradition grew from the work of
Havelock Ellis and Freud and his students. It was extended by writers such
as Wilhelm Reich, Margaret Mead, and Erik Erikson, and by the members
of the Frankfurt school including Herbert Marcuse. This was the strand of
social theory that examined the relationship of sexuality to society, of
repression to civilization, and of the individual psychic formation to the

creation and reproduction (or transformation) of the social order.[12]

One could refer to these three traditions as explorations of three areas of freedom: political, economic, and sexual. In my view, feminism draws on all of these traditions. At the same time, it transforms them, because what is at issue is the winning of these rights, for the first time, for women. It is in the elaboration of what that victory would mean for society as a whole that the complexity of feminist thought, and the controversies within feminism, take their shape.

Intention to demonstrate that feminism is on the left

One of my purposes in writing this book has been to give some of the grounds for my conviction that feminism, even "bourgeois" feminism, is to the left of the political spectrum. I want to defend feminists against the charge of being only interested in the liberation of privileged women. Some have argued that feminism is only a product of, or an element in, an ideological defense of the status quo.[13] But I would argue that in the range of writing on contemporary feminist theory, a set of propositions are set forth that, taken together, can only be described as revolutionary. In describing some of these ideas, I want to reclaim the revolutionary potential of feminism. In so doing, I want to contribute to the effort to link the demand for women's rights to other struggles for social justice around the globe. The new backlash from the political right explicitly connects women's rights—for example, the right to abortion and to freedom from forced sterilization—to other radical left causes such as social welfare and the campaign for a nuclear freeze. But some analysts see feminism either as isolated from other fights for social justice, or as a centrist political position.[14] I think that ultimately this is a misreading of feminism.

In the early years feminists made extravagant claims about the universality and the identical characteristics of the oppression of women at all times and in all places. More recently, there has been something of a retreat from universalism, and an acknowledgment of the diversity of women's experience and situation with respect to race, class, nationality, religion, and other specificities. This is a healthy development.[15] The future evolution of feminist thought must take account of the complexity of women's experience. The voices of women of color, women from developing nations, and working-class women, have now begun to articulate what a feminist or liberationist perspective would mean to them. This dialogue is crucial to the development of a truly international women's movement.

It is, however, a confusion of the issues, I believe, to argue that, because of its origins in the writings of women in a relatively privileged situation, feminist theory cannot by definition be revolutionary. It is true that much of the theory of the second wave came from the pens of women who in the majority were white and who had access to public print. But Marx was hardly a scion of the working class. Revolutionary potential lies, not in the color and social class of the writer, but in the content of the ideas expressed, and in the uses to which they are ultimately put.

I do not mean to imply that I uncritically accept all feminist theory as politically radical. In part, I wish to counter some recent feminist statements that explicitly disavow any connection to radical or left politics and traditions. But I am arguing that the achievement of full freedom for women (all women, not a privileged few) presupposes such profound economic, social, and political changes that, were such a historical development to take place, the present status quo could not and would not survive. Herbert Gintis has taken Marxist writers to task for criticizing feminists, blacks, gays, and other groups for their failure to adhere to a recognizably Marxist rhetoric and world view, and for clinging, instead, to a vocabulary of democratic liberalism. Instead of accusing them of false consciousness, Marxists should be aware of the process by which these groups have stretched the language of liberalism well beyond its original limits.[16] The argument, I think, goes beyond issues of discourse. Ought one to castigate feminism because it is insufficiently revolutionary and geared to the concerns of the working class? Or ought one to take a longer view, and ask, what would become of present social arrangements, in the capitalist West and indeed, in most societies, capitalist and communist, if all of the demands of the women's movement were met with respect to all women?

The politics of feminist theory:
against the new essentialism

That feminism has the potential to be a force for progressive social change does not mean that it is automatically such a force. Indeed, the success of the women's movement, in relative terms, has produced many political varieties of feminist views. As Alix Kates Shulman has noted, "feminism is not a monolith; there are many different, even at times contradictory, positions which may spring from good feminist motives."[17] In tracing the history of the development of feminist thought since 1970, my intention is to look carefully at the politics of feminist theory, and to raise the question of the social and political implications of texts, even where these issues are not directly addressed by their authors.

I am sympathetic to the notion of letting a hundred or a thousand flowers bloom. As Shulman writes, "[f]or better or worse, any large political or social movement, powered by passion, must eventually sustain internal debates, divisions, factions, and splits."[18] But I think it is of great importance to be clear about what some of the differences are, and to discuss them openly. It is only by assessing the present of feminist theory and practice that one can move into the future with some degree of clarity. As I indicated at the beginning of the introduction, in the shape of contemporary feminist thought I believe that there are some reactionary tendencies. In the account presented here, I argue that feminist theory has moved from an emphasis on the elimination of gender difference to a celebration of that difference as a source of moral values. A woman-centered analysis presupposes the centrality, normality, and value of women's experience and women's culture. The development of a woman-centered perspective in recent years owes a good deal to the work of feminist historians of nineteenth-century American women. Kathryn Kish Sklar, Carroll Smith-Rosenberg, and others have given renewed importance to the world of women and to the culture of domesticity. Within their enforced separation from the world of paid work, produced by the development of industrialism, elite women created an interesting and complex world of their own.[19]

In the late twentieth century, women have been forced in large numbers back out of the domestic sphere and into the paid workforce. A good deal of the energy of contemporary feminist theory derives from the contradictions engendered by these changes in women's estate. Yet some exponents of the woman-centered perspective are creating a new version of woman's sphere, in which, depressed by the apparently overwhelming power of patriarchy, women can retreat to an imagined safety. Connected to this development is the growing popularity of the ideology characterized by Monique Wittig as "woman is wonderful."[20] In this view of the world, women are intrinsically good, and men, intrinsically evil. Women must therefore withdraw from the world built by men, and, by implication, withdraw from the struggle to change that world for the better. As Nancy Chodorow has pointed out, this view conceals a new biologism: it encapsulates a belief that women are superior beings to men, by virtue of their physical identity as female.[21]

In saying this, I am by no means arguing against the establishment of a separate women's culture, or of an autonomous women's movement. The wonderful variety of creations—from the *Dinner Party* by Judy Chicago to the flourishing independent lesbian communities in many cities[22]—are visible products of the new sense of positive identity among women fostered by the second wave. They are, in themselves, a form of social change, creating the space—emotional and physical—for the development of women's energies and strength. In this, they partake in a practical way of the utopian quality of feminist thought.

Further, the core of the woman-centered perspective, in my view, is not only legitimate, but essential to the foundation of a newly just society. The socially constructed virtues of women, the result of their long subordination, have redeeming qualities for all human beings. Women's capacities to nurture, to affiliate with others, to work collectively, all are crucial characteristics. But to posit that these grow uniquely out of biology, rather than out of culture and history, is to me, a betrayal of the feminist tradition. At the heart of feminism is an egalitarian impulse, seeking to free women from oppression by removing all of the obstacles to their political, economic, and sexual self-determination. To erect a doctrine of female superiority to men, by virtue of some essential quality of biology or spirit, is to my view a dangerous step backward.

Method, categories, conceptualization

Finally, a word on method. This book is a history of ideas, rather than a history of the women's movement. To some extent, the texts I discuss form a self-referential body of thought: Susan Brownmiller and Mary Daly develop ideas set forth by Millett and Firestone. But of course ideas do not evolve in a vacuum. I thus allude to certain developments in the women's movement, as background to the discussion, but I do not cover them in detail. I therefore assume some knowledge in the reader of the political, social, and economic changes of the past fifteen years or so since the second wave broke on the shores of Western industrial societies.[23] Further, although I have mentioned the importance of placing feminist theory into the context of the rest of Western social and political thought, I have not undertaken that rather formidable task here.[24]

The book is organized on the basis of a set of themes, generally, although not invariably, according to the chronological order in which these themes were introduced into feminist debate. For this purpose, I examine a number of texts, under the rubrics indicated by the table of contents. I have deliberately not proceeded, in the manner of some other studies, by organizing the book along the lines of a categorization of feminist thought into left, right, and center; liberal versus radical; or, in the most common categorization, socialist feminist, radical feminist, and liberal feminist.[25]

Obviously, some of these categories are useful. In particular, recent analysts seem to agree on the distinction between radical feminism, which holds that gender oppression is the oldest and most profound form of exploitation, which predates and underlies all other forms including those of race and class; and socialist feminism, which argues that class, race, and gender oppression interact in a complex way, that class oppression stems from capitalism, and that capitalism must be eliminated for women to be liberated. Both of these, in turn, would be distinguished from a liberal or bourgeois feminist view, which would argue that women's liberation can be fully achieved without any major alterations to the economic and political structures of contemporary capitalist democracies. A final category would be a cultural feminist position, which eschewed an explicit political or economic program altogether and concentrated on the development of a separate women's culture.

In recent years, however, the lines between these definitions have begun to blur somewhat, as feminist practice outstrips feminist theory: in the current women's movement, there are probably more subcategories and variations than these definitions can encompass.[26] But the concepts that I examine here are, in some cases, common to all current feminist positions, and in others, form part of their common vocabulary of debate and disagreement. Generally speaking, as noted, I address myself to the body of thought known as radical feminism, and to its evolution over the period since 1970. My use of the term to apply to writers like Chodorow and Dinnerstein may be controversial; but one of the themes of my argument is the shift in the meaning and application of the word "radical" from its use by Shulamith Firestone to its use by Mary Daly. If the discussion encourages a clarification in the meaning of this and other terms, then it will have served a useful purpose.

Finally, the choice of texts here is somewhat arbitrary. I discuss only works published since 1970, and, with one exception, only works originally published in the United States. This has eliminated such obvious choices as Simone de Beauvoir's *The Second Sex,* Betty Friedan's *The Feminine Mystique,* and Germaine Greer's *The Female Eunuch.* Since they are well known, I assume some knowledge of these feminist classics in the reader.[27] Given that the selection of texts is subjective, my discussion of them is an interpretation or reading, rather than a scientific or objective overview. But I do not subscribe to the belief that knowledge necessarily stems from detachment and measurement, carried out from some fictive Archimedean point "outside" of the reality under consideration. Rather, I side with those who believe that understanding springs from immersion, from empathy, involvement, and commitment.

I Uncovering the Patriarchal Power Structure

Prologue

Simone de Beauvoir's analysis of women's subordination proceeded from the assumption that men viewed women as fundamentally different from themselves. In being so defined, women were reduced to the status of the second sex. In her words,

> just as for the ancients there was an absolute vertical with reference to which the oblique was defined, so there is an absolute human type, the masculine. . . . Thus humanity is male and man defines woman not in herself but as relative to him; she is not regarded as an autonomous being. . . . She is defined and differentiated with reference to man and not he with reference to her; she is the incidental, the inessential as opposed to the essential. He is the Subject, he is the Absolute—she is the Other.[1]

Many of the best-known writings of the second wave could be seen as a set of variations on this theme. In a number of ways, Kate Millett, Shulamith Firestone, and others expressed the view that women's differences from men were the chief mechanism of their oppression.[2] These differences were an artifact of patriarchy, designed to exclude women from full participation in the world outside of the home. Although not the only argument of the new radical feminists, the issue of difference came to symbolize their views in the mind of the public. The implications were disturbing. Did these writers want to abolish the difference between men and women, and thereby to put an end to sex, love, the family, motherhood, civilization altogether? Those who dissented from their views found them unnatural. As Joan Didion commented, with indignation, "[a]ll one's actual apprehension of what it is like to be a woman, the irreconcilable difference of it—that sense of living one's deepest life underwater, that dark involvement with blood and birth and death—could now be declared invalid, unnecessary, *one never felt it at all.*"[3]

Part I examines the analysis set forth by Kate Millett and others, which placed the "actual apprehension" of being a woman into its social and political context. Chapter 1 assesses the work of Millett, particularly her account of the phenomenon of patriarchy, and that of Elizabeth Janeway on the social conditioning of women into conventional sex role behavior. Chapter 2 considers the attempt by Shulamith Firestone to establish a materialist basis for feminist theory, and the critique of this attempt by Juliet Mitchell. It also examines the work of the anthropologists Sherry Ortner and the late Michelle Z. Rosaldo on the universal sexual division of labor between the public and domestic realms. Chapter 3 explores Susan Brownmiller's hypothesis that the threat of rape serves to preserve male control of women in all societies. Finally, chapter 4 reviews the process of consciousness-raising, a means of recording and analyzing female experience and oppression.[4]

I

Patriarchy and the Rediscovery of Sex Roles

In 1970, when Kate Millett published her now classic work, *Sexual Politics,* [1] she used a word which has become part of the standard vocabulary of feminist writing, although in recent years its meaning and even its legitimacy as a concept have come in for considerable criticism. To refer to the fact that, in many parts of the world (and, some would argue, everywhere), men exert control over women, Millett spoke of "patriarchy," literally, from the Greek, the rule of the father. [2]

The word "patriarchy" might at first glance seem an inappropriate term to characterize the situation of women in the modern world, at least, in Western industrialized countries. But users of the term argued that, despite many differences of detail distinguishing the lives of women in the West from those of their sisters both in the developed socialist countries and in the underdeveloped Third World, the fundamental fact of male domination over women could be discerned in all societies. The term "patriarchy" was therefore justified by this fact, that of the "universal" oppression of women by men. As Adrienne Rich wrote,

> Patriarchy is the power of the fathers: a familial-social, ideological, political system in which men—by force, direct pressure, or through ritual, tradition, law, and language, customs, etiquette, education, and the division of labor, determine what part women shall or shall not play, and in which the female is everywhere subsumed under the male. . . . Under patriarchy, I may live in *purdah* or drive a truck; . . . I may serve my husband his early-morning coffee within the clay walls of a Berber village or march in an academic procession; whatever my status or situation, my derived economic class, or my sexual preference, I live under the power of the fathers, and I have access only to so much of privilege or influence as the patriarchy is willing to accede to me, and only for so long as I will pay the price for male approval. [3]

Or, in Kate Millett's more succinct formulation:

> [O]ur society, like all other historical civilizations, is a patriarchy. The
> fact is evident at once if one recalls that the military, industry,
> technology, universities, science, political office, and finance—in
> short, every avenue of power within the society, including the coer-
> cive force of the police, is entirely in male hands.[4]

Given the constraints of religious belief and social custom, it might seem
clear, at least to Western eyes, how the oppression of women could be
perpetuated in more traditional societies. But, Millett asked, how was it
possible for patriarchy to continue in a world in which women had education, access to financial resources and extensive civil and political rights,
and were not visibly subject to forms of direct coercion?[5] The answer, she
suggested, lay in psychology. The social control of women in a "free"
society such as the United States was not carried out through a rigid,
authoritarian system of force. Rather, it took place by means of the
engineering of consent among women themselves. Instead of being openly
coerced into accepting their secondary status, women were conditioned
into embracing it by the process of sex-role stereotyping. From early
childhood, women were trained to accept a system which divided society
into male and female spheres, with appropriate roles for each, and which
allocated public power exclusively to the male sphere.[6]

How could such a division be accepted by women? What were the
elements of the system of sex-role socialization and how did they operate?
Millett's view of the subordination of Western women was historical and
dialectical. She traced the history of the first wave of feminism, from the
campaign for women's rights arising from the movement for the abolition of
slavery to the winning of suffrage for women in the United States in 1920.
She then documented how, in the years since women won the vote, a vast
counteroffensive had been launched against them, using the weapons of
psychology, literature, and culture, broadly defined. All of these were used
to convince women, against at least the evidence of recent history, that
they were not in fact the equals of men.

The villains of Millett's piece were many, including notably Sigmund
Freud, and psychoanalytic thought as it had developed following him. Like
Betty Friedan, Millett accused Freud of helping to organize a counterrevolution against the emancipation of women.[7] The theory of "penis
envy" was devised, she argued, to stigmatize women who sought to
escape the confines of socially correct "feminine" behavior.

> The theory of penis envy shifts the blame of her suffering to the female for daring to aspire to a biologically impossible state. Any hankering for a less humiliating and circumscribed existence is immediately ascribed to unnatural and unrealistic deviation from her genetic identity and therefore her fate. A woman who resists "femininity," e.g. feminine temperament, status, and role, is thought to court neurosis, for femininity is her fate as "anatomy is destiny." (189)

In addition to Freud himself, Millett blamed the academics in social psychology who had helped to create what was essentially an ideology of sex roles. This was a set of rigid role prescriptions that served to keep women from deviating from the behavior expected of them, for fear of being thought abnormal, or undesirable, or finally, mad. Sex roles, and sex-role stereotyping, were, then, the means by which an entire society kept women subject to the rules of the patriarchy.

In her analysis, Millett drew upon the language and concepts of sociology and social psychology. In particular, she relied on the work of Robert Stoller, John Money, and others on "core gender identity." In this work, Stoller and other researchers into the psychology of gender convincingly demonstrated that biological sex and social gender were separable concepts, from a developmental point of view. Biologically, the sex of a normal baby was obvious from anatomical details at birth. Psychologically, however, the acquisition of a sense of one's own sexual identity as male or female, as a "boy" or "girl," could be dated fairly precisely at the age of around eighteen months. That is, it could be shown to be acquired culturally. Further, research showed that this sense of gender—this "cognitive sense of gendered self," as Nancy Chodorow has called it[8]—was acquired independently of, and in exceptional cases in opposition to, the anatomical "facts."

The sense of one's gender, in short, was arrived at in response to the environment of the family, to the interaction between parents and child. It was produced psychologically and socially, rather than physiologically, in an automatic response triggered by mechanical or physical means. Conceptually, then, it was possible to make a distinction between sex and gender. Sex meant the biological sex of a child—was it born anatomically a male or a female member of the human species? Gender was the culturally and socially shaped cluster of expectations, attributes, and behaviors assigned to that category of human being by the society into which the child was born.

The significance of the distinction between sex and gender depended, in part, on the prior knowledge that expectations of behavior and even character formation for men and women varied widely from culture to culture. In this, feminist theory built on the work of Margaret Mead and other anthropological researchers in the 1920s and 1930s. In *Sex and Temperament in Three Primitive Societies* (1935), Mead had sought to demonstrate that, in other societies around the world, the attributes assigned to and expected of males and females differed widely from those of Western culture. There were cultures, for example, in which men were expected to be, and were, peace-loving, while women were expected to be, and were, warlike. Cross-cultural research of this kind built up evidence for the argument that gender behavior was a social artifact.[9] The attributes that Western societies considered normal and natural for women and men, respectively, were in fact, created by means of social pressures, in short, by what psychologists called "conditioning."

What, then, was the cluster of attributes that had been assigned to women in contemporary Western culture? What was considered to be "normal" for the gender "female" as opposed to the gender "male"? How did these attributes contribute to the continuation of patriarchy? Millett took her evidence on these questions from the work of social psychologists, who for years had been busy setting forth a catalog of normal gender behavior. Millett demonstrated that for female, "normal" meant passive, while for male, it meant active. Men had instrumental traits: they were tenacious, aggressive, curious, ambitious, planful, responsible, original, and competitive. Women had expressive traits: they were affectionate, obedient, responsive to sympathy and approval, cheerful, kind, and friendly.[10] Social pressure kept women conforming to the expressive role expected of them, a role that dictated conformity and obedience, while men occupied the instrumental role of rationality and power.

In arguing that sex could be separated, at least conceptually, from gender, and that expectations for sex roles, or more accurately, gender roles radically differentiated men from women, Millett implied that it was above all the psychology of women that kept them subject to the rule of patriarchy. She itemized a number of realms and modes within which patriarchy operated. Besides the categories of ideological, biological, sociological, class, economic, and educational, she included a category "force," under which she listed rape, hostility, and ridicule. But in the wake of the "counterrevolution" against the first "sexual revolution" from 1830 to 1930, patriarchy in modern times was upheld chiefly by attitudes, more than by political and/or economic structures. In her words,

[i]t must be clearly understood that the arena of sexual revolution is within human consciousness even more pre-eminently than it is within human institutions. So deeply embedded is patriarchy that the character structure it creates in both sexes is perhaps even more a habit of mind and a way of life than a political system. (63)

What accounted for the strength and the persistence of the system of male domination in the modern era? What were the elements in the system of sex roles that kept women in their place? Another account based on social roles was that offered by Elizabeth Janeway, in *Man's World, Woman's Place.* [11] Eschewing the word "patriarchy" Janeway spoke instead of "social mythology." She traced the origins and the persistence of the notion that "woman's place is in the home," by way of exploring the discrepancy of power between the sexes, or, as she put it, the "subordination of woman to man" (51).

Like Millett, Janeway took social scientists to task for their pronouncements, disguised as scientific description, on what and how women ought to be. From Erik Erikson's famous studies of girls and "inner space" in the late 1930s to the work of Talcott Parsons and David McClelland in the 1950s and 1960s social psychologists and sociologists had persistently substituted "prescription" for "description," explaining how women ought to be, rather than how they were. These analysts argued that the limitations placed upon women by their "natural" inclinations toward domesticity and the role of wife and mother were dictated by a biologically based psychology. If this was the case, then what need was there for exhortation, for impassioned pleas to women to remain as they naturally were? Janeway exposed the contradiction between *is* and *ought* in these writers. If women were naturally inclined to be domestic and subordinate, why then did these and other writers protest so much? It was, she argued, precisely because on this matter of woman's "nature" one was not dealing with a fact of nature and biology, but with a social mythology. She defined this as a normative set of beliefs and practices intended to shape social life according to a particular set of values.

The social mythology outlined by Janeway rested on a set of beliefs about roles. She traced the historical development of the idea that women belonged in the domestic sphere, pointing out that the "home" of the adage was a relatively modern invention, dating approximately from the eighteenth century as was the nuclear family, to which women were assigned as their major duty. From these fairly recent historical developments emerged the concept of the woman's "role," which, Janeway pointed out, had no direct counterpart to any man's role. Thus the role of

mother, homemaker (or housewife or houseworker), and wife was said to
define what a woman was in ways that were directly related to her being
female. No such strictures related to men, who were more likely to be
defined by what they did in the public world of work than by what sex they
were.[12]

Janeway argued that the strength of sex role differentiation derived in
part from male propaganda. Ideas about women's place appeared with
alarming frequency in all the venues that served to make ideology public,
from scientific journals to the popular media, including especially women's
magazines. But these ideas were also internalized by women, and perpetuated by them in large measure. The "psychology" of women was not
entirely invented and imposed by men. Were there, then, elements in the
social mythology that women found useful, helpful, or even compelling?
Janeway argued that many women had, in fact, "bought in" to the mythology, on the ground that it held certain rewards for them. In her view, these
women, in accepting their subordinate place in the modern world, had
essentially made a secret bargain with men: they had agreed to exchange
"private power in return for public submission. That is the regular, or-
thodox bargain by which men rule the world and allow women to rule in
their own place" (56). The power exerted by women in the domestic
sphere over the lives of their children and in the sexual arena of the
marriage bed was, emotionally, enough of an inducement to some women
to keep them from exerting any kind of claim upon the realms of other kinds
of power—intellectual, economic, political—available in the public sphere.

Although different in tone and emphasis, the accounts of Millett and
Janeway converged in their analysis: in the subordination of modern
women the influence of sex roles was a key factor. It is important to
understand that the concept of sex roles was by no means the invention of
contemporary feminists: it was a convention of long-standing within the
discipline of sociology. But in sociological usage, "sex roles" contained
none of the irony or potentially explosive meaning lent to the concept by
contemporary feminism. It referred, simply, to the appropriate social
functions fulfilled, respectively, by males and females, and to the matching
temperamental traits and qualities that accompanied these functions. As
codified by Talcott Parsons and other writers on the sociology of the family
in the 1950s, male or masculine behavior was that cluster of psychological
traits thought to be suited to the "role" of breadwinner—aggression,
initiative, rationality, objectivity, in short, "instrumental" characteristics.
Female or feminine behavior was the cluster suited to the "role" of

homemaker—passivity, obedience, emotionalism, subjectivity, in short, "affective" characteristics.

If, as Millett did, one contrasted this array of "correct" or "appropriate" sex roles with the findings of Stoller and Money on sex and gender, it could be demonstrated that the literature on sex roles in fact represented, not a pure scientific description, but a set of cultural directives for what constituted the gender expectations of the society under scrutiny. In effect, Millett and Janeway argued, this was a comprehensive ideology of behavior, created to justify and support the argument that "woman's place was in the home," after the experience of World War II, when women had been drawn out of the home and into the labor market.[13] In this sense, the ideology of sex roles, promulgated by social scientists and popularized in the media, was a major element in the continued subordination of women. However, part of the point of Janeway's book was to demonstrate that the ideology—or social mythology, as she referred to it—was being reinstituted or reinforced, in a number of quarters, precisely at the moment, historically, when the social reality (particularly, the attitudes and behavior of large numbers of women reentering the labor market) was beginning to belie the mythology.

To recapitulate, then: in the feminist analysis set forth by Millett and Janeway, the meaning of "sex roles" became transformed. What had been presented by (male) social scientists as "value-free" description now encapsulated a critique.[14] In conventional sociological terms, "sex role" was a social role dictated by the biological sex of the actor. In the hands of feminists, "sex role" became a role assigned to the actor because of the gender-associated behavior linked by society (more or less arbitrarily) with that biological sex. To a feminist like Millett or Janeway, sex roles—that is, roles assigned because of biological sex—were a form of oppression, keeping women restricted and limited in their scope.

The oppression of women rested upon more than the establishment of sex roles. Kate Millett argued that a major pillar of patriarchy was what she called "sexual politics." This was the system of interpersonal power by means of which individual men dominated individual women. Conventionally, she said, politics had been defined by political scientists as the arena of public power, that is, chiefly electoral politics. Academic analysis concentrated on the issue of how the pie of political power was divided among those holding or seeking public office, and those seeking to influence them. Millett introduced a different, expanded definition of politics, one that incorporated a notion of the political nature of the relationships between men and women. Like the relationships of men to one another in political life, this was also a relationship of domination and subordination, in the Hegelian sense. But it was expressed in and through the medium of sexual relationships, conventionally referred to as connections of love, rather than power. Much of *Sexual Politics* was devoted to a devastating analysis and deconstruction of the erotic descriptions in four major male writers: D. H. Lawrence, Henry Miller, Norman Mailer, and Jean Genet. Millett wanted to expose the crude expression of power relationships, of the intention to dominate, in the vision of modern sexuality as set forth in these "modern classics."[15]

"The personal is the political" was an important slogan of the second wave of the women's movement. Coined by Carol Hanisch, it had many layers of meaning.[16] In Millett's analysis, the chief of these meanings was the sense in which sexual relationships between men and women, at the most intimate and personal level, embodied a political dimension. The domination of one woman by her husband or lover, through the "conquest" enacted repeatedly in the sexual act between them, was part of the social control of all women by all men exerted under patriarchy. Thus the class of women, the group of all women, in a given society, was kept subordinate to the class of men, the group of all men in that society, by a variety of means: economic, psychological, legal, and ideological. But this control was ultimately exerted at the private, personal level, in the bedroom.

In the literary criticism making up the bulk of her book, Millett was thus attempting a process of demystification. The writers that she analyzed were part of the much-admired twentieth-century achievement of bringing sex and sexuality, explicitly depicted, into the center of modern literature. But what were the ideological implications of the depiction of sexual behavior these books presented? They were, Millett argued, precisely, that of the power relationship contained in and expressed through the sexual act itself. In a widely circulated and reprinted paper, Anne Koedt undertook a similar task. In "The Myth of the Vaginal Orgasm,"[17] Koedt sought to demonstrate how men controlled women by means of their control over the sexual act. The ideology surrounding this relation of power was the myth that, for women to achieve "true" orgasm, they must experience penetration by a penis. Along the same lines, Millett quoted the work of Mary Jane Sherfey, who had demonstrated that the orgasmic potential of women far exceeded that usually experienced under conditions of ordinary heterosexual intercourse, during which initiative and control remained in male hands.[18]

}

In Millett's view, however, the political aspect of sexual intercourse was not limited to heterosexual couplings. That the relation of power had no necessary connection to the players being male and female was the burden of Millett's analysis of the writing of Jean Genet. The same dynamic of conquest—of winner and loser, dominant and subordinate—could be seen to be operating in the sexual relations between man and man, in a homosexual relationship where all parties were reduced to relative power-lessness: in prison. This, she argued, was a "pure" case, which, in the absence of "real" women, created "pseudo" women out of the men who assumed the passive role, the role of the conquered or dominated partner. This was, in a sense, the exception that proved the rule: relations of sexuality were used as relations of power, and the balance of power lay with men.[19]

This, of course, was in the eyes of some men only to redress the balance, to compensate for what they saw as the already inordinate power of women. Norman Mailer's remarkably frank reply to Millett inadvertently illustrated the accuracy of her analysis. Mailer spoke of

> man's sense of awe before women, his dread of her position one step closer to eternity . . . which made men detest women, revile them, humiliate them, defecate symbolically upon them, do everything to reduce them. . . . So do men look to destroy every quality in a woman which will give her the powers of a male, for she is in their eyes already armed with the power that she brought them forth. . . .[20]

Shulamith Firestone took the analysis one step further. She examined the phenomenon of "love," which she called "the pivot of women's oppression."[21] Firestone argued that the concept of love was a kind of ideological coverup or disguise of the relations of power that prevailed in heterosexual relationships. In this sense, the emotion of love, as experienced by men and women alike, served to disguise the actual political meaning of sex by putting it within the context of a confusing and misleading set of expectations.

> A man must idealize one woman over the rest in order to justify his descent to a lower caste. . . . [T]his idealization process acts to artificially equalize the two parties. . . . *Thus "falling in love" is no more than the process of alteration of male vision—through idealization, mystification, glorification—that renders void the woman's class inferiority.*[22]

The subordination of women under patriarchy in the Western industrial countries, then, was a complex matter. As Millett and others pointed out, the rule of men was not enforced by means of visible coercion, but rather through the continued reproduction of an ideology that reinforced a separation between male and female roles, and then created or sustained a set of beliefs about the roles thus created. Among these beliefs were the most cherished of ideas, namely, that of physical and emotional love between men and women. Sexual love was revealed as a crucial part of the ideological structure that perpetuated male power over women, with their full participation. For women, to fall in love with men was no metaphor, but an action that each time it was repeated reinforced their subordination, both individually and collectively.

2

The Public/Domestic Dichotomy and the Universal Oppression of Women

What were the underpinnings of patriarchy? Was the cultural, sociological, and psychological analysis of the oppression of women sufficient to explain it? Or was there another layer of reality that needed examination, as well? Theorists of the second wave looked for evidence that the basis of patriarchy lay in material conditions. But on this point, there was considerable variation in the interpretation of the term material, and in the degree of significance accorded to material factors.

Marxism, of course, claimed the title deeds to materialism as a scientific theory of society. But Shulamith Firestone disputed this claim on behalf of feminism. In *The Dialectic of Sex,* she announced that she was launching a new materialist theory of history, that would go beyond and complete the theoretical work of Marx and Engels. She recalled that in setting forth the theory of historical materialism, Marx and Engels had intended to supersede what they called derisively "utopian socialism," which moralized ineffectually about social inequities. "Scientific socialism," in contrast, would be able to analyze the sources of injustice, predict and guide revolutionary change, and eventually institute genuine social justice. In their theory, said Firestone, they had correctly focused upon economic class and the class struggle as the motor of history. But they had paid inadequate attention to sex, or what Firestone termed "sex class."[1] She proposed to remedy this omission by developing "a materialist view of history based on sex itself" (5), which could lead to the true and final revolution in which women would seize control of the means of reproduction. In this "expanded" definition of historical materialism, the basic division in society, and the motor of history, was not economic class but sex class. Firestone "rephrased" Engels' definition from *Socialism, Utopian and Scientific,* to read:

> Historical materialism is that view of the course of history which
> seeks the ultimate cause and the great moving power of all historic
> events in the dialectic of sex: the division of society into two distinct
> biological classes for procreative reproduction, and the struggles of
> these classes with one another; in the changes in the modes of
> marriage, reproduction and childcare. . . ; in the connected de-
> velopment of other physically-differentiated classes (castes); and in
> the first division of labor based on sex which developed into the
> (economic-cultural) class system. (12)

In *The Origin of the Family, Private Property and the State,* Engels had
propounded the original insight that the first division of labor was that
between men and women, and the first expropriation of labor that of
women by men, in the reproduction of the human species. This truth had
since been allowed to disappear from the center of Marxist theory, where,
in Firestone's view, it properly belonged.

Firestone held that the historical basis of patriarchy was indeed "material." Marx and Engels had defined "materialism" to signify a relation to the
economic development of society, via changes in the modes of production
and exchange, with the resulting creation of classes and of class struggle.
Thus, in the broad sense, "materialist" designated a relation to economic
conditions. In Firestone's version, however, the "material" basis of history
was the physical realities of female and male biology, along with those
political and cultural structures erected to ensure that biology would
remain determinative of the social order. She argued that the fundamental
inequality between men and women could be traced, not to the differences
between them, but to the reproductive functions of these differences.

> Unlike economic class, sex class sprang directly from a biological
> reality: men and women were created different, and not equally
> privileged. Although, as de Beauvoir points out, this difference of
> itself did not necessitate the development of a class system—the
> domination of one group by another—the reproductive *functions* of
> these differences did. The biological family is an inherently unequal
> power distribution. (8)

The power difference between men and women, then, was embodied in
what Firestone called the "biological family." This contained the following
four "fundamental—if not immutable" elements: (1) the physical dependency of women upon men for survival, because of the debilitating effects
of childbirth (at least, before the availability of birth control—although
Firestone included here "menstruation, menopause, and 'female ills'" as
well); (2) the long period of dependency of human infants; (3) the

psychological effects of this "mother/child interdependency"; and (4) the division of labor between the sexes, based on the "natural reproductive difference" between them (8–9). The feminist revolution would come about, therefore, only by means of the final dissolution of the "biological" family, through the creation of conditions whereby "genital differences between human beings would no longer matter culturally" (11). That is, the physical realities of reproduction and childcare would be overcome, through establishing the option of "artificial reproduction," and the socialization of childcare (that is, sharing the work among all members of the society). Only with the abolition of women's physical and psychological responsibility for the reproduction of the species could women's liberation be accomplished.

It is relevant to note that the claim of the Firestone theory to a materialist base rested, as this account has indicated, on the physical realities of reproductive biology. But Firestone argued that it was the psychological effects that were at the root of the social ills she diagnosed.

> [U]nless revolution uproots the basic social organization, the biological family—the vinculum through which the psychology of power can always be smuggled—the tapeworm of exploitation can never be annihilated. We shall need a sexual revolution much larger than—inclusive of—a socialist one to truly eradicate all class systems. (12)

Ultimately, then, the materialism of this theory depended upon an implicit notion of causality that apparently differed considerably from the materialism of Marx and Engels. Firestone did not make clear what was the dialectical relation between the physical or biological, on the one hand, and the psychological or social, on the other. How did the one in some sense produce the other? Firestone did not use the term reproduction in its full Marxist sense, to refer not only to biological reproduction, but also to the daily maintenance of the labor force, and to social reproduction, that is, the perpetuation of social systems. Her focus was upon the reproduction of the species in the narrow sense, that is, on childrearing.[2] In Firestone's view, to change society, was it sufficient to change biology? The details of her feminist revolution—sexual, social, biological—remained vague. But one point was clear: for women to be liberated, motherhood and the family in their current forms would have to be abolished.

In *Woman's Estate,* Juliet Mitchell rejected the claim of Firestone to have created a new historical materialism.[3] While she agreed that her "invigorating book" (87) contained a materialist theory, it was in Mitchell's view neither historical nor dialectical.

> To say that sex dualism was the first oppression and that it underlies
> all oppression may be true, but it is a general, non-specific truth, it is
> simplistic materialism, no more. After all we can say there has always
> been a master class and a servant class, but it does matter *how* these
> function. . . ; there have always been classes, as there have always
> been sexes, how do these operate within any given, specific society?
> Without such knowledge (historical materialism) we have not the
> means of overcoming them. (90)

Mitchell criticized Firestone, and radical feminism generally, for not
speaking of women's oppression in a historically specific way. In order to
account for the situation of women, and the changes in this situation over
time, Mitchell argued, an adequate account must be given of the elements
that made women's situation unique. Among the oppressed social groups
of the world, what distinguished women, "half of the human species," was
that women had historically inhabited two worlds, and had been subject to
oppression in both: the world of production, that is, the labor market; and
the world of reproduction, that is, the family. While Mitchell cited biological
reproduction, that is, childbearing, as one of the elements in the oppression of women, she argued that this was only one of four "structures" that
an analysis would need to take into account. These were: production, that
is, women's role in economic production; reproduction of children; sexuality, and its regulation and control (since historically this meant the regulation and control of *women's* sexuality, predominantly); and the socialization
of children (120). Women's oppression depended on a number of elements
created by her situation of straddling two worlds, home and work, and of
being caught in the contradictions produced by both. As Mitchell remarked, "Women's position in society is in the home—and outside it, in
production" (173). The analysis, then, of the oppression of women could
not focus only upon biology and reproduction. It must examine, too, the
economic and psychological realities that stemmed from women's place in
the labor force, in production, and her place in the family, in the reproduction of children, and (via their socialization) of culture and ideology.

In practical terms, this meant an examination of women's participation in
the labor force, the use of women as a reserve army of labor, the kinds of
work women did or did not get paid to do, and the historical changes in what
was considered "women's work." Mitchell argued that one needed to
examine these changes in the Western, capitalist economies, and in the
socialist, postrevolutionary economies as well, to see what changes had or
had not been made in the position of women as participants in production.
Similarly, one needed a history of reproduction: what was the impact of

contraception, "an innovation of world-historic importance"? (108). What about the ideology of parenthood, the "social cult of maternity," in which the woman's activity of bearing and raising children came to be seen as a replacement for work, and the child became "an object created by the mother, in the same way as a commodity is created by a worker"? (109). Similarly, for sexuality, whose history, said Mitchell, had been virtually ignored by socialists, and distorted by liberal "ideologues." She called for cross-cultural accounts that would explore the relationship between degrees of sexual freedom, on the one hand, and variations in the position and dignity of women, on the other. And finally, like Firestone, Millett, and Janeway, Mitchell emphasized the importance of demystifying the ideologies governing the socialization of children: the notion of instrumental versus expressive roles assigned to male and female parents, respectively; and the obsession with correct childrearing (always the responsibility of the mother).

Mitchell wrote that socialist countries had assumed, rather simplistically, that the liberation of women would flow automatically from their inclusion as full members of the work force. Thus the experiments of Russia and China had failed to free women, because they had concentrated only upon the element of production, while they had systematically inhibited or prevented changes in the other three areas. But in bourgeois capitalist countries, she argued, radical feminists were stressing only the structures relative to women's "private," domestic experience. Only a "transformation of *all* the structures into which [women] are integrated, and all the contradictions" coalescing and exploding—"a *unité de rupture*"—would bring about the "authentic liberation of women" (121–22).

What Mitchell was pointing to was the complexity of the relationship between women and economic production, and the importance of the changes in the historic relations between the two over time. Whatever their disagreements, Mitchell and Firestone agreed on one point, and that was the relation of women's oppression to the ideological association of women with the private sphere. (I am using the word "ideological" here to mean insistence upon an idea, whether or not it accords with the reality.) In this, they seconded the analysis of Elizabeth Janeway, who had argued that the fact that "woman's place" was adjudged to be in the home, and only in the home, was a key element in the social mythology that helped to keep women relatively powerless. Janeway traced the history of the family, following Philippe Ariès and others, to show that the very concepts of the "home," the domestic "hearth," and the nuclear family, as "woman's sphere," were all fairly recent historical developments. The role of women in the process of the production of goods, which had been substantial in the pre-industrial period, had been drastically reduced with the advent of industrialization, which moved most areas of production out of the home into the factories. Even after this development, early factory work in England and the United States was largely carried out by women and children. But gradually, as a result of many historical forces the importance of women's role in the paid labor force had been reduced. Women's economic contributions, in the majority, were limited to home rather than workplace, after marriage, from the mid-nineteenth century onward. The trend only began to be reversed during World War II; accelerating in the 1950s, this reversal was doubtless one of the major factors in the revival of the feminist movement in the 1960s.[4]

In the meantime, the association of women with the private sphere and of men with the public had hardened into a truism and an ideology. Men had become associated with what was public: the workplace, politics, religion in its institutional forms, intellectual and cultural life, and in general terms, the exercise of power and authority; women, with what was private: the home, children, domestic life, sexuality (or its repression). The split between public and private, or domestic, appeared, then, as a major, even universal characteristic of how men and women, maleness and femaleness, were viewed.

In the connection of women to the "private" or "domestic" sphere, the most obvious element was, of course, their reproductive function. Not just the fact that women bore children, but their apparently "natural" association with children in rearing them, appeared to be the factor that connected women to the domestic realm. This was the view set forth in an influential essay by the anthropologist Michelle Rosaldo. Rosaldo offered the hypothesis that the assignment of women to the domestic sphere and of men to the public one was characteristic of all societies. This was the thread that linked all known human societies, from the most primitive to the most complex, and that underlay the universal oppression of women, despite the variety of forms that this took worldwide.[5]

Rosaldo proposed that, despite all of the variations that could be observed cross-culturally in the roles assigned to the sexes, all cultures distinguished between male and female, and assigned appropriate behaviors and tasks to each. Further, she observed that in all cases, no matter what form the sexual division of labor took, the tasks and roles assigned to men were given greater significance and importance. "[M]ale, as opposed to female, activities," she wrote, "are always recognized as predominantly important, and cultural systems give authority and value to

the roles and activities of men. . . . An asymmetry in the cultural evalua-
tion of male and female, in the importance assigned to women and men,
appears to be universal" (19).

Rosaldo distinguished between authority, and power and influence,
using the definitions first proposed by Max Weber. Women were not
without certain forms of power, she argued, and in some societies were
able to exert a good deal of influence in social decision making. But even in
the most apparently egalitarian of societies, authority, the source of legitimacy in the exercise of power, lay with men. Rosaldo traced this authority
to the importance granted male activities, as opposed to female activities,
in a given society. "[M]en," she wrote, "are the locus of cultural value"
(20).

What was the basis of this assignment of "cultural value" to men? For
Rosaldo, it lay in the differentiation between the "domestic" and "public"
spheres. This, in turn, stemmed from women's activities and responsibilities in childrearing. Rosaldo offered the following definitions of
"domestic" and "public":

> "Domestic" . . . refers to those minimal institutions and modes of
> activity that are organized immediately around one or more mothers
> and their children; "public" refers to activities, institutions, and forms
> of association that link, rank, organize, or subsume particular
> mother-child groups. (23)

Rosaldo rejected the view, based on Engels, that the relegation of women
to the domestic sphere was a relatively recent historical phenomenon,
growing out of the development of industrial capitalism, which had pushed
women out of the area of "social production." She held, instead, that "a
domestic/public asymmetry is general in economic forms of human organization as in other forms. Advanced and capitalistic societies, although they
are extreme in this regard, are not unique" (35).

Part of the basis of male authority, for Rosaldo, was the ability of men to
maintain distance from the domestic sphere. She proposed a direct relationship between the degree of the subordination of women in a given
society, and the degree to which the realms of public and domestic were
separated. Drawing on the example of the Philippine society of the Ilon-
gots, whom she had studied, she pointed out that where men were more
closely involved in domestic life, the distance between men and women,
and the degree of authority that men exerted over women, appeared to
diminish. "Societies that do not elaborate the opposition of male and
female," she suggested,

and place positive value on the conjugal relationship and the involvement of both men and women in the home seem to be most egalitarian
in terms of sex roles. When a man is involved in domestic labor, in
child care and cooking, he cannot establish an aura of authority and
distance. And when public decisions are made in the household,
women may have a legitimate public role. (39)

A parallel interpretation was advanced by Sherry Ortner.[6] Unlike Firestone, she located women's oppression in culture rather than in biology.
But, with Simone de Beauvoir, she saw the relegation of women to the
private sphere as arising out of an interpretation of biology: the association
of women with nature, and of men with culture, civilization, and the control
of nature (including, therefore, of women).

In Ortner's interpretation, in all cultures, world wide, women were
"considered inferior to men." Although this devaluation of women took
different forms, it was indisputably universal. "I would flatly assert," she
wrote, "that we find women subordinated to men in every known society.
The search for a genuinely egalitarian, let alone matriarchal culture, has
proved fruitless" (70). If the subordination of women was universal, so,
too, then must be the cause of this subordination. Ortner argued that one
element characterizing every known society was the process by which
human consciousness created what anthropologists term "culture." In this
process, Ortner said, every society recognized a distinction between
"culture" and "nature" (although as she noted both of these terms referred
to "conceptual categories" rather than aspects of "reality"). Culture, as
expressed in ritual, was an expression of the need to regulate and control,
"rather than passively move with and be moved by, the givens of natural
existence." In other words, Ortner argued, "We may . . . broadly equate
culture with the notion of human consciousness (i.e. systems of thought
and technology), by means of which humanity attempts to assert control
over nature" (72). In the distinction between "culture" and "nature," then,
"culture" was seen not only as separate from, but as superior to, "nature,"
because of its ability to control and transform the natural environment.

In this universal scheme, what, then, was the place of women? Ortner
argued that the devaluation of women grew out of the association of women
with nature, and more specifically, out of the belief that women were
"closer" than men to the natural world, "less transcendental of nature."
This connection of women to nature had three aspects. First, women's
mammalian work as bearer of human young. Ortner argued, with de
Beauvoir, that woman's "enslavement to the species" was one source of

her oppression. Women merely participated in the animallike repetitive tasks of carrying on the reproduction of the human race. But men participated in the project of culture, of creating the new. While "woman's body," she wrote, "seems to doom her to mere reproduction of life[,]" the male "must (or has the opportunity to) assert his creativity externally, 'artificially,' through the medium of technology and symbols. In so doing, he creates relatively lasting, eternal transcendent objects, while the woman creates only perishables—human beings" (75). In other words, because women gave birth, men created culture: "Woman creates naturally from within her own being, whereas man is free to, or forced to, create artificially, that is, through cultural means, and in such a way as to sustain culture" (77). Presumably Ortner's point of view throughout this analysis was intended to be critical of the nature/culture dichotomy. But her language in this and similar passages was unfortunately close to that of many prefeminist tracts of the 1950s, and of many antifeminists still extant: poor men, forced into cultural production because they can't make babies! Note, in the passages cited here, her repeated ambiguous statement as to whether men are "free to" or "forced to" make culture.

The second aspect was the association of women with the home or the "domestic circle." Because of lactation, and of the long period of maturation in the human infant, the relationship of mother with child was extended beyond birth, first, for the number of months occupied with breast-feeding, and then for the years required to socialize the child into the culture of the society. The need to supervise children, to teach them language, to provide them with food, all occupied the mother and kept her close to home. Ortner noted the irony that, while because of this association with the domestic, the woman was viewed as more distant from culture than the man, nonetheless it was the woman who in fact introduced the children to culture via language. Yet at a certain age, children would be taken from the mother in order to complete the process of socialization: "[M]ost cultures have initiation rites for adolescents (primarily for boys . . .), the point of which is to move the child ritually from a less than fully human state into full participation in society and culture . . ." (78).

In all cultures, said Ortner, there was a division between domestic and public life. Lévi-Strauss had argued in *The Elementary Structures of Kinship* that in every society, "the domestic unit—the biological family charged with reproducing and socializing new members of the society—is opposed to the public entity—the superimposed network of alliances and relationships that *is* the society . . ." (78). Given that

> domestic units are allied with one another through the enactment of
> rules that are logically at a higher level than the units themselves[,]
> this creates an emergent unit—society—that is logically at a higher
> level than the domestic units of which it is composed. (79)

Because the domestic (or private) sphere was associated with the female,
it was inevitable that women became associated with "a lower order of
social/cultural organization." Ortner considered the Lévi-Straussian equation of family = female = biology = nature "too simple." Rather, she said, the
realm of family "(and hence woman) represents lower-level, socially frag-
menting, particularistic sort of concerns, as opposed to interfamilial relations representing higher-level, integrative, universalistic sorts of concerns" (79). Family, domestic, and female, then, tended to be associated
with a lower order—closer to nature—while public and male tended to be
associated with a higher order, where culture—law, religion, ritual, and
politics—prevailed. It is noteworthy that in these passages, Ortner used
the terms "higher" and "lower" to refer to a number of overlapping
concepts: superior and inferior in value; logically prior to and logically
subsequent to; and general and particular. Presumably Ortner did not
clarify the relationships between these three sets of meanings because she
considered the connections among them to be self-evident. But it is
arguable that this would only be the case in the context of Western culture,
whereas she was arguing for their universal application across all cultures.

The third aspect was that women's "psyche" itself was seen as closer to
nature than men's. Here, Ortner acknowledged that she was on dangerous
ground, as she was willing to argue that in fact women did seem to have a
different "psychic structure" from that of men. She was not arguing for a
physiological cause of this difference. Rather, she saw it as a product of the
differential socialization of women. "Nonetheless," she wrote, "if we grant
the empirical near universality of a 'feminine psyche' with certain specific
characteristics, these characteristics would add weight to the cultural view
of woman as closer to nature" (81).

Up until this point in her argument, Ortner had been saying that,
because of certain physiological givens, certain culturally defined characteristics were universally attributed to women, namely, their supposed
closeness to "nature." At this point, she slipped into the position of saying
that certain psychological characteristics, universally attributed to women, were in fact characteristics that women display. That is, in her view,
the social conditions that women experienced acted to create a genuine
artifact known as the "feminine personality," good at interpersonal par-

ticularism, but not at universal generalizing. This was a condition from which presumably only a few, highly trained female anthropologists were able to escape. Ortner did not specify in her article any of the empirical research that would make the existence of a universal "feminine psyche" such a certainty.

Drawing on the work of Nancy Chodorow, Ortner argued that the "feminine" psyche was characterized in all societies by a relative "concreteness," rather than abstractness, as compared to men. Because of their role as socializers of the young, women tended to develop a personality that was immediate, interpersonal, subjective, that is, that was connected to the particular rather than to the general. In this, as in the other aspects cited by Ortner, women thus appeared to be more "like nature"— that is, as immanent, embedded in things, rather than "like culture"—that is, transcendent, and transforming of things. Women seemed, in their very psychic makeup, to be more unmediated and direct, less mediated than men by categories of abstraction. (In this part of her argument, Ortner did not define "psyche" and so it is hard to judge exactly what she meant.)

Ortner concluded that, because of all these aspects—women's "body and its functions," her "social roles," and her "psychic structure" (73–74)—women were seen to be closer to nature than men, and intermediary between nature and culture, while men were the controllers and manipulators of culture itself. Until this set of associations could be disassembled, the universal subordination of women would continue. While none of these associations of women with nature was "true," taken together they constituted a "(sadly) efficient feedback system," in which "various aspects of woman's situation (physical, social, psychological) contribute to her being seen as closer to nature, while the view of her as closer to nature is in turn embodied in institutional forms that reproduce her situation" (87). Both institutions and cultural assumptions would have to be transformed, in order for "both men and women . . . [to] be equally involved in projects of creativity and transcendence" (87).

Juliet Mitchell had underlined the importance of cross-cultural studies, and had emphasized the need to look at all aspects of women's experience—in production as well as reproduction—in order to arrive at a correct interpretation of woman's estate. It is noteworthy that in seeking the causes of the "universal" oppression of women, both Rosaldo and Ortner gave short shrift to the Marxist conception of the sexual division of labor—a focus of much work by socialist feminist writers—in favor of an examination of the cultural and symbolic significance of reproduction and the domestic sphere. In so doing, they lent some of the authority of anthropological theory to the hypothesis of Firestone, namely, that women's connection to biological reproduction was the root cause of their oppression.[7]

Whatever the interpretation—whether one saw the association of women with the domestic sphere as universal and defining of their situation in all cultures like Ortner, Rosaldo, and Firestone, or whether one saw this association as having developed in a historically specific moment like Janeway and Mitchell—it was clear that an analysis of the oppression of women must take account of more than one level of reality. The biological realities of women's lives—specifically, their reproductive capacities—interacted with the psychological and the cultural, that is, the meanings attributed to them. Similarly, the economic roles performed by women interacted with the ideological accounts of these roles. Whether one talked about production and reproduction, or public and private realms, the perpetuation of male power over women was a complex phenomenon. It seemed as though the analysis of the origins of women's oppression presented a kind of chicken-and-egg dilemma. In the dialectic between biology and culture, which came first?

3

Rape and the Male Protection Racket

In her search for the origins of patriarchy, Shulamith Firestone focused upon the biology of reproduction. Childbirth, with its attending physical limitations, seemed to her the major source of women's age-old subordination. But in the realm of biology, there was an alternative hypothesis: this was the theory of rape. In Susan Brownmiller's influential book, *Against Our Will: Men, Women and Rape*, she argued that rape, the act of forcing a woman to have sexual intercourse against her will, was the secret of patriarchy. Both the possibility and the actuality of rape served as the main agent of "the perpetuation of male domination over women by force."[1]

It might seem curious to label the Brownmiller hypothesis a biological one. The description is belied both by the material making up the bulk of the book, and by Brownmiller's own explicit statement of purpose. The account ranged over wide areas of legal history, sociology, and criminology, going back into the furthest reaches of recorded history for the evidence of attitudes toward rape among the first civilizations whose legal codes survive, such as Babylon, and using anthropological evidence for comparative purposes. Brownmiller stated that she gathered this vast array of material on the legal and moral status of rape in order to "give rape its history" (404). "Critical to our study," she wrote, "is the recognition that rape has a history, and that through the tools of historical analysis we may learn what we need to know about our current condition" (12).

Given this approach, one might assume that Brownmiller intended to show rape in its cultural setting, that is, how it had become a weapon against women in the context of attitudes toward women that had developed historically. In large measure this is what she did. Brownmiller suggested that the meaning of rape was connected to the concept of women as property. The legal framework of punishment for rape, as she traced it from the Babylonian code through Hebrew law and into the English common-law tradition, was that punishment for rape was an action brought by one man against another for damage to his property. It was a form of compensation for the loss incurred through a daughter, or a wife, whose value, either for exchange in marriage or as a possession, had been thus reduced or destroyed (16–30).

A comparable account of rape, Brownmiller argued, could be derived from examining it as a "normal" component of warfare. In this context, rape was considered by men to be an inevitable accompaniment of conquest. In the case of war, the "enemy" was to be humiliated by any means necessary. The particular use of rape was for the purpose of showing that the conquered side no longer controlled what had belonged to it: neither land, nor goods, nor women. Brownmiller dissociated herself somewhat from the view that women in war were raped because they were enemy women: "it is in the nature of any institution in which men are set apart from women and given the extra power of the gun that the accruing power may be used against all women, for a female victim of rape in war is chosen *not* because she is a representative of the enemy, but precisely because she is a woman and *therefore* an enemy" (64). But she argued that, like looting, rape in war was a matter of public policy, whether carried out by Nazis, or Allied soldiers in World War II, the conquerors of Bangladesh, or the American soldiers in Vietnam (31–113).

Brownmiller's analysis of rape in legal history and in war, then, presented it as a cultural and social phenomenon, institutionalized in law and custom. But at base, her account rested on a view of rape as a fact of human society neither cultural nor historical but physiological in origin. In her view, the rape by men of women stemmed, in the first instance, from two facts about the evolution of human biology. In the first place, unlike their primate ancestors, human beings did not copulate in response to the female estrous cycle. Mating in monkeys, chimpanzees, and other nonhuman primates was controlled by the female's receptivity to the male, and took place only upon the female's invitation and willingness for it to occur. In humans, the sexual urge had become separated from its connection to reproduction, and could occur all year around. "Without a biologically determined mating season," Brownmiller wrote,

> a human male can evince sexual interest in a human female at any time he pleases, and his psychologic urge is not dependent in the slightest on her biologic readiness or receptivity. What it all boils down to is that the human male can rape. (13)

In the second place, Brownmiller cited the facts of anatomy. Human beings copulated by means of the penis entering the vagina:

> Man's structural capacity to rape and woman's corresponding struc-
> tural vulnerability are as basic to the physiology of both our sexes as
> the primal act of sex itself. Had it not been for this accident of biology,
> an accommodation requiring the locking together of two separate
> parts, penis into vagina, there would be neither copulation nor rape as
> we know it. (13–4).

In Brownmiller's account, the step between the possibility of forced intercourse and the reality of it was imperceptible. Implicit in her argument was
the acknowledgment (and the assumption) of superior muscular force in
men, which permitted them to overpower women, individually and collectively. Implicit also was a notion that the person with superior power would
necessarily use it against a person with inferior power. Brownmiller introduced the notion of the "ideology" of rape, a concept she attributed to
Wilhelm Reich.[2] In this analysis the physical capacity to rape became the
basis of the decision to rape.

> [I]n terms of human anatomy the possibility of forcible intercourse
> incontrovertibly exists. This single factor may have been sufficient to
> have caused the creation of a male ideology of rape. When men
> discovered that they could rape, they proceeded to do it. (14)

By "the ideology of rape," however, Brownmiller meant something
more sweeping and general than her notion of the connection between the
capacity to rape and its use in particular cases on particular women. It was
her contention that once "discovered" by men, rape had been, and continued to be, used as a means to control women, both actually and
potentially, by means of the fear that it inspired. Brownmiller speculated
that, if the first rape in prehistory took place by accident, as part of a battle
over sexual access in which the woman lost, the second rape must have
been planned, probably as a gang rape, with many men against one woman.
In her imagined version of the history of primitive society, the point of this
action was to demonstrate that all women could be thus conquered. As a
result, Brownmiller argued, "rape became . . . man's basic weapon of
force against women, the principal agent of his will and her fear." "Man's
discovery," she wrote,

> that his genitalia could serve as a weapon to generate fear must rank
> as one of the most important discoveries of prehistoric times, along
> with the use of fire and the first crude stone axe. From prehistoric
> times to the present, I believe, rape has played a critical function. It is
> nothing more or less than a conscious process of intimidation by which
> *all men* keep *all women* in a state of fear. (14–15)

Brownmiller's sweeping view of the world history of rape was, of course, highly speculative. But it is arguable that it was no more speculative or ill-founded than some previous writing in what might be termed the "aggression" school of anthropology. In a sense, Brownmiller's interpretation of prehistory was a riposte to the body of work by Robin Fox, Lionel Tiger, and others, which interpreted the persistence of male domination in human society as a genetic inevitability.[3]

The ideology of rape, then, meant the notion that the actions of some men—in modern times, a minority—took place on behalf of all men. In the minds of women, the knowledge of the possibility of rape acted as a powerful form of social control. To keep this knowledge alive, it was not necessary for all men to rape all women. This work could be carried out by only a few men, those whom society called "rapists." Brownmiller reviewed the literature on rape, most of it written by criminologists. She drew particular attention to the work of Menachem Amir, whose extensive study of rapists had produced a "profile," a portrait, of the "average" or typical rapist, as revealed through psychological testing, and the sociological data available about the men covered in his research. To Brownmiller, the significant fact emerging from this work was the finding that, among criminals, in general terms, the convicted rapist was not an abnormal, peculiar, or aberrational type. Both psychologically and sociologically, he was in the middle of the scale, very much in the center of the range of characteristics that psychologists would consider "normal" for members of the "sub-culture of violence."[4] In the light of her hypothesis, this fact was of enormous significance. In real life, the rapist was not a deviant, or an aberrant person, but an ordinary, even a typical man. To be sure, he was a criminal; but the typical rapist, the man whom she called "the police-blotter rapist," was not discernibly different from other criminals, except to the degree that he "acted out" a certain kind of violence against women.

In Brownmiller's view, the criminal activities of this small group of men had a particular social function, hitherto unremarked. "[O]n the shoulders of these unthinking, predictable, insensitive, violence-prone young men," Brownmiller wrote,

> there rests an age-old burden that amounts to an historic mission: the perpetuation of male domination over women by force. . . . Myrmidons to the cause of male dominance, police-blotter rapists have performed their duty well, so well in fact that the true meaning of their act has gone largely unnoticed. Rather than society's aberrants or "spoilers of purity," men who commit rape have served in effect as

front-line masculine shock troops, terrorist guerillas in the longest
sustained battle the world has ever known. (209)

In arguing that rape was a major agency in the social control and
domination of women, Susan Brownmiller was not alone. In a widely read
article, published in 1971, Susan Griffin characterized rape in similar
terms.[5] Griffin called rape "the all-American crime." Rape, she argued,
was a crime carried out by a few men on behalf of many. Griffin outlined
what she took to be the procedure by which most men in the United States
made use of the fear of rape in women. It was, she said, a "male protection
racket." Women alone were vulnerable and liable to be raped. They were
in danger at all times, but especially on the streets at night. Therefore, a
man could argue, a woman needed protection (by him) from every other
man. Thus the need of men in women was reinforced. Each man could
maintain his hold on "his" woman by threatening her with what could be
done to her, in the absence of his protection, by the rest of the men. Each
of these of course could make the same argument to "his" woman. By this
primitive system, the law of the urban jungle, no woman could afford to be
without her "protector." What the system omitted to make explicit, need-
less to say, was that often, a woman's "protector" could become her rapist
as well.

Griffin made the connection between the crime of rape, at home, and the
American crimes being committed abroad against other countries, especially Vietnam. The idea that rape and imperialism had elements in common
was played down in Brownmiller's analysis, which instead made the argument that rape was a symptom of the universal war of men against women.
More than Griffin, Brownmiller stressed the primacy of male enmity
toward women, and, as I have argued, the biological origins of this enmity.
Whatever the variations in their interpretation of the phenomenon,
Brownmiller and other writers on rape were making a crucial point. They
were drawing attention to the role played by rape, and the fear of rape, in
the power that men exerted over women's lives.[6] In so doing, they were
making an interpretation of rape that viewed it, not as deviant or abnormal
behavior, but as normal and even typical. The act of rape, in this view, was
paradigmatic of male attitudes toward women, if not in practice, then at
least in theory. This did not mean that, in a reversal of the dogma of popular
culture that all women wanted to be raped, all men wanted to rape women.
But it did mean that, although rape was performed as an actual act only by
some men, all men in some sense benefited by their actions. To the degree
that they were not active and visible opponents of rape, all men were

therefore complicit in these actions. By extension, then, one could speak of "the pervasive male ideology of rape (the mass psychology of the conqueror)" (324) as Brownmiller did, or even, as the title of a later film put it, of "rape culture." This meant a cultural atmosphere in which the raping of women was taken to be normal, even expected, and in which male attitudes toward women, and those of women toward themselves and other women, were colored by this assumption.[7]

In saying this, Brownmiller and Griffin were of course arguing that rape culture and the ideology of rape were, in fact, not normal, but were socially produced. It took a feminist perspective to argue that this set of attitudes stemmed from a profound contempt for, and fear of, women, and that it was not an inevitable fact of human culture. In this, Brownmiller's position contained its own contradictions. Brownmiller's view of rape, like Firestone's of childbirth, was a form of biological materialism. Biology was the base, culture the superstructure: the facts of human anatomy and physiology had produced, given rise to, certain patterns of ideology and social organization. But in Brownmiller's theory, unlike those of Marx, Engels, and Firestone, a change in society and culture did not have to await a change in the material base—in this case, the structure of human genitals.

Brownmiller's book ended on a positive note. She drew attention to the fact that, as one outcome of the renewal of feminism in the 1970s, women in large numbers were learning techniques of self-defense, were organizing rape crisis centers, and were holding "speak-outs" on rape.[8] Having written her book to give rape its history, she expressed the hope that women could deny rape a future (404). The very optimism of her closing words belied the apparent determinism of her theory. Although she had argued that the ideology of rape stemmed from the biological facts of genital anatomy, Brownmiller believed that it could be changed by means of the social activity of women, through feminist organization. Yet at another level, she was being consistent. Because men could rape women, they would and did. Hence to stop rape, women had to make it impossible, by defending themselves against it.

To the extent that rape expressed the unequal distribution of power between men and women, and the exercise of their extra power by men, the only way to deny rape its future was to increase the power of women to the point where it was equal to that of men. To the extent that women were trained by their upbringing to be victims, women, too, participated in rape culture. If rape was the secret of patriarchy, then women must demystify it, by naming it, describing how it operated, and above all, by fighting it openly, individually and collectively. In this way, women could begin to break the power of men over them, which, in this view, appeared both as the cause and the effect of rape.

The very sweep and scope of Brownmiller's book inevitably raised more questions than it answered. Placing the issue of rape thus squarely on the feminist agenda had a number of implications, some theoretical, and some practical. From the point of view of activists, the legal issue of rape was a major focus for political work. The elements in the law that retained the perspective disclosed by Brownmiller and others had to be isolated, and then changed. Thus the requirement that rape, unlike other crimes involving assault, have witnesses other than the victim, stemmed from the assumption that women were always "asking for it," and embodied in the law a fundamental distrust of woman and their sexuality. Similarly, the usual procedure of questioning a rape victim about her previous sexual activity. The law that exempted husbands from punishment for raping their wives was a remnant of the legal history, traced by Brownmiller, that instituted penalties for rape only because, as she argued, it was an assault on another man's property. A man had, implicitly, the right to do as he liked with his own property. These and other reforms of rape law were sought by feminist activists, with some success.[9]

At the theoretical level, the issue of rape placed radical feminism squarely at odds with other perspectives, specifically, a socialist view of the centrality of class, and a black view of the centrality of race and racism. Brownmiller's account of rape in relation to American racism drew sharp criticism from black women writers for its oversimplification of a complicated history, and its insensitivity to the use of rape charges as a political weapon by the criminal justice system against the black community.[10] The controversy aroused by the early radical feminist discussions of rape in New Left circles is dramatized in Marge Piercy's novel, *Vida,* in a conversation between the heroine, Vida Asch, and her feminist sister, Natalie:

> "My god, Natty, I hope you don't go around saying in your women's group that a Black man raped you! He was probably incredibly oppressed. . . . You want to sound like some Southern-belle racist?"
> "Now, you listen, Davida!" Natalie clutched her hand hard. Her eyes were burning, and she looked close to tears. "I spent as much time getting my ass kicked in civil rights as you did. And I am not a racist! But I'm not going to lie about my experiences anymore. I'm not!"[11]

The experience of rape appeared to cut across class lines and lines of race. It was a form of oppression known to women because of the fact of

being women, no matter what their background or individual circum-
stances. At the time Brownmiller published her book, this was still a
hypothesis. Only further inquiry would show whether or not rape did,
indeed, function as a universal institution that oppressed women
worldwide.[12] But that the question was asked, that it was raised for
discussion in the first place, was the achievement of the women's movement. In particular, it was due to those writers and organizers who first
spoke of rape as an issue for the consideration of social theory, rather than
of criminology, and of the ideology of rape as a phenomenon that needed
explanation, rather than as a natural fact of social life.

4

Consciousness-Raising:
The Personal as Political

Feminist theorists argued that, although the effects of patriarchy were everywhere palpable, they were not necessarily visible to most women. Indeed, one of the features of patriarchy, Kate Millett held, was its very invisibility, its ability to masquerade as the "natural" and inevitable form of social organization.[1] To become aware of the effects of male domination, women had to undergo a process of education, or reconceptualization,[2] known as "consciousness-raising." Developed by radical feminists in the late 1960s, and modeled on a practice used by the revolutionary Chinese called "speaking bitterness," consciousness-raising was a means of sharing reliable information about female experience. As described by Alix Kates Shulman, who participated in the early meetings which elaborated the technique,

> [t]hose early CR sessions were really fact-gathering sessions, research sessions on our feelings. We wanted to get at the truth about how women felt, how we viewed our lives, what was done to us, and how we functioned in the world. Not how we were *supposed* to feel but how we really did feel. This knowledge, gained through honest examination of our own personal experience, we would pool to help us figure out how to change the situation of women.[3]

Once the technique was codified in print and broadly circulated, consciousness-raising became a widespread practice among newly recruited feminists.[4] In this context, consciousness-raising was a way of learning to see and to feel the previously invisible effects of patriarchy. Raising one's consciousness meant heightening one's awareness, becoming attuned to the evidence of male domination to which previously one paid little attention, or ignored altogether. The metaphor evoked the idea of raising or bringing "up" into consciousness things previously known or understood only at the unconscious level. It meant becoming aware, at a conscious level, of things that one knew, but had repressed. The analogy (by implication) was with a Freudian or psychoanalytic model, in which the unconscious was "below" the conscious mind and in which unbearable knowledge or experience was kept unconscious via repression, in order to allow daily life to continue unchanged. To raise one's consciousness, then, was to become aware of knowledge one would have preferred to keep hidden or unconscious, of one's own subordination or oppression as a woman, and the impact that this had on one's life. As de Beauvoir wrote, "one is not born, but rather becomes a woman."[5] By means of consciousness-raising, women learned to see this process in operation. In exchanging information about their lives and experiences, participants threw light upon the cues, expectations, remarks, and reactions that formed, and then reinforced, correctly female, that is, feminine, behavior.

Despite some superficial points of resemblance, consciousness-raising or CR was not a form of group therapy. To be sure it was carried on in small groups, although composed only of women, and the content of the discussion was the personal experience of the participants. But unlike a therapy group, a CR group had no leader or authority figure. At least theoretically, all women in the group were equal participants. Further, the intention governing the sharing of information was radically different. In group therapy, information was exchanged in order to promote the healing of individuals: they could get better, get beyond their "illness," by using the group process on their own behalf. But in CR, the point of sharing information about personal life and personal experience was to connect these into something that could transcend the personal. A crucial function of CR was to enable women to connect the personal with the political. Once shared in a small group with other women, individual pain and suffering appeared in a different light. It could be seen that these were not personal, idiosyncratic problems, but ones which fell into a pattern that, with variations, characterized other women's lives as well. As Juliet Mitchell wrote,

> what they thought was an individual dilemma [was] a social predicament and hence a political problem. The process of transforming the hidden, individual fears of women into a shared awareness of the meaning of them as social problems, the release of anger, anxiety, the struggle of proclaiming the painful and transforming it into the political—this process is *consciousness-raising.*[6]

Jo Freeman and others have written about the history of CR and its significance as a method for developing a feminist awareness in individual women and groups of women.[7] I want to focus here on the process of consciousness-raising as an element in the construction of feminist theory. What were the principles or axioms of consciousness-raising that contribute to a feminist perspective or world view? What did consciousness-raising contribute to a theory of patriarchy? Equally or perhaps more importantly, how did the process of consciousness-raising help women to move, individually and collectively, from a focus on their oppression and their victimization to a concern with their own worth and a sense of their own agency?

A first assumption of consciousness-raising was that what women had to say about the details of their daily lives, about their personal experiences and histories, mattered, it had significance, and above all, it had validity. This meant that the source of authority, of legitimacy and validity, about the lives of women, and the significance of what they experienced was the individual woman herself. Rather than being the objects of study by psychologists and social scientists, women were the experts, the authorities, the sources of knowledge about themselves. This expertise stemmed, to borrow the title of a work of feminist criticism, from "the authority of experience." A woman knew something to be true because she lived through it, and had her own feelings and reactions, rather than the feelings she was supposed to have, or even, that she herself expected to have.[8]

The validity of the knowledge was underscored by the corroboration of the other women in the group. The heart of CR was the discovery that one was not alone, that other women had comparable feelings and experiences. Many of the crucial elements of the new knowledge about women's situation contributed by the women's movement were accumulated through accounts first garnered in consciousness-raising groups.[9] The number of women who had had abortions, when this was illegal and a taboo subject for discussion; the number of women who had been raped, often by people well-known to them and trusted; the number of women who had experienced incest, or sexual molestation, within their families, by fathers, brothers, uncles, or other male relatives; the number of women who had been beaten or otherwise physically abused by their husbands—all of these intimate and "shameful" facts about the lives of individual women, by means of the process of consciousness-raising, and the principles of sharing personal experience, could be seen in a different light. These were not isolated phenomena, illustrating the individual failure of an individual woman within her own family to direct her own life correctly. They were the symptoms of a society-wide structure of power and powerlessness, in which the victimization of women by the men holding the power of official authority, whether husband or public official, was hidden from public view by the mechanism of privatization.

The CR process bridged the gap between the public and the private realms. It was private, in that it took place among a small group of six to twelve women, usually in a place such as a living room or a women's movement office—a private setting. It was private, too, among women, as men were excluded. But it was public, in the sense that it opened up personal secrets: these became knowledge shared with others. Once spoken aloud, women's private experience could become the stuff of public campaigns, and the basis of political organization around the issues thus exposed. In this sense the transition from the personal to the political had two facets. First, the facts of individual oppression came to be perceived as political and social, that is, as the effects of the forces operating in the society at large to perpetuate the subordination of women as a class. Second, these facts could then become elements of political organizing. They could become the substance of the politics of the women's movement.

A further contribution of CR to feminist theory was the notion of the commonality underlying the diversity of women's experience. The individual lives of the women in a consciousness-raising group could vary considerably. Their situation in their family of origin—number of and sex of siblings; their birth order; their age, and the generation that they belonged to; their class—their own and that of their family of origin; their racial and/or ethnic and religious background, and the customs governing the lives of women in that tradition; their history of work experience and education; their sexual history, and their sexual orientation; their relation to marriage and divorce; whether or not they had children—all of these were variables that made for great diversity in the details and nuances of each woman's personal experience. Nonetheless, despite the differences, certain common elements could be discerned, which could be summarized as the variety of effects and consequences stemming from the fact of being a woman and being treated as and considered a woman by others. Thus the experience of CR gave concrete form to the concept of women as a "sex class" (Shulamith Firestone's term). The condition of being female was a defining characteristic, cutting across differences of class, race, and sexual orientation.

In some cases, the process of CR had the effect of bringing women to see and to understand that they belonged to the category "all women" whether they liked it or not. This effect was particularly visible in the case of women with high aspirations for intellectual or professional achievement, women who had made some considerable inroads into a male-dominated profession. These "exceptional" women, like Simone de Beauvoir before her conversion to feminism, thought of themselves as having escaped from the constraints of the female condition. Were they not inevitably told, in what was intended as a compliment from their male colleagues, that they thought "like a man"? The exceptional woman saw herself as being apart from other women, and as superior to them. In a CR group, she learned the falsity of this stance.

The moment of truth, in consciousness-raising, came at the point where the "exceptional woman" understood that to be told, "You think like a man" was to be told, "You are not a 'real' woman," and (simultaneously), "Real women are inferior to men." That this particular mechanism of exclusion had worked on her, psychologically, meant that she had agreed to, acquiesced in, the negative judgment about all women, and that this, by definition, included herself. The self-hatred and self-rejection required of the "exceptional woman" were thus laid bare.

The impact of this experience was a kind of transformation of consciousness, a redefinition of identity, in which a woman's sense of herself became readjusted to fit the new reality that she encountered. To see this mechanism at work upon oneself—to see that the price of acceptance in a male-dominated arena was the rejection of identification with other women, and simultaneously, of one's own sexual identity—was to relinquish the status, in one's mind, of "exceptional." It became clear that this was simply one category of women, one way of dividing women from one another, and from a sense of connection to the group of all women. Thus paradoxically the "exceptional woman" came to see how ordinary, how regular and systematic was the process by which she and her sisters with similar experiences were categorized, and by virtue of this categorization, isolated and controlled.[10]

Finally, the CR group represented a social experiment in microcosm. The mode of relationships within the group was itself a statement of feminist principles, an attempt to put theory into practice. What women tried to develop in the group was a kind of model, or mini-society, that could serve as an alternative and a contrast to the reality experienced by the members in their other activities and roles, from work to marriage to parenting. As Pamela Allen characterized it, it was a "free space," within which women were not subject to the pressures exerted upon them by their daily obligations. The agreement to meet regularly at a set time was the first element in the creation of the space. The preservation of an ongoing group depended upon the establishment of reliability and of trust among the members. The establishment of trust could then be extended to the idea of "sharing" and "opening up," Allen's terms, that is, of beginning to learn how to tell each other and oneself the truth.[11]

Equally important was the concept that, within the group, women could be equals. The techniques of consciousness-raising included provisions intended to overcome inequalities of power among the women in the group, at least insofar as these were expressed by measureable criteria such as time spent in holding the floor. Thus, the convention was that each woman would have a turn to speak, and that she would be allowed to complete her statement without interruption. Similarly, in commenting on someone else's contribution, the attempt was made to avoid invidious comparisons, or to sit in judgment on what had been said. The implication here was that the members of the group were equals, and that no one person's experience had more validity, or more importance, than that of any other member. Other means were developed to achieve similar ends. Some women's groups gave everyone an equal number of chips, or slips of paper. Each time one person spoke, she surrendered one of her chips. When these were used up, that person could no longer contribute to the discussion.[12]

Obviously these structures had their limitations. Creating equal opportunities to speak was not the same as ensuring that these opportunities would be equally distributed, or equally utilized. Nancy Hartsock pointed to some of the difficulties encountered in one group when middle-class and working-class women attempted to work together on an equal basis. Because the terms of debate had been set by the women from a middle-class background, the very differences created by the differentials of education and cultural background ensured that those who were middle-class were free to be articulate, confident, to speak readily, while those who were working-class felt less confident in that company, and were hesitant to express themselves. Thus the inequality of class was replicated in, and could almost be measured by, the time each took to speak and to make herself heard.[13] But one can distinguish between intent and outcome. Clearly the aspiration to create a setting of equality was part of the structure of consciousness-raising, whether or not this goal was actually achieved in a given group.

Overall, then, CR had a double aspect. On the one hand, it examined the means by which women were oppressed. It extended and developed

the analysis of the workings of patriarchy, using data and materials gener-
ated from reports of individual participants' experiences. On the other
hand, and simultaneously, it validated those experiences. It sought to
create a small piece of the world in which that experience of women
mattered, had authority, and was directly useful to other women. The CR
group was therapeutic, in that by encouraging women to "speak bitterness," it helped them to heal some of the wounds inflicted by their
experiences. It was utopian, in that it carved out a space within which the
effects of patriarchy could be remedied. And it opened up new horizons: as
women exchanged information and knowledge, they glimpsed the possibility of seeing positive value and richness in women's experience.

II Developing a Woman-Centered Analysis

Prologue

Despite important divergences in focus and emphasis, the theorists of the second wave examined in part I agreed on one point: female difference was a primary source of women's oppression. For Janeway, Ortner, and Rosaldo, the crucial element in female difference was the association of the female with the domestic sphere, and hence, the exclusion of women from public life. For Firestone, it was the childbearing function of women. For Brownmiller, it was the genital difference that gave men the phallic power to penetrate women. For Mitchell, it was the complex connection of women as a group to the two worlds of production and reproduction. And for Millett, it was sex-role differences that limited and constrained women. But all of these writers dwelt upon the dangers of difference for women. Patriarchy, it seemed, was built upon the exaggeration and the maintenance of women's otherness from men.

The view that women's differences were the source of female oppression led—via a number of paths—to a focus upon those differences and their points of origin. Indeed, the second wave initiated an unprecedented examination of women's experience. Juliet Mitchell had argued that in order to explicate women's estate and condition, it would be necessary to examine it in detail, from a number of different aspects. Her work, and that of Millett, Firestone, and others, legitimized gender as a focus of inquiry. Whether a "class," a caste, or a "minority," women were a generic grouping, unified despite differences of class, race, and nationality by their long experience of oppression.[1] Mitchell's call to research was virtually a blueprint for the new field of Women's Studies, which began to establish itself as an interdisciplinary area of study in a number of colleges and universities in the late 1960s and early 1970s.

The premise of Women's Studies as a discipline was that women's experience was different from that of men, because of their long oppression. One aspect of that oppression was the exclusion of women from universities and from the creation of scholarship. Traditional definitions of knowledge were derived from, and set by, the experience of men. Thus in every discipline, from sociology and psychology to economics and religion, the world of women's knowledge and experience was omitted, and the knowledge transmitted—of necessity partial and distorted—was in fact male knowledge only. Women's Studies, then, focused upon female experience, on the differences found in women.

Consciousness-raising, too, focused the attention of women upon themselves. As Alix Shulman has noted, CR was a process of data collection, a look at women's experience in and of itself. Although CR served to spotlight women's oppression, it also began a process of illuminating and validating women's experience. As women's self-esteem increased, the differences that had appeared defects began to be viewed in a new light, as elements of strength.

Paradoxically, then, the focus on female difference and the examination of that difference gradually led to a change in the terms of debate from those set by de Beauvoir and extended by the early writers of the second wave. One could begin to discern a shift in emphasis to another view, which gained widespread expression at about the middle of the 1970s. Rather than considering women's differences from men as a form of inadequacy and a source of inferiority, this view considered these differences to be a source of pride and of confidence.

Some voices from the early publications of the second wave prefigured such a set of arguments with reference to female sexuality. The discussion of clitoral orgasm by Anne Koedt, Mary Jane Sherfey, and others had laid the groundwork for this view. These writers argued that female sexual capacity was radically different from, and superior to, that of men, pointing especially to women's seemingly infinite capacity for orgasm.[2] In the context of this discussion, it was noted that the original condition of all fetuses was female, and that male genitalia only developed upon the addition of certain hormones.[3] The implication of these arguments was that, in fact, one could begin to consider the possibility that femaleness was normative, while maleness was a deviation.

By the mid-1970s, Gerda Lerner, Adrienne Rich, Susan Griffin, and other feminist writers were referring to the concept of a woman-centered analysis or perspective, that is, the view that female experience ought to be the major focus of study and the source of dominant values for the culture as a whole.[4] Part II examines the development of this perspective. Chapter 5 locates one of its original sources in writing on lesbian feminism by the Radicalesbians, and the development of the critique of heterosexism by Charlotte Bunch and Adrienne Rich. Chapter 6 considers the evolution of feminist psychology in the work of Phyllis Chesler and Jean Baker Miller. Chapter 7 assesses the gynocentric reexamination of the institution of motherhood by Rich. Chapter 8 considers the analysis by Dorothy Dinnerstein, locating the origins of male anger toward women in the female monopoly of childrearing. Chapter 9 analyzes the work of Nancy Chodorow, which extended the discussion of the relation between female mothering and the construction of gender identity. Finally, chapter 10 discusses the critique by Chodorow and Evelyn Fox Keller of the values embodied in masculinity.

5

Lesbianism and the Woman-Identified Woman

The woman-centered perspective drew, in the first instance, upon the theoretical writings of lesbian feminism in the early 1970s. If women as a group were oppressed, then surely among the most oppressed of women were lesbians, whose very invisibility as a group was testimony to the taboo status of their identity.[1] The women's movement of the 1960s and 1970s comprised large numbers of lesbians, who devoted their energy to writing, organizing, and participating in the development of feminist theory and practice. Yet initially there was a strong reluctance to acknowledge their presence, let alone their centrality. The fear of the label "lesbian" among women who sought to establish a powerful and effective force for changing the status of all women was ironic testimony to the power of that label to isolate and to silence those to whom it was applied.[2]

In the controversies that ensued, lesbian theorists argued that lesbianism was much more than a matter of individual sexual preference. It was a political commitment as well. As Jill Johnston wrote,

> [t]he word lesbian has expanded so much through political definition that it should no longer refer exclusively to a woman simply in sexual relation to another woman. . . . The word is now a generic term signifying activism and resistance and the envisioned goal of a woman commited state.[3]

Johnston and others argued that, among women, it was lesbians who were most likely to focus personal attention and energy on women rather than on men. A woman who sought and received validation from other women was not hostage to male approval. If the personal was the political, then the choice to give primacy to a woman in one's personal relationships was of great political significance. Putting women first was a basic organizing principle for an autonomous women's movement.

Further, the argument was made that to accept the attempts by the media to divide and to discredit the women's movement by using the label of "lesbian" was to betray the essence of the feminist project. The impact of this "sexual McCarthyism" was to lose sight of what the women's movement shared with the movement for gay liberation. Both had a common goal: "a society free from defining and categorizing people by virtue of gender and/or sexual preference. . . . A woman is called a Lesbian when she functions autonomously. Women's autonomy is what Women's Liberation is all about."[4]

The philosopher Ti-Grace Atkinson carried this point further. Atkinson drew an analogy between the second wave of the women's movement and the American labor movement during the early years of the twentieth century.[5] During one of the periods of its greatest militancy, the labor movement had been accused of harboring Communists, and of espousing Communist, that is, radical social ideas. Among many influential labor leaders, the response to this accusation was to refute it by purging from the ranks of labor unions those militants suspected of Communist sympathies. Faced with a barrage of "red-baiting," the leaders chose to accept, implicitly, the legitimacy of these accusations. They agreed to get rid of those considered to be the offenders—often the most radical and militant among the union members—and thereby to prove that those who remained were acceptable and loyal to the powers that be. As a result, Atkinson wrote, not only was the American labor movement badly split and weakened: the loss of its most militant members meant that the policies of the labor movement would be set thereafter by the political beliefs of the leaders who remained. That is, they would become reformist, destined to accommodate themselves to the political and economic status quo. Thus the expulsion of Communists, as a response to "red-baiting," had the effect of taming the labor movement, keeping it from becoming politically militant, not to speak of revolutionary.

As "Communism" was to the labor movement, said Ti-Grace Atkinson, so "lesbianism" was to the women's movement. The practice of "lesbian-baiting" was designed to contain the women's movement, very much as "red-baiting" had been designed to tame the labor movement. The form that this took was the accusation that all women concerned with women's liberation were lesbians. If women who considered themselves to be "straight," that is, heterosexual, were to dissociate themselves from lesbians and lesbianism, to deny the accusation, they would be in effect consenting to a split in the women's movement. At the same time, if they agreed to "purge" lesbians from the women's movement, and to insist on its heterosexual character, they would be acquiescing in a concept of the women's movement that was basically reformist, rather than radical, and that, like the labor movement that preceded it, could be easily accommodated within the status quo.

Atkinson was thus taking the position that an acceptance of the lesbian perspective was not just a matter of defending civil liberties, or even freedom of sexual expression. It was a crucial element in the development of a complete feminist theory. Her argument was based on an axiom from the sociology of knowledge. What lesbians could imagine for women grew out of their situation of marginality and difference. In a way she was turning the argument of women's liberation upon itself. If the perspective of women on society differed radically from that of men, then by the same token, the perspective of a lesbian differed from that of a straight woman, or even a straight feminist.

Atkinson saw lesbians as the radicals—the extreme left—of the feminist movement. By virtue of their lack of sexual ties to men, and therefore, of their freedom from conventional heterosexual commitments, especially marriage, lesbians were placed sociologically in a situation of great freedom. Because of their sexual and social choices, they rejected the stereotypes about women. Thus they could think radically and profoundly about the possibility of social change with reference to gender arrangements. But if the heterosexual majority of the women's movement allowed itself to be intimidated by the accusation of lesbianism, and therefore rejected both lesbians and their social perspective, then the movement itself would be crippled by this action. It would be forced to accept compromise. The goal of total liberation for all women would never be attained.

It was important to see, then, that the tactic of lesbian-baiting was dangerous to the women's movement. It was a strategy of divide and conquer. On the individual level, as well, the accusation of lesbianism was used to keep women from moving toward a feminist analysis. As the Radicalesbians wrote,

> [l]esbian is the word, the label, the condition that holds women in line. When a woman hears this word tossed her way, she knows . . . that she has crossed the terrible boundary of her sex role. . . . Lesbian is a label invented by the Man to throw at any woman who dares to be his equal, who dares to challenge his prerogatives . . . , who dares to assert the primacy of her own needs.[6]

The negative connotations of the label lesbian could thus be understood politically—as yet another means of establishing effective social control over women. But the Radicalesbians argued that the word also contained a positive connotation. In their view, a lesbian was a model for any woman seeking her freedom. "What is a lesbian?" they asked rhetorically. She is

> the rage of all women condensed to the point of explosion. She is the woman who, often beginning at an extremely early age, acts in accordance with her inner compulsion to be a more complete and freer human being than her society . . . cares to allow her. . . . She may not be fully conscious of the political implications of what for her began as personal necessity, but on some level she has not been able to accept the limitations and oppression laid on her by the most basic role of her society—the female role.[7]

In other words, a lesbian was someone who had withdrawn herself from the conventional definitions of femininity. She had refused to buy into the limitations and restrictions placed upon her by the social expectations of acting like a "true woman."

What then was a "true woman?" The Radicalesbians argued that she was someone who accepted and internalized the view of herself dictated by male society and culture. The "true woman" was consigned "to sexual and family functions," and was excluded from "defining and shaping the terms of" her own life. The bargain made by women, in agreeing to stay within what was fundamentally a limiting and subservient position in life, was that they, in turn, received a stamp of approval, of legitimacy, from the men to whom they agreed to be subordinated:

> In exchange for our psychic servicing and for performing society's non-profitmaking functions, the man confers on us just one thing: the slave status which makes us legitimate in the eyes of the society in which we live. This is called "femininity" or "being a real woman" in our cultural lingo. (244)

In other words, a true or authentic woman was a woman who committed herself to a man for the sake of receiving, not only his name, but the legitimacy conferred in the reflection of his power, his status, and his accomplishments, by virtue of becoming an extension of him. She was "authentic, legitimate, real to the extent that" she was "the property of some man" whose name she bore. By this definition, the "true woman" was male-identified. That is, she identified herself "with the oppressor, living through him, gaining status and identity from his ego, his power, his accomplishments" (244).

The "true woman" concealed from herself the real truth about her own existence. Beneath the facade of male-derived identity, the Radicalesbians argued, there lay "an enormous reservoir of self-hate." If her entire validity as a person derived from the man to whom she was attached, then she was nothing, in and of herself. Her own value was entirely derived from his. Therefore, she alone had no value, was worthless. The proof of this was the status of the woman without a male source of identity: "[t]o be a woman who belongs to no man is to be invisible, pathetic, inauthentic, unreal." The identification with the male served to conceal this self-knowledge, or at least, to keep it hidden "beneath the edge of . . . consciousness. . . ."

This is why, the analysis continued, most women would resist a direct relationship with other women. To confront another woman directly meant to encounter, as in a mirror, the reality of one's own true self.

> Women resist relating on all levels to other women who will reflect their own oppression, their own secondary status, their own self-hate. For to confront another woman is finally to confront one's self—the self we have gone to such lengths to avoid. And in that mirror we know we cannot really respect and love that which we have been made to be. (244)

The Radicalesbians argued that women could not let the situation continue in which they depended, for their validity, upon the approval and the legitimation of men. This, they pointed out, was not necessarily a prescription for all women to end their emotional attachment to men and become lesbians in their personal lives. "[W]hat is crucial," they held,

> is that women begin disengaging from male-defined response patterns. In the privacy of our own psyches, we must cut those cords to the core. For irrespective of where our love and sexual energies flow, if we are male-identified in our heads, we cannot realize our autonomy as human beings. (243–44)

This, then, was the lesson taught by lesbianism to other women. Because of their sexual orientation, lesbian women were free to seek emotional and psychological sustenance from women rather than from men. But in addition, by being connected primarily to women, they escaped from, and indeed, renounced, the definition of "woman" as secondary, derivative, or second-best to men. That is, they accorded to one another that primacy and importance that most women accorded only to men. "Until women see in each other the possibility of a primal commitment which includes sexual love," the Radicalesbians argued, "they will be denying themselves the love and value they readily accord to men, thus affirming their second-class status" (243).

The belief in the primacy of women was the source of a new sense of female validity. And this, in turn, grew out of the encounter with other women. In dialectical fashion, the confrontation with women—the look into the mirror—which evoked the realization of women's degradation, was at the same time, the source of its remedy. As its first result, the encounter with other women produced the realization of how devalued women were, and how brutalizing was the attitude of self-rejection that was developed in women as a result of their socialization as female. But as its second result, the encounter raised the possibility of a new definition of female identity.

"Only women," the Radicalesbians wrote, "can give to each other a new sense of self. That identity we have to develop with reference to ourselves, and not in relation to men" (245). The connection of women with one another began a healing process in which one could overcome the self-hatred inherited from a male-identified self-definition, and build a new sense of one's value as a woman. The alienation and lack of authenticity, the sense of lacking reality and substance, that the Radicalesbians diagnosed as the symptoms of the "real woman," could be diminished, and in their place a reconstructed definition of womanhood could be created, that of the "woman-identified woman." In a lyrical passage, the Radicalesbians described this process of healing and transcendence.

> Together we must find, reinforce, and validate our authentic selves. As we do this, we confirm in each other that struggling, incipient sense of pride and strength, the divisive barriers begin to melt, we feel this growing solidarity with our sisters. We see ourselves as prime, find our centers inside of ourselves. We find receding the sense of alienation, of being cut off, of being behind a locked window, of being unable to get out what we know is inside. We feel a real-ness, feel at last we are coinciding with ourselves. (245)

The concept of the primacy of women, their importance, their position as the primary focus of attention and commitment what was the Radicalesbians considered to be the core of feminism. "It is the primacy of women relating to women, of women creating a new consciousness of and with each other, which is at the heart of women's liberation. . . ." The new identity, that of woman-identified woman, was to be the source of revolutionary change. "This consciousness," they wrote, "is the revolutionary force from which all else must follow . . ." (245). In this sense, then, all feminists had to learn to be woman-identified, whether or not they chose to express this commitment sexually. Psychologically, both straight women and lesbians needed to make the transition to the notion of the primacy of women, and of women's connections to one another.

Lesbianism, then, was not merely about sexual connections among some women. It was a source of an alternative model for female identity. Some argued, however, that the significance of lesbianism for feminist theory went further than issues of psychological self-definition. Charlotte Bunch explained that a lesbian feminist perspective was persistently misunderstood in the feminist community. "[M]ost feminists" she wrote, "still view lesbianism as a personal decision, or, at best, as a civil rights concern or a cultural phenomenon." To be sure, discrimination against lesbians was "real," and the struggle against it was important. Similarly, lesbianism was a major element in the creation of women's culture. But above all, it was a theoretical position. "Lesbian feminist politics is a political critique of the institution and ideology of heterosexuality as a cornerstone of male supremacy. It is an extension of the analysis of sexual politics to an analysis of sexuality itself as an institution."[8]

Heterosexuality was simply defined: it meant "men first." "[E]very woman is defined by and is the property of men," with a right to "her body, her services, her children. . . ." Those who questioned this definition of the world were "queer," no matter who they slept with. The definition of women as secondary, as marginal, was basic to their location in the workplace, and in the household:

> The original imperialist assumption of the right of men to the bodies and services of women has been translated into a whole variety of forms of domination throughout this society. And as long as people accept that initial assumption—and question everything *but* that assumption—it is impossible to challenge the other forms of domination. (69–70)

Because of their marginality, and because of their renunciation of "heterosexual privilege," lesbian women were exposed to the realities of what that privilege procured for women in the way of protection and safety. The perception therefore of the operations of heterosexuality as an institution was therefore more apparent to lesbians, "not," Bunch wrote, "because we are more moral, but because our reality is different—and it is a *materially* different reality" (71). A feminist analysis, then, in Charlotte Bunch's view, needed to incorporate the insights into women's oppression afforded by lesbian experience; in particular, it required an understanding of the way in which heterosexuality supported male domination.

In an elaboration of this point, Adrienne Rich charged feminist theorists with the responsibility of looking as carefully at heterosexuality as they did at motherhood, the family, and other social institutions.[9] "[T]he failure to examine heterosexuality as an institution," Rich wrote, "is like failing to admit that the economic system called capitalism or the caste system of racism is maintained by a variety of forces, including both physical violence and false consciousness."[10] Despite their best efforts, she wrote, many feminist analyses were weakened by a failure to treat heterosexuality as a political institution, and to ask the question of what forces imposed this on women.

Rich posited a fundamental attachment of women to women, possibly born out of an infantile connection to the mother, early source of "emotional caring and physical nurture for both female and male children. . . ." If the "search" for "tenderness" by both men and women originally turned to women, one would have to raise the question of *"why in fact women would ever redirect that search . . ."* (637), and of what "societal forces" could "wrench women's emotional and erotic energies away from themselves and other women and from woman-identified values" (637–8).

To answer the question, Rich proposed a concept of "compulsory heterosexuality." She argued that a heterosexual preference was inculcated and then enforced in women by a variety of mechanisms, all of them serving to reinforce male power. A range of means, from rape, sexual slavery, and physical violence to the ideology of romantic love served to enforce heterosexuality "for women as a means of assuring male right of physical, economical, and emotional access" (647). One crucial means, she argued, was the continued "invisibility or marginality" of lesbian existence (647).

Rich expanded the definition of lesbianism to refer, on the one hand, to lesbian experience—the historical and contemporary existence of lesbians—and on the other to what she termed the "lesbian continuum," that is,

> a range—through each woman's life and throughout history—of woman-identified experience; not simply the fact that a woman has had or consciously desired genital sexual experience with another woman . . .[but also] many more forms of primary intensity between and among women. . . . (648)

In the latter meaning, Rich argued, one could uncover a rich history of women, from the women's school of Sappho in the seventh century B.C. and the Beguines of the Middle Ages to the economic and social sororities among African women and the Chinese "marriage resistance sisterhoods" prior to the revolution. All of these women could be seen as proto-feminist, and their histories as instances and forms of resistance to male power.

"If we consider the possibility," Rich wrote,

> that all women—from the infant suckling her mother's breast, to the grown woman experiencing orgasmic sensations while suckling her own child, perhaps recalling her mother's milk-smell in her own; to two women, like Virginia Woolf's Chloe and Olivia, who share a laboratory; to the woman dying at ninety, touched and handled by women—exist on a lesbian continuum, we can see ourselves as moving in and out of this continuum, whether we identify ourselves as lesbian or not. (650–51)

Such a redefinition would render the concept of lesbianism a part of normal female experience, and heterosexuality would thus come to be seen, not as normal and inevitable, but as a system imposed upon women, out of the fear by men of their loss of women. What men most dreaded, Rich wrote, was not women's sexuality or their maternal power, but "that women could be indifferent to them altogether, that men could be allowed sexual and emotional—therefore economic—access to women *only* on women's terms, otherwise being left on the periphery of the matrix" (643). Rich called upon "heterosexually identified feminists" to have the "special quality of courage" to "do the intellectual and emotional work" of looking at heterosexuality as, not a "preference," but "something that has had to be imposed, managed, organized, propagandized, and maintained by force . . ." (648).

Rich's redefinition of lesbianism was controversial. Some lesbians might feel that in her attempt to be all-inclusive of women, she was minimizing or overlooking the particular requirements of courage and the specific kinds of anguish experienced by lesbian women (in cases of child custody, for example) that straight women could avoid. In addition, her implicit hypothesis of universal, if suppressed, lesbianism among all women throughout history might strain the credulity of even the most earnest of "heterosexually identified feminists," including this writer.[11] But certainly Rich's conclusion made sense: until the full reality of lesbian experience was made an explicit part of history and common discourse, women, in the absence of choice, would have "no collective power to determine the meaning and place of sexuality in their lives" (659).

The process of consciousness-raising was based on the assumption that women's experience was a legitimate source of knowledge. Ignored, trivialized, or suppressed by a male-dominated society and culture, it was now being explored and developed as a crucial source of feminist theory.[12]

The articulation of lesbian consciousness carried this process one step further. The concept of the woman-identified woman gave weight to relations among women, and to female experience, unmediated by male definitions and male control. In this sense, a lesbian perspective was crucial to the development of a woman-centered analysis.

6

Androgyny and the
Psychology of Women

If lesbian feminism was one source of the woman-centered perspective, another was the debate over the psychology of women. An early focus of contemporary feminist thought was the psychological damage done to women by the system of sex-role stereotyping. Their traditional role prescribed a character structure and a set of values for women that evoked contempt from men toward women, and from women toward themselves. The condition of being subordinated by and to men had turned women into an inferior "species." Women had fulfilled their role expectations all too successfully. As a result, they were genuinely ill-fitted for equality with men. By a kind of self-fulfilling prophecy, women had become the poor creatures that men thought they were.

An influential exponent of this point of view was the psychologist Phyllis Chesler. In *Women and Madness,* she documented the results, among women, of the social process of conditioning for appropriate sex-role behavior.[1] Chesler took the argument from sex roles to its logical conclusion. Millett, Janeway, Naomi Weisstein, and others had pointed out that, in the division of characteristics that governed sex-role stereotyping, women had received the worst of the deal. In establishing such a rigid difference between "male" and "female," society appeared to have allocated to "female" all of the qualities that males thought were undesirable.[2] If the evidence from the practice of psychoanalysts was to be credited, it appeared that expectations for normal behavior in males—for so-called "masculinity"—were the same as expectations for normal behavior in human beings generally. But expectations for normal behavior in females—for so-called "femininity"—if abstracted from their connection to women, were in fact expectations for abnormal or nonfunctioning human beings.[3] In other words, if a man acted like a woman (or, more precisely, in the manner expected of a woman), he would be adjudged to be sick or disturbed, and would be treated accordingly. But if a woman acted like a woman, this identical behavior in her case would be adjudged to be "normal" and as expected.

What, then, was society saying about women? It was saying, said Chesler, that women were supposed to be sick. For women, sickness—and specifically, mental illness—was an expected condition, part of the definition of what and how women were. To conform to the stereotype of "womanly" or "feminine" meant to display those characteristics that distinguished women from men. It meant, therefore, behavior that was passive or weak, compliant, and indecisive. It meant being easily moved to tears ("hysterical"), susceptible to suggestion from others, easily led or persuaded. It meant being nonaggressive and noncompetitive, and dependent, in need of direction, as well as companionship and affection. In short, women were meant to be inadequate, self-doubting, and essentially incapable of a strong, independent, and autonomous existence. The sex-role stereotype for women, Chesler maintained, was a prescription for failure, for victimization, and in extreme cases, for severe mental illness.

What about the woman who refused to conform to the social and familial expectations that she encountered, who declined to become "feminine"? Chesler argued that the rebellious woman—whether lesbian or straight—was likely to be caught in the worst kind of no-win situation, a kind of "Catch-22." Society, and society's representatives and guardians, the members of the psychological profession, would punish such a woman severely for her failure to conform. They would label her "deviant," abnormal or mentally ill, and would attempt to bring her back to the kind of behavior and attitudes deemed suitable for women. Thus a lesbian woman would find her psychologist attempting to "cure" her of her sexual preference for women and persuade her to learn how to "need" men. Similarly, a straight woman with ambitions for a career in a male-dominated profession would find her therapist arguing that she should learn to give up her abnormally high rate of aspirations and learn to become a good wife. Thus, to be a "normal" woman was to be sick or mad, and to be an "abnormal" woman was to be called, and treated as, sick or mad. Often, Chesler argued, these kinds of reactions could in fact drive rebellious women mad, that is, back to normality for women, which, she said, was inevitably madness.[4]

What, then, was the way out for women? How could they emerge from the cultural and psychological trap set for them by the prescribed feminine role? What less damaging alternatives for women could be imagined? Consciousness-raising, to be sure, was a first step: becoming aware of the limits and dangers of femininity, both as an individual psychological state, and as a wider social phenomenon, was a prerequisite for change. But where did women go from there?

One suggestion, much debated among feminists, feminist-influenced academics, and popularizers of feminism in the early 1970s was a return to the ancient concept of androgyny. Carolyn Heilbrun argued that, in Western literature and mythology, there was a long-standing tradition defining the human as combining the best qualities of men and women. The exaggerated and polarized traits of conventional masculinity and femininity that characterized modern culture could be replaced with a balanced vision drawing on the best of each. Androgyny, an

> ancient Greek word—from *andro* (male) and *gyn* (female)— . . .
> seeks to liberate the individual from the confines of the appro-
> priate. . . . [It] suggests . . . a full range of experience open to
> individuals who may, as women, be aggressive, as men, tender; it
> suggests a spectrum upon which human beings choose their places
> without regard to propriety or custom.[5]

While Heilbrun traced the path of the "hidden river" of androgyny through the Western tradition from Plato to Virginia Woolf, others turned their attention to institutionalizing the concept in the practice of contemporary psychology. As Phyllis Chesler and others had noted, psychology made radical distinctions between expectations for males and females. These expectations were enshrined in personality tests, used widely to judge the "normality" or "abnormality" of a given subject. Standardized separate sets of criteria were used to check for normality in males and females, respectively. Sandra Bem designed what she termed an "androgynous" test, one that would blend the traits usually allocated to "masculine" and "feminine" subjects into a series of traits that were both crucial to the mental health of any individual, male or female. On her new androgynous personality scale, the Bem Sex-Role Inventory (BSRI), the most healthy and well-adjusted subjects, male or female, registered the most extensive and complete range of traits traditionally considered "normal" for male and female. That is, the well-adjusted, androgynous person registered on the scale as possessing the full range of so-called female qualities—nurturance, compassion, tenderness, sensitivity, affiliativeness, cooperativeness—along with the full range of so-called masculine qualities—aggressiveness, leadership, initiative, competitiveness—all at the same time. Bem reported that it was the brightest and most accomplished people (using other criteria such as intelligence testing and educational achievement) who measured as most androgynous, that is, as least reflective of traditional male or female sex-role stereotypes.[6]

In the thinking of Bem and like-minded psychologists, the problems created by sex-role stereotyping—what Heilbrun called "the macho-sex-kitten dichotomy, the inevitable quarterback-cheerleader assignment of life's roles"[7]—could be eliminated by means of the concept of androgyny. In a new "psychology of androgyny," sex-role stereotypes would be set aside. Alternative criteria of mental health would separate sex from gender once and for all. In this new world maleness and femaleness would be experienced as elements of one's physical awareness—one would be conscious of inhabiting a body supplied with the biological capacities and characteristics of male or female—but in no other way. In Bem's view,

> a healthy sense of maleness or femaleness involves little more than being able to look into the mirror and to be perfectly comfortable with the body that one sees there. . . . But beyond being comfortable with one's body, one's gender need have no other influence on one's behavior or life style.[8]

In Bem's analysis, the problem that had so troubled Shulamith Firestone—that of the biological capacity of women to bear children—became a nonproblem. Once "all people" had become "psychologically androgynous," the relationship of women to child-bearing would be a simple matter of free choice: "although I would suggest that a woman ought to feel comfortable about the fact that she can bear children if she wants to, this does not imply that she ought to want to bear children, nor that she ought to stay home with any children that she does bear."[9] Presumably, under the regime of androgyny, any problems of childcare could be solved by tapping men's newly developed nurturant instincts.

Popularized versions of the androgyny model received widespread attention and a good deal of apparent acceptance. Media interpretations such as Marlo Thomas's *Free to Be . . . You and Me,* in book, record, and film form, with Roosevelt Grier giving the example of a symbolic black football hero not embarrassed about crying, and the children's book about a gender-free child named "X," about whom no one could form rigid gender-expectations, helped to publicize the concept.[10] Adrienne Rich remarked that "[a]ndrogyny has recently become a "good" word (like "motherhood" itself!) implying many things to many people, from bisexuality to a vague freedom from imposed sexual roles."[11]

On one level, androgyny was a solution to the problem of sex-role stereotyping. Logically speaking, there was a certain inevitability in the progression from the analysis of sex-role stereotypes to the endorsement of psychological androgyny. If the problems encountered by women stemmed primarily from their allocation to a limiting feminine sex role, then the abolition of sex-role stereotyping was a plausible solution. If the major element in the oppression of women was the enforcement of their differences from men, that is, the exaggeration of femininity as different from or other than masculinity, then it made sense to argue for the psychological homogenization of the two sexes.

Critics of androgyny among feminists, however, queried just how radical a model it was, in the form presented by Heilbrun, Bem, and others. Some noted that, while masquerading as a progressive concept, it still contained a reactionary core, in that it enshrined, and perpetuated, the association of certain traits with women and others with men. The androgynous ideal hoped to put back together that which had been split asunder by culture, like the beings in the Platonic myth, who, cut in half and severed from their mates, wandered the world seeking to be reunited and become once again a complete human being. But in this idealized reunification of what should never have been artificially separated, the androgynous ideal remained a static concept, in which traditional notions of the masculine and the feminine were simply stitched back together, in a "split-level hybrid or integration model. . . ."[12] Catharine Stimpson pointed out that "the androgyne still fundamentally thinks in terms of 'feminine' and 'masculine.' It fails to conceptualize the world and to organize phenomena in a new way that leaves 'feminine' and 'masculine' behind."[13]

In fact, the concept of psychological androgyny had a certain congruency, on the psychic level, with the demands of bourgeois feminism on the economic level. Feminist activists were fighting for the abolition of sex-linked job qualifications, and for the right of women to have access to all areas of the paid workforce. As Janeway, Millett, and others had pointed out, distinctions about women's capacities in the workforce were often linked to the allegedly intrinsic differences between women and men, which had been used to keep women out of male-dominated jobs. If women wished to have the full range of work opened to them, one way to accomplish this was to show that women had or could develop all of the important "male" characteristics demanded by employers.

Psychological androgyny meant that women, like men, could exercise hitherto masculine qualities: they could be "aggressive, ambitious, analytical, assertive, athletic, competitive, . . . dominant, forceful, . . . self-reliant, . . . willing to take risks. . . ."[14] Of course, proponents of androgyny pointed out the value of males acquiring the "feminine" values, as well, such as being "affectionate, cheerful, childlike, compassionate, . . .

flatterable, gentle, gullible, . . . sensitive to the needs of others, . . . understanding, warm, yielding."[15] But these qualities tended to have less of a market value. The impact of the androgynous ideal in the capitalist marketplace appeared to be the demonstration that, in the competition for access to all areas of work, in particular, in the competition for access to positions of power, leadership, and authority, women were as good as men. That men could be as good as women did not, in this context, appear to be an important consideration.

In fact, the argument that, by means of psychological androgyny, women could be or become as good as men assumed that, in itself, the socialization of men left nothing to be desired. To be sure, according to the androgynous ideal, men were to learn to develop those parts of themselves left under-developed in their socialization as men. They were to learn, like Rosie Grier, to cry, to express their pent up feelings, and they were to legitimize their nurturing instincts. But the suggestion was that these traits would be added on, as a welcome addition to or enrichment of the male character. The BSRI revealed no critique of male characteristics. Indeed, the an-drogynous concept embodied an uncritical vision of maleness and of mascu-linity: the qualities of aggression, competitiveness, leadership, and so on were taken to be good in themselves, and therefore important for all people to acquire.

Above all, the androgynous ideal appeared to ignore or to gloss over issues of power. It held out a promise of social change via individual psychological transformation. There was no room in the androgyny con-cept for market forces or other material factors. And there certainly was little or no acknowledgment of the political dimension of relations between women and men. As Janice Raymond wrote, "the language and imagery of androgyny is the language of dominance and servitude combined. One would not put master and slave language or imagery together to define a free person."[16] As with much of the academic literature on sex roles, the fundamental feminist critique of male dominance over women tended to disappear from the debate. Jean Baker Miller remarked that combining aspects of maleness and femaleness might appear to be an appealing conceit. But "[t]he idea remains a fanciful notion unless we ask seriously who really runs the world. . . ."[17]

Instead of androgyny, Miller, a psychoanalyst, proposed an alternative: a new psychology of women.[18] Miller began with the feminist premise that women had been what she called "subordinates," and men "dominants," and that this arrangement had only come into question in recent times. But, she asked, what if one chose to regard women's historic oppression as a potential source of strength and power for women? Miller proposed to think about the victimization of women dialectically (although she did not use this term). She sought to examine not only what had been done to women by virtue of their subordination to men, but also, what women had become, and made of themselves, in response to this condition. Was it possible that the attribution to women by men of certain psychological characteristics had not been an entirely negative phenomenon, needing to be remedied by the "adding-on" of "masculine" characteristics, but rather that this process had had positive, life-enhancing effects as well? Were there aspects of woman's condition that had some intrinsic psychological and social value?

In Miller's analysis, the historic subordination of women was a fundamental underpinning of Western civilization. Freud had maintained that civilization was built upon the repression of sexuality. In Miller's elaboration of Freud, the male "dominants" had repressed not only sexuality, but that group with whom they associated, and onto whom they projected the idea of sexuality, namely, women. In all societies, she argued, those who held the dominant position determined what aspects of life and culture had the most importance and the greatest value, and then took charge of those aspects for themselves. The other aspects, those deemed to be of lower value or of lesser importance, or those that the dominants wished to be relieved of, to keep buried and out of sight, would be assigned to the subordinates. In Western culture, the ruling groups valued and kept for themselves intellectual and managerial functions, and above all, abilities "related to 'managing' and overcoming the perceived hazards of the physical environment." The aspects that the dominants would assign to subordinates would be those that were "perceived as uncontrollable or as evidence of weakness and helplessness." These would include sexuality; "the realm of 'object relations,'" that is, intense interpersonal relationships; and things associated with the physical and bodily functions, generally. All of these aspects of human experience, Miller held, had been relegated to subordinates, and specifically, to women. Thus "women . . . [became] the 'carriers' for society of certain aspects of the total human experience . . ." (22–23).

Psychoanalysis itself, Miller suggested, had only become necessary because of this act of dissociation and repression by the dominant male culture. That is, the division of labor which resulted in the assignment of these realms to women, themselves subordinated in the culture as a whole, made it necessary to create a special science to dredge up that which had been so repressed and buried among the male dominants.

> It seems possible that Freud had to discover the very specialized
> technique of psychoanalysis because there were crucial parts of the
> human experience that were not well provided for in fully acceptable
> and socially open ways within the culture of the dominant group. That
> is, they were not well provided for by the dominants *for* the dominants
> *themselves.* (22)

Thus, in Miller's view, the things "assigned" to women were human skills
crucial to the functioning of a healthy human society. These had been in
some sense cast off by men, and relegated to women. At the same time,
these necessary qualities were devalued, as "women's" and therefore
inferior. This process distorted the human realities, according to a system
of values that governed a very distorted culture.

Miller's analysis led to a reinterpretation, for example, of the conventional division between "rational" and "emotional" faculties. Men cultivated rationality, and attempted to diminish their vulnerability to emotions.
Women, on the other hand, were encouraged to be attuned to emotions,
especially those of others. As she put it, "[m]en are encouraged from early
life to be active and rational; women are trained to be involved with
emotions and with the feelings occurring in the course of all activity" (39).
Women learned their emotional skills at least to some degree as a result of
their subordination.

> Most women do have a much greater sense of the emotional compo-
> nents of all human activity than most men. This is, in part, a result of
> their training as subordinates; for anyone in a subordinate position
> must learn to be attuned to the vicissitudes of mood, pleasure, and
> displeasure of the dominant group. Black writers have made this point
> very clearly. (38)

But in Miller's view the devaluing of emotions was a serious cultural error.
The skills often dismissed as "womanly intuition" or "womanly wiles," she
argued, were in fact evidence of women's possessing "a basic ability that is
very valuable. It can hardly be denied that emotions are essential aspects
of human life" (39).

In Miller's concept, the contemporary psychological condition of women
pointed in two directions. She grouped some of the capacities and characteristics currently *"more highly developed in women as a group"* (27) in a
chapter labeled "Strengths," even though she pointed out that those
characteristics had traditionally been called "weaknesses." Specifically,
women's ability to express vulnerability, weakness, and helplessness;
their capacity to experience, express, and interpret emotions; their capac-

ity to cultivate cooperativeness, and to encourage coordination and working together, especially in the family—all of these, said Miller, were "two-sided" qualities.

> *In a situation of inequality and powerlessness, these characteristics can lead to subservience and to complex psychological problems. . . . On the other hand, the dialogue is always with the future. These same characteristics represent potentials that can provide a new framework, one which would have to be inevitably different from that of the dominant male society. (27)*

In a society that was differently organized, Miller was suggesting, the very facts about women's psychology that had been treated as aspects of their inferiority could become the building blocks of a new and more humane culture.

Miller's view of the way out for women was, then, rather different from that proposed by the androgynous ideal. She was not proposing some kind of amalgam of "masculine" and "feminine" to create a new, "whole" personality that could be comfortably inhabited by men and women alike. Rather, she was suggesting that in the creation of the new woman—the woman produced by feminism—the crucial ingredients would come from the traditional strengths of women developed during the long period of their subordination. She believed that what women had learned in subordination would be the "psychic starting point" for "an entirely different (and more advanced) approach to living and functioning—very different, that is, from the approach fostered by the dominant culture" (83).[19] Thus, for Miller, women were *not* in need of being "cured" of their disabilities as developed under the debilitating impact of a male-dominated culture. Rather, the culture itself was desperately in need of those qualities that it had foolishly relegated only to women.

On one level, Miller's view of the damage done to women was not that different from that of Phyllis Chesler. She acknowledged the pain and the difficulty that women encountered in attempting to fill their traditional roles of wife and mother, as well as the fears and terrors experienced by the women who were attempting to step out of these roles into a new sense of self-definition and self-concept. Where she differed from Chesler was in the weight and importance that she attributed to the strengths of women, in the struggle for self-determination that they were undertaking under the influence of feminist ideas. In these traditional qualities of women, Miller saw the seeds of a new set of social values. The goal for women, she argued, should by no means be to learn to act like, think like, and adopt the values of, men and the male-dominant culture. Rather, concepts such as autonomy, power, authenticity, self-determination—all of these should be reexamined and redefined by women, in order to incorporate within them some of the features of their "old" strengths while acquiring new ones. In the new psychology of women envisioned by Miller, some of the dichotomies decreed by male culture, and the traditional psychology it had produced—aggressiveness versus passivity; leadership, independence, and autonomy versus affiliativeness; power versus powerlessness—could be dissolved or transcended. Thus, for example, the concept of autonomy as it had been developed to apply to men was, she argued, inappropriate for women.

> [A] word like *autonomy*, which many of us have used and liked, may need revamping for women. It carries the implication—and for women therefore the threat—that one should be able to pay the price of giving up affiliations in order to become a separate and self-directed individual. (94)

Being autonomous, for men, usually meant the enhancement, rather than the sacrifice, of relationships, while for women it could in fact mean the opposite, given the usual reluctance of most men to tolerate a self-directed woman in intimate relationship. But, in addition, Miller argued that women needed a broadened concept of autonomy, or even, a more "complete" notion than autonomy. "Women are quite validly seeking something more complete than autonomy as it is defined for men, a fuller not a lesser ability to encompass relationships to others, *simultaneous with the fullest development of oneself*" (95; my italics). For women, then, a new concept of autonomy would mean a sense of self-direction and self-determination that grew in relation to, and with the help of, a sense of affiliation and connection with others, rather than in competition against them.[20] Thus autonomy, in the new psychology of women, would be unhooked from its links to aggression and violence toward others.

The "new psychology of women," then, meant in general a development that took as its base the psychological characteristics that had been fostered in women while they were "subordinates." It built on this base a set of strengths growing out of women's new aspiration to be equals. Miller saw that the major resources for women's growth in the era of feminism would come from women's own experience in an era of subordination. She did not prescribe to women that they should abandon what they knew, as defective and faulty, now that they sought equality. Rather, she called upon them to remember it, because it was their experience, rather than that of men, that in her view held the seeds for a possible human future. Miller's interpretation of the psychology of women, then, was an important expression of a woman-centered analysis. Not only did she focus on women rather than men as her object of study: she took the condition of women as potentially normative for all human beings.

7

The Cultural Meaning of Mothering:
I. As Experience and Institution

Woman-centered analysis underwent a further, major development with the emergence, in the mid-1970s, of a feminist reexamination of motherhood. Of all the differences between men and women, the most immutable appeared to be women's reproductive capacities. To Simone de Beauvoir and others the mammalian responsibility of women was the difference that most condemned women to an unfree existence. That feminism and motherhood were in diametrical opposition had seemed almost axiomatic in the early 1970s. But in the second half of the decade, this axiom was challenged by a spate of publications that reopened the question of the relation of feminism to mothering.[1]

In the early years of the second wave, feminists who were mothers felt somewhat out of place. In the late 1960s, Alix Kates Shulman was the only member of her consciousness-raising group who was a mother, and because of this singularity was treated as something of a curiosity by her "sisters."[2] This was the case not only because many members of the movement chose not to be mothers, but because motherhood—the bearing and raising of children—seemed to be rather more a barrier to self-fulfillment in women than a vehicle for it. Feminists reacted against the propaganda of the 1950s, which had decreed that femininity lay in clinging to the role of wife and mother. With Shulamith Firestone, they argued that biological motherhood lay at the heart of women's oppression. Firestone held that it was only with the advent of a woman-controlled technology, which would free women from *the tyranny of their biology by any means available,"* that the ultimate revolution freeing women could take place.[3]

It is arguable that the political struggles over the right of women to cheap and safe abortions (which at this writing continue to rage in most Western countries), had to do with the perception that control over termination of pregnancy was somehow central to the future of women and women's place. The right of women to decide not to mother children continued to stir up the most passionate of political and religious reactions among conservatives and those they could influence in positions of political power. The views of the Roman Catholic Church on this point were explicit: abortion and "artificial" means of contraception were against God's law for women. Control of reproduction was thus necessarily a crucial feminist issue, and as Linda Gordon demonstrated, had always been essentially a political struggle over the right of women to win self-determination.[4]

Politically, then, the right not to become a mother was central to feminist analysis. But there were other elements in the feminist reaction against compulsory motherhood. Many feminists felt enormous anger against their own mothers, whom they saw as the major agents of their socialization into a passive "female" role. Very little anger was directed, initially, against their fathers, whose role in the process was much less visible.[5] That the core of feminism meant freedom from reproductive obligations was illustrated by the furor aroused by the article published by the sociologist Alice Rossi, suggesting that feminists might have gone too far in their rejection of women's nurturing role. Her analysis of the "biosocial" aspects of parenting drew sharp criticism from some members of the feminist academic community.[6]

In this context, what could be the content of a feminist analysis of motherhood? Adrienne Rich undertook to make such an analysis by dividing the concept of motherhood into two halves, which she named "experience" and "institution," respectively. The point of this distinction was to enable her to discuss what had been done to women as mothers under patriarchy, as separate from what might be the experience of women in motherhood when it could be detached from, and freed of, the bondage imposed by male domination. "Throughout this book," she wrote,

> I try to distinguish between two meanings of motherhood, one superimposed on the other: the *potential relationship* of any woman to her powers of reproduction and to children; and the *institution*, which aims at ensuring that that potential—and all women—shall remain under male control.[7]

Rich sought to recuperate the question of motherhood for feminist theory. She defended the area of inquiry thus: "This book is not an attack on the family or on mothering, *except as defined and restricted under patriarchy*" (14). The distinction between "experience" and "institution" is crucial to an understanding of Rich's theoretical position. She differed substantially on the question of motherhood from Shulamith Firestone.

While acknowledging the importance of her analysis, Rich criticized Fire-stone for accepting and reproducing a patriarchal, male-influenced notion of childbirth:

> Firestone sees childbearing . . . as purely and simply the victimizing experience it has often been under patriarchy. "Pregnancy is barbaric," she declares; "Childbirth *hurts.*" . . . Her attitudes toward pregnancy ("the husband's guilty waning of sexual desire; the woman's tears in front of the mirror at eight months") are male-derived. (174, quoting *Dialectic of Sex,* 198–99)

She took Firestone to task for being "so eager to move on to technology," and especially, for her failure to imagine what transformations might occur in the experience of childbirth, should the present realities surrounding it be changed: "[Firestone] discards biological motherhood from this shallow and unexamined point of view, without taking full account of what the experience of biological pregnancy and birth might be in a wholly different political and emotional context" (174). Rich did not rule out the Firestone solution, that of "artificial reproduction," as part of a possible future for women. She thought, though, that women ought to have the choice between it and biological childbirth, in that ideal world, just as they would have the choice whether or not to have children in the first place. But she also found Firestone's account of childbirth wanting in its analysis of the present. Firestone, she said, had failed "to explore the relationship be-tween maternity and sensuality, pain and female alienation." Without a full and profound exploration of the experience of motherhood under patriar-chy, she argued, women would never be able to transcend the present and move into the future.

> I do not think we can project any such idea onto the future—and hope to realize it—without examining the shadow-images we carry out of the magical thinking of Eve's curse and the social victimization of women-as-mothers. To do so is to deny aspects of ourselves which will rise up sooner or later to claim recognition. (175)

Motherhood involved suffering and deprivation for most women under patriarchy. Indeed, maternity was, as Rich put it, a "keystone of the most diverse social and political systems" of male control (13). Yet even under these conditions, the experience of motherhood could suggest an alterna-tive: it contained within itself the potential for great creativity and joy. It was not, then, the fact of women's capacity to reproduce that was the basis of women's enslavement, in Rich's view, but the mode by which that fact had become integrated into the system of male political and economic power over women. Once that system had been dismantled, Rich argued, then motherhood itself would become a transformed and a transforming experience for women. Thus, to "destroy the institution" of motherhood, Rich wrote, "is not to abolish motherhood. It is to release the creation and sustenance of life into the same realm of decision, struggle, surprise, imagination, and conscious intelligence, as any other difficult, but freely chosen work" (280).

What, then, were the definitions and restrictions that had made mother-hood into an institution? "When we think of an institution," Rich wrote, "we can usually see it as embodied in a building: the Vatican, the Pentagon, the Sorbonne, the Treasury, the Massachusetts Institute of Technology, the Kremlin, the Supreme Court" (274). Motherhood had no such "symbolic architecture," no such "visible embodiment of authority, power, or of potential or actual violence." And indeed, in ordinary thinking, she argued, the realities of motherhood were obscured by the associations brought to it: of lovely paintings of madonnas, of affectionate memories of one's own mother, or of the homes in which other mothers, in the mind's eye, took care of their children. That is, the emotional associations with motherhood evoked either an idealized state of being, a cultural icon of womanhood, or private experiences as child or parent and, in an extension of private experience, the imagined private experiences of other families. Motherhood was not conceptualized in its public, political aspect, as a fact of life subject to legal and economic controls and to enormously powerful cultural sanctions.

Even with visible institutions, Rich pointed out, it was not in their "symbolic architecture" that true power lay, but in

> the ways in which power is maintained and transferred behind the walls and beneath the domes, the invisible understandings which guarantee that it shall reside in certain hands but not in others, that information shall be transmitted to this one but not to that one, the hidden collusions and connections with other institutions of which it is supposedly independent. (274)

Thus, with motherhood: by virtue of law, culture, medicine, and profes-sional expertise from intellectuals and psychoanalysts, this structure of power effectively controlled women. In the absence of a monument sym-bolizing motherhood as an institution, Rich painted her own word-picture, to evoke the reality of it so that, she wrote, "women never again forget that our many fragments of lived experience belong to a whole which is not of our creation." The elements of the institution, as ennumerated by Rich, were:

> Rape, and its aftermath; marriage as economic dependence, as the guarantee to a man of "his" children; the theft of childbirth from women; the concept of the "illegitimacy" of a child born out of wedlock; the laws regulating contraception and abortion; the cavalier marketing of dangerous birth-control devices; the denial that work done by women at home is a part of "production"; the chaining of women in links of love and guilt; the absence of social benefits for mothers; the inadequacy of child-care facilities in most parts of the world; the unequal pay women receive as wage-earners, forcing them often into dependence on a man; the solitary confinement of "full-time motherhood"; the token nature of fatherhood, which gives a man rights and privileges over children toward whom he assumes minimal responsibility; the psychoanalytic castigation of the mother; the pediatric assumption that the mother is inadequate and ignorant; the burden of emotional work borne by women in the family. . . . (276)

The list of elements—what Rich called the "connecting fibers of this invisible institution" (276)—blended together the physical or material, the legal, the economic, and the psychosocial, including in the latter category both the attitudes of experts toward mothers, and the attitudes internalized by mothers toward themselves. It was, in short, the kind of web of power that both Rich and Kate Millett evoked in their descriptions of patriarchy and how it enforced its rule: a blend of coercion by legal and extralegal means with the creation of consent through socialization.[8]

Within the web, though, women were by no means entirely powerless. Rich marveled at what women had been able to keep for themselves of the experience of motherhood, despite the enormity of the constraints upon them, and the degree to which they had managed to continue to be human in the grip of an inhuman situation. "What is astonishing," she wrote, ". . . is all that we have managed to salvage, of ourselves, for our children, even within the destructiveness of the institution: the tenderness, the passion, the trust in our instincts, the evocation of a courage we did not know we owned . . ." (279–80). The experience of motherhood had not been entirely formed or controlled by the institution. Women had retained and developed capacities of resistance to male power.

Rich's view of world history in *Of Woman Born* was, in fact, of an ongoing struggle in which male civilization had sought to contain and to diminish the power of women. She abjured any belief in a mythical period of female rule or matriarchy. But Rich did argue, with Elizabeth Gould Davis and others, that there had been a time in the distant past when culture and politics had been what she called "gynocentric," that is, sharing "certain kinds of woman-centered beliefs and woman-centered social organization" (93). During the period of the worship of the Great Goddess, Rich held, women, and particularly, their capacity to give birth, had been held in respect and awe. Femaleness had been associated with fertility and with power. "In the earliest artifacts we know, we encounter the female as primal power" (93)[9]

This gynocentric perspective had been buried by centuries of patriarchal rule. So powerful was its influence that the very question raised by her book was simply not a question scholars considered worthy of raising, let alone addressing. The impact on civilization of the fact that all human beings were "of woman born" was not an issue for patriarchal scholarship. To the extent that her book was based on research, as well as on her own personal experience (a combination of sources and of perspectives that angered some of her critics considerably),[10] Rich immersed herself in the available scholarship relevant to her subject matter. She described the experience of reading and absorbing this body of materials, produced mostly by men:

> I . . . began to sense a fundamental perceptual difficulty among male scholars (and some female ones) for which "sexism" is too facile a term. It is really an intellectual defect, which might be named "patrivincialism" or "patriochialism": the assumption that women are a subgroup, that "man's world" is the "real" world, that patriarchy is equivalent to culture and culture to patriarchy, . . . that generalizations about "man," "humankind," "children," "blacks," "parents," "the working class" hold true for women, mothers, daughters, sisters, wet-nurses, infant girls, and can include them with no more than a glancing reference here and there, usually to some specialized function like breast-feeding. . . . Female sources are rarely cited . . .; there are virtually no primary sources from women-as-mothers; and all this is presented as objective scholarship. (16)

Rich placed her work within the new tradition of feminist scholarship, citing the writings of the historians Gerda Lerner, Carroll Smith-Rosenberg, and Joan Kelly, as examples of work that began from the premise that, until recent times, women and womankind had been studied and written about largely by men, and that women and their experience had been treated as secondary. Yet women were not some kind of "subgroup" or minority, a special category to be included only in footnotes, or in a special chapter on "women" or "the family;" as Gerda Lerner wrote, "the key to understanding women's history is in accepting—painful though it may be—that it is the history of the *majority* of mankind. . . . History, as written and perceived up to now, is the history of a minority, who may well turn out to be the 'subgroup'" (16–17, citing Lerner).

Rich's concept of "patrivincialism" or "patriochialism"—the provincial and parochial character of patriarchal thought—encapsulated the basic critique of scholarship from the feminist perspective. Patriarchal thought was provincial and parochical because it stemmed from a false, or limited, premise, namely, that the male point of view was a correct and adequate vantage point from which to view and to explain the world of human experience. Yet this limited, and therefore nonobjective, vision had dominated thinking about women, in that it dominated culture in general, even to the point of governing thinking itself. As Rich put this, it was the "omnipresence of patriarchal bias . . . [which] affects even the categories in which we think, and which has made of even the most educated and privileged woman an outsider, a nonparticipant, in the moulding of culture" (56–57n.). This domination was part of Rich's definition of patriarchy, a system of power that extended even to "the language in which we try to describe it"; as Brigitte Berger, the sociologist, wrote: "until now a primarily masculine intellect and spirit have dominated in the interpretation of society and culture—whether this interpretation is carried out by males or females . . . fundamentally masculine assumptions have shaped our whole moral and intellectual history" (58, quoting Berger).

Because of the strength of the patriarchal tradition, the gynocentric perspective was difficult to recapture in modern times. But if it were possible for patriarchal rule to be overthrown, Rich argued, women would possess a particular set of strengths which, if explored and cultivated, could contribute something new to the history of culture. Rich's argument contained a fundamental ambiguity about the capacities of women. It was not clear whether she believed that these capacities had once been fully exerted, were then suppressed, and were now being in a sense rediscovered, or whether she saw the modern era as entirely unprecedented in women's history. Elsewhere in the book, she was extremely critical of modern obstetrics and gynecology. Yet she argued that it was only upon the arrival of a fully free choice for women, with reference to childbirth, that the creativity she attributed to women could be exercised. In the ancient gynocentric period, did women die regularly in childbirth? Was the concept of individual creativity that Rich evoked for women in the late twentieth century relevant to, or descriptive of, any member, male or female, of that ancient family of cultures? Part of the difficulty in answering these questions lay with Rich's style, which was a blend of meticulous scholarship and poetic, and thus exaggerated, language. But partly, too, it lay with her concept of patriarchy, which, as with some other writers, was an ahistorical construction that tended to gloss over the specificity of particular times and places, and to obscure the process of historical development both of institutions and of ideas.[11]

In speaking of women's untapped capacities, Rich did not refer in the manner of Jean Baker Miller to women's psychological strengths, but rather to a potential epistemological revolution that she saw as stemming from the physiology of women. Rich believed, in fact, that women saw the world differently from men. In particular, she held that the dualism that had characterized Western philosophy for so much of its long history, the "mind-body" split, was a product of the male objectification of women. That is, men separated themselves from the "physical," and exalted the abstract, or rational, as characteristically human. The physical or bodily, they projected onto women, and rejected as lesser, or less "real": "The dominant male culture, in separating man as knower from both woman and from nature as the objects of knowledge, evolved certain intellectual polarities which still have the power to blind our imaginations" (62). The "even more fundamental" dualism, of "inner" and "outer," of "me-not me," as expressed by Freud—the fundamental organization of the (male) ego—seemed to Rich not to apply to female experience: "The boundaries of the ego seem to me much less crudely definable than the words 'inner' and 'outer' suggest. I do not perceive myself as a walled city into which certain emissaries are received and from which others are excluded" (63, commenting on quote from Freud's essay "On Negation"). Women, she argued, had been subjected to dualism—to the alienation of consciousness from physical reality and experience—by the impact of male culture.

If the institution of motherhood could be destroyed, then the particular physiological organization of women, which had for so long been inexorably linked only to their reproductive functions, could be freed for other uses. Women would become free to explore new possibilities, to think with their bodies for the first time.

> In arguing that we have by no means yet explored or understood our biological grounding, the miracle and paradox of the female body and its spiritual and political meanings, I am really asking whether women cannot begin, at last, to *think through the body,* to connect what has

been so cruelly disorganized—our great mental capacities, hardly
used; our highly developed tactile sense; our genius for close observation; our complicated, pain-enduring, multi-pleasured physicality.
(284)

If this development were to take place, Rich claimed for it potentially
more world-historical importance than any possible socialist revolution:
"The repossession by women of our bodies will bring far more essential
change to human society," she wrote, "than the seizing of the means of
production by workers" (285). Women freed from the institution of
motherhood, Rich thought, would become the creators of a new "relationship to the universe," transforming not only thinking but "[s]exuality,
politics, intelligence, power, motherhood, work, community" and "intimacy" (286).

Rich outlined several prerequisites for the new organization of culture
that she anticipated from women. First, women would have to be freed
from the "shackles" of motherhood. Provided with the necessary economic, social, and psychological systems of support, women could view
mothering as one choice among many. Second, as a consequence of this
change, women would be freed mentally from the sense of themselves as
only, or primarily, mothers or nonmothers, along with the complex of guilt
and limits accompanying these categories under patriarchy.[12] Third, a
woman-centered or gynocentric consciousness had to emerge among
women, providing them with sufficient interest in and respect for themselves to prompt the exploration of their own experiences. Liberated by
this process, women would being "thinking through the body," rather than
in patriarchal categories. All of these changes, in Rich's view, would
produce a utopian alternative, a new world vision, and from this a new
culture and world.

The revolution envisaged by Rich was a revolution of consciousness,
although to be sure it was to be made by a consciousness newly linked to
the body. Like Jean Baker Miller, she saw women as the source of a
world-saving set of values, which she associated with women's physiological richness of experience and with their capacity to mother. But were
women endowed with this virtuous and loving capacity by their biology?
Did Rich think that women were immune to the use and abuse of patriarchal
forms of power, once taken into their own hands? She explicitly disavowed
any belief in the intrinsic goodness of women. She rejected any formula
that would "fix upon 'nurturance' as a special strength of women, which
need only be released into the larger society to create a new human order."

Rich did not believe in women as unambiguously good or pure. In fact, she argued that "[t]heories of female power and female ascendancy must reckon fully with the ambiguities of our being, and with the continuum of our consciousness, the potentialities for both creative and destructive energy in each of us" (283). Yet she apparently placed great hope in the kind of thought that would emerge from women once they undertook to unify mind and body. But the basis of her belief that women would use these new powers for good, rather than for evil, remained unexplored.

8

The Cultural Meaning of Mothering:
II. The Mermaid and the Megamachine

The feminist reexamination of mothering took a new direction with the work of Dorothy Dinnerstein. If, in *Of Woman Born,* Adrienne Rich had considered the effects of motherhood as an institution upon women, Dinnerstein, in a more global task, undertook to analyze the effects of motherhood upon human society. Given that women remained *"almost universally in charge of infant and early child care,"*[1] Dinnerstein asked, what influence did this arrangement have on human character development, in men and women, and on the development of culture? Elizabeth Janeway suggested that the issue of power between mothers and children might be a major source of the issue of power between men and women, and that infantile experience of the overwhelming, life-and-death power of mothers might be at the core of male anger toward women in adult life.[2] Expanding on this insight, Dinnerstein argued that women's monopoly of mothering was the central cause of the human malaise endangering the continuation of life in the late twentieth century.

Dinnerstein, a psychologist, did not identify herself specifically as a feminist, although she associated herself with what she called the feminist project of dismantling current gender arrangements. In fact, she worried (on paper) as to whether her book might run the danger of being misunderstood by feminists, and be wrongly taken as an attempt to shore up the system they opposed. But, said Dinnerstein, to understand was not to justify. She intended to further the feminist project, by showing some of the reasons for the difficulty that women had been encountering in their search for liberation.

> Any reader who has pushed in a practical way against the legal or economic or other institutional barriers blocking change in some specific part of our overall male-female situation—even quite modest, limited change—knows how sturdy these concrete societal barriers are, and how fiercely defended. But what must be recognized is that

these external problems are insoluble unless we grapple at the same
time with internal problems, of feeling and understanding, that are at
least equally formidable. (12)

Dinnerstein assumed that her reader had read and absorbed the basic
feminist texts and had become convinced of the need for radical change.
"[I]t is not my aim here," she wrote, *"to help spell out what is intolerable in
our gender arrangements.* Other writers have for some time been handling
that task very well indeed. . . . *My aim is to help clarify the reasons why
people go on consenting to such arrangements"* (6).

By gender arrangements, Dinnerstein referred to the division of "responsibility, opportunity, and privilege" between men and women, and to
"the patterns of psychological interdependence . . . implicit in this division" (4). She referred, also, to the emotional "symbiosis" between men
and women that resulted. The division of psychological characteristics
resulted in the symbolic roles of the mermaid and the minotaur:

> The treacherous mermaid, seductive and impenetrable female repre-
> sentative of the dark and magic underwater world from which our life
> comes and in which we cannot live, lures voyagers to their doom. The
> fearsome minotaur, gigantic and eternally infantile offspring of a
> mother's unnatural lust, male representative of mindless, greedy
> power, insatiably devours live human flesh. (5)

Both of these images—"semi-human, monstrous"—grew out of the un-
healthy and dangerous symbiosis between male and female, and were
symptoms of a larger human disease: the growing inability of the human
animal to live in harmony with its own species, and with the natural
environment. Like Jean Baker Miller, Dinnerstein saw the human gender
arrangements as related to a planetary crisis that threatened the future.
But she also saw deep psychological reasons for the reluctance of human
beings, particularly men, to relinquish the sexual symbiosis, and the
subordination of women that it entailed. The burden of her book, then, was
an attempt to diagnose these reasons for reluctance to change, in the hope
that making them explicit and, thereby, conscious in the reader, would be a
contribution to bringing that change a step closer.

The core of Dinnerstein's analysis was her contention that the experience of human infancy shaped later consciousness, most acutely in the
realm of sexuality, and that presiding over that infancy, for all human
beings, was the presence of a woman. Following Melanie Klein, Dinnerstein held that, by definition, the mothering of an infant involved a less
than complete satisfaction of a child's wants and needs.[3] It was from this

preverbal experience that the infant formed her/his impressions of profound pleasure and bodily satisfaction in feeding and being washed and changed. And it was from this same experience that the child first felt discomfort, frustration, and anger. Inevitably, the mother did not, and could not, satisfy all of the infant's needs immediately, and in some cases she could not or would not satisfy them at all. Thus the child's first experiences both of intense joy and pleasure and of extreme anger and dissatisfaction were felt in relation to the person who was initially his/her entire universe. From this fundamental fact of the first human relationship, many consequences flowed.

Among them, Dinnerstein argued, was the familiar association analyzed by Simone de Beauvoir of women with nature. The object world experienced by the child was in the first instance a continuum of sensations, which encompassed its own body and the mother's body, along with their connections through touching and feeding. As the child learned to distinguish "I" from "not-I," the boundaries of its own body from the "surround," the first lesson was of the independent existence of the mother, who, presumably, had first appeared to the child as coextensive with the universe. As a representative of the universe, she was capricious, unreliable, and unpredictable. Sometimes she was the source of pleasure, while at other times she was, or appeared to be, the source of discomfort or pain. The mother's body, wrote Dinnerstein, was "the first important piece of the physical world that we encounter, and the events for which she seems responsible the first instances of fate" (95).

This experience of the infant took place in the earliest months of life, and had the most profound effects on human beings: "[W]oman is the creature we encounter before we are able to distinguish between a center of sentience and an impersonal force of nature: it seems extremely unlikely that the flavor of this early encounter could fail to survive as a prominent ingredient of our later feeling for her" (105–6). The child's encounter with the father was different in kind. This was because, given the usual monopoly over childcare by women, the father became a significant and known quantity to the child much later in its development, usually after the concept of an independent "I" figure had begun to be established in the child's mind. According to Dinnerstein, the father was perceived clearly by the child only at the point where the notion of an independent subjectivity like its own had already begun to be formed. Thus he/she could "see" Daddy as a separate person with much less difficulty.

This part of Dinnerstein's analysis tended to eliminate the father from any significant daily contact with the infant during its first six months or so

of life. Yet even in households with very conservative gender arrangements, surely the father would have some regular physical contact with a
baby from the day it arrived. Dinnerstein's account assumed that these
exchanges either did not take place, or were without psychological impact,
an assumption that seems questionable. In any case, she argued that the
subjectivity, the independent existence and will of Mommy were experienced at a time in the child's development that preceded its consciousness
of "I-ness," so that these impinged upon it with a force, and an unpredicta-
bility, that had no conceptual counterpart in the infant's mental life.

These sensations of mother as out of control and unpredictable continued throughout later life with relation to all women, where they found
expression in terms such as Lady Luck, the (now superseded) custom of
naming hurricanes after women, and references to Mother Nature (95).
Because of their experience in infancy, Dinnerstein held, men experienced
an overwhelming need to control women in later life. The autonomy of
women, in sexual expression and in other areas of life such as work, was
profoundly threatening to men. It was for this reason that they sought to
dominate women in personal relationships, and excluded them from the
major areas of life—work and culture—that lay outside of the family.

For their part, women acquiesced in these arrangements, because of
their own sexual formation. Dinnerstein's view of patriarchy—what she
termed "women's exclusion from history"—stemmed from her analysis of
the sexual formation of males and females in childhood, and the creation,
thereby, of the double standard in sexuality. By virtue of being nurtured by
a woman, men tended to become polygamous—that is, attached to many
women—while women turned out monogamous—attached to one
man—in their preferences. Chiefly this was because, as a result of their
memory of the precariousness of maternal availability, men found their
need for women so overwhelming, and so threatening, that they had to
keep it under control. This they accomplished by separating sex from love,
and by thus avoiding a replication of the intense need of one woman
experienced in infancy. The need of women, and the feared trauma of
repeating the loss of early childhood over and over again, made men
institute a fierce control over women and of their sexuality, while at the
same time refusing to permit, in themselves, the depth of commitment to
and involvement with one woman that might endanger them in this primitive way.

Conversely, she argued, the need of their mothers was muted in women, partly by means of the conversion to sexual attachment to the
opposite sex, and partly because women carried in themselves a sense of

the "maternal richness" that the mother had embodied. Women experienced less anxiety about losing the mother, because they "became" the mother themselves: they were "more self-sufficient than the mother-raised man: what is inside oneself cannot be directly taken away by a rival" (42). For this reason, Dinnerstein hypothesized, a woman was likely to be less devastated than a man by sexual rivals, and could tolerate male infidelity, as long as the man always acknowledged his need of her and returned to her in the end. (She also argued that women could "return" to the mother through the homoerotic feelings aroused by the vicarious connection to the "other woman.") But for males, jealousy was an intolerable, survival-threatening emotion: hence, the need to keep women under control, and their sexuality, and thus their freedom of sexual expression and choice, muted.

Dinnerstein's account of women's lack of need for their mothers was in sharp contrast to that of Adrienne Rich. In her discussion of mothers and daughters,[4] Rich spoke of the "loss of the daughter to the mother, the mother to the daughter" as the "essential female tragedy" (237). Under patriarchy, most women were severely deprived of their mother's love and acceptance. Because of the limits placed upon women, daughters grew up, Rich wrote, feeling "wildly unmothered" (225).

> Many daughters live in rage at their mothers for having accepted, too readily and passively, "whatever comes." A mother's victimization does not merely humiliate her, it mutilates the daughter who watches her for clues as to what it means to be a woman. Like the traditional foot-bound Chinese woman, she passes on her own affliction. The mother's self-hatred and low expectations are the binding-rags for the psyche of the daughter. (243)

Dinnerstein's assumption—perhaps related to her own experience—of women's easy access to "maternal richness" led to the connected hypothesis, that women suffered less than men from jealousy of their rivals. But this view corresponds neither to this writer's experience nor to the folk wisdom of the blues. Precisely because women derive much of their legitimacy and value from their attachment to a man, in a male-dominated society, the loss of a partner's loyalty is much more grave for women than for men. This is true in social terms, and, I would argue, therefore in psychological terms as well. On both of these points, Dinnerstein's account of women's experience, and of their "investment" in current gender arrangements, seemed unconvincing.

The double standard of sexuality, as described by Dinnerstein, underlay the rule of men over women, and the exclusion of women from power and

from history. Men enjoyed greater sexual freedom, coming and going—
"geographically or psychologically" (208)—from the intimate home base.
Women were content to acquiesce in their role as "she-goddess," embodying the magic power of the mother. In this role, they acted as the witness,
and reputed source of strength, for men at home, whence they went out to
"perform." Women learned to be a part of nature, of that which is to be
controlled, while men learned to be active in the world and to attempt to
control it. Men made history, identified with the denial of mortality and of
the corruptibility of the body. Women, representatives of carnality and the
flesh, were excluded from history. Each of these sexual roles, Dinnerstein
wrote, was a "bluff." Men were not the heroes of worldly activity they
pretended to be, any more than women were goddesses and storers of
magical powers. But there was a tacit agreement between the sexes not to
call one another's bluff (209).

The hatred and fear of women would continue, Dinnerstein argued, as
long as women maintained their monopoly over childrearing. Women were
used as a "scapegoat-idol" for all of the ills of human existence.

> That we are born mortal now gets its meaning from other grievances
> against the body [that is, the frustrations experienced in preverbal
> infancy], which develop before we discover that it was born and will
> therefore die, and which later melt together with this discovery into
> one global rage. For this rage woman, who both bore and raised the
> body, is at present the natural target.

The only way out of this impasse was for men to take an equal share in the
task of nurturing infants. In this way, the blame and anger that now went
exclusively to women would be distributed equally to both genders. The
frustrations and limitations of the human condition would be perceived as
an inevitable fact, rather than seeming the fault and responsibility of
women.

> When these early grievances develop as much under male as under
> female auspices, when they can no longer be foisted off on the female
> and must be integrated instead, their character, and therefore the
> character with which they later endow the fact of mortality, will be
> cleaner, less necrophilic. When our love for the mortal flesh has
> learned to incorporate our hate for it, we will have learned to live
> without marching to meet death halfway. (149)

From a change to shared parenting, Dinnerstein predicted a second
result: the end of male dominance. Male rule in the world stemmed from
female rule of the cradle. Everyone, she argued, accepted male power,

and even male despotism, as preferable to what people feared most: sinking back into the "helplessness of infancy," presided over by female power which, she said, is *"under present conditions the earliest and pro-foundest prototype of absolute power"* (161). The particular quality of wom-anly power over the growing child was an unbearable blend of intimacy with frustration and humiliation at the inevitable thwarting of the child's will. Paternal power, in contrast, appeared as a *"sanctuary from maternal authority"* (176). But this was a deceptive sanctuary, an escape only into limited freedom. The psychology of patriarchy involved a profound self-deception; having escaped the maternal power, most people, argued Dinnerstein, "exhausted" their "impulse toward autonomy": "In some part of ourselves we do not really want to be our own bosses; all we want is to be bossed a little more finitely and comprehensibly" (189).

The impulse to freedom, then, Dinnerstein argued, was doomed to be frustrated, in that it always contained its own limits. It presupposed the revolt against the power of women, which threatened—psychologically—to reassert itself. Thus "brotherhood" slipped back into patriarchy, over and over again. And, she said, this would continue

> until we start outgrowing the original dependency, the original terror of eternal helplessness, instead of trying all our lives to keep it at bay. And we will take on this emotional task only when we no longer have the option, at the beginning, of shirking it by running for refuge from the first tyrant to another of a new gender. When we can not run away from the task we will face it: we will then put tyranny in its place instead of trying to keep woman in hers. The project of brotherhood cannot be achieved until it includes sisters. (197)

The final point of Dinnerstein's argument converged with that of Jean Baker Miller: the division of sexual arrangements concealed an agreement about the nature of culture itself.[5] The world as we know it, said Din-nerstein, rested on the exclusion of women, and what women repre-sented, from culture. Therein lay its ultimate danger, which she saw as the danger of human extinction. Citing the analysis of Lewis Mumford, Din-nerstein called the essential illness of modern culture the "megamachine" myth: the increasing attempt to extend human control via rationality and to turn the world into a machine. The "megamachine," "the final embodiment of the self-contemptuous human impulse toward worship of dead automatic things and disrespect for what lives" (218), was driven by the spirit of "the male realm," the pursuit of power and profit. Thus the division of the world into male and female, and the assignment of life and growth to women, meant that culture was doomed unless the fateful symbiosis of minotaur and mermaid could be ended, and until all human beings, male and female, could learn to embody all aspects of the human within themselves. Unless men and women both renounced the symbiotic gender arrangements that allowed neither sex to take full, adult responsibility for the direction of human society, the megamachine would continue on its inexorable path: this was the "basic pathology shaping our species' stance toward itself and nature . . . whose chances of killing us off quite soon, if we cannot manage to outgrow it first, are very good indeed" (4).

Ironically, Dinnerstein's analysis seemed to imply that the threatened imminent destruction of world civilization by a male-developed and controlled technology was caused, ultimately, by female control over childrearing. But this encapsulation of her argument does not do justice to its complexity. Dinnerstein was suggesting that in the struggle of women to enter history, the social and political resistance they encountered had its roots in the preconscious infantile memories of both women and men. Opposition to feminism had both rational and prerational elements. In addition, Dinnerstein's analysis pointed to the significance of feminism for social and political change. The perpetuation of the current gender arrangements was linked to the dominance of a dangerous and possibly self-destructive technologically based culture. The integration of women, and of a woman-centered perspective, into world politics was therefore a matter of simple survival.

9

The Cultural Meaning of Mothering:
III. The Construction of Gender Identity

Like Adrienne Rich and Dorothy Dinnerstein, Nancy Chodorow asked new feminist questions about mothering and motherhood. Perhaps the most fundamental question was, why did women mother? Chodorow pointed out that mothering by women was by no means inevitable. Rather than being an unremarkable aspect of women's "nature," it was a phenomenon in need of explanation. Chodorow therefore raised the question of the "reproduction" of mothering: how did one account for the fact that women continued to want to mother children, to see themselves as mothers or potential mothers, and to carry out the tasks of mothering, largely to the exclusion of men?

Chodorow argued that women came to be mothers, or to want to be mothers, by means of a profound process of psychological character formation. She rejected two widely held views of why women mothered, the first a theory that women were somehow suited by "nature" and evolution for mothering, and the second, the feminist conventional wisdom that women were forced into mothering by ideology and the pressure of sex-role stereotyping. Chodorow refuted the idea that women's mothering was in some sense innate, a result of the evolution of the species from its formative period as hunters and gatherers in the earliest years of human society. There was no convincing evidence, she wrote, that mothers in the late twentieth century chose this role as a result of "instincts," or of some form of genetic programming, despite the arguments of the members of what Chodorow referred to as the "functional-cum-bio-evolutionary" school of thought. It might very well have been the case that when human beings relied for survival on hunting and gathering, the rational and most efficient use of human resources dictated that women should rear as well as bear children, and gather food close to the home base, while men did the hunting further afield. But this division of labor applied to one form of human social organization, no longer appropriate in the modern world. And certainly the evidence adduced for some survival of this social organization in the genetic makeup of modern human beings was fragmentary and unconvincing.[1]

Nor did Chodorow find convincing the arguments set forth by other feminist writers about "role formation," the notion that women became mothers because they were responding to a pervasive social ideology about the correct role for women. This theory presupposed that women accepted the persuasion of conventional attitudes about femininity as laid down by the media, by educational institutions, by religious and cultural organizations, and by families. The theory of gender-role formation was flawed, said Chodorow, because, in explaining women's behavior, it relied on intentionality, the idea that because society wanted women to conform to a certain role, women somehow voluntarily agreed to play that role.

Role theory was flawed because, in Chodorow's account, mothering was not an activity that women simply decided to take on and then carried out. Nor was it an activity that, if women did not choose to do, they could be forced into or coerced to perform. Mothering was reproduced, Chodorow argued, both at the level of social organization and at the level of individual development by a complex system that depended upon the family for its continuity. Chodorow drew on the theoretical perspectives of, on the one hand, Talcott Parsons, and on the other, the writers of the Frankfurt school, whom, she held, converged in this theoretical point despite the differences in their political perspectives. She pointed to the family as the institution within which the economic and social requirements of the whole society were met by means of the creation of appropriate personality structures for the roles to be played within it. It was in the family that children learned to be men and women, and that women learned to be mothers. But the quality of this learning, for both sexes, was not by means of identification and the learning of a role by imitation. Rather, it was by means of the development of a psychic structure, the very shape of personality. "The capacities and orientations I describe must be built into personality; they are not behavioral acquisitions. Women's capacities for mothering and abilities to get gratification from it are strongly internalized and psychologically enforced, and are built developmentally into the feminine psychic structure" (39).

The proof that role theory was inadequate to explain mothering in women lay in the theory of object-relations, on which Chodorow relied for her account. The theorists of object-relations, a branch of psychoanalysis that drew heavily on the original theories of Freud, but was strongly critical of some of the fundamental principles of Freudian analysis, had argued that for a child to develop normally, it must receive what D. W. Winnicott had termed "good-enough mothering." This was mothering, or nurturing (although Chodorow drew attention to the conflation of these two terms: that anyone besides women might do "mothering" was never taken into consideration) that met the needs of a child for developing a clearly defined and ongoing sense of self. The qualities for successful nurturance (nurturance that created a healthy, rather than a psychotic, child) were, said Chodorow, embedded in personality—specifically, in female personality—and could not be learned as an act of the will, or merely through imitation of others. "[T]he mothering that women do," wrote Chodorow,

> is not something that can be taught simply by giving a girl dolls or telling her that she ought to mother. It is not something that a girl can learn by behavioral imitation, or by deciding that she wants to do what girls do. Nor can men's power over women explain women's mothering. Whether or not men in particular or society at large—through media, income distribution, welfare policies, and schools—enforce women's mothering, and expect or require a woman to care for her child, they cannot require or force her to provide adequate parenting unless she, *to some degree* and *on some unconscious or conscious level*, has the capacity and sense of self as maternal to do so. (33)

Although in the accounts that Chodorow drew upon, the question of why women (rather than men) mother was almost never raised, she found that in object-relations theory, there were embedded the elements of an analysis of who it was that could provide "good-enough mothering." These writers held that, for an infant to develop normally, it had to move over time through a series of stages. From an initial psychological sense of oneness and unity with the parent, the infant acquired gradually a realization of the reality of the parent as a separate entity, and thereby, concomitantly, a sense of its own separateness and integrity. The failure of this process meant that the child failed to develop such a sense, a lapse to which these analysts traced major mental illnesses.[2] The complex process was by no means automatic, although it depended, in part, on the normal physiological development of the child, so that its physical capacities could provide the basis of its increasing psychological awareness. It depended principally on the capacity of the parent to interact with the child in an appropriate way at each point in the process, and to participate with it in this growth. This capacity, in turn, depended upon the ability of the parent to empathize with the infant, and, indeed, to return—to "regress," in analytic language—to the state of "primary identification," the sense of oneness, from which the infant began its development. Only through this reciprocity of experience could the parent-child relationship develop gradually, and in stages, to the point where the child acquired the sense of its own separation and autonomy.

According to object-relations theory, all children began life with the experience of unity and oneness with the parent. But not all children developed a healthy sense of self, because not all parents were able to carry out their side of the developmental process. In this theory, to give "good enough" parenting, one had to have received it originally oneself. Theoretically, then, said Chodorow, anyone who had participated in such a successful parent-child relationship as an infant could reproduce it with his or her own children: "[A]nyone—boy or girl—who has participated in a 'good-enough' mother-infant relationship has the relational basis of the capacity for parenting" (87–88). Why was it, then, that only women reproduced mothering, while men remained in the relatively distant role of fathering? Chodorow argued that the answer to this question lay in the "differential object-relational experiences" that girls had as infants. The very process described by object-relations theorists by which infants acquired the most fundamental sense of self was, in fact, a process that differentiated girls from boys, and determined that girls, rather than boys, retained the capacity for parenting. As infants, girls and boys underwent "different psychological reactions, needs, and experiences, which," said Chodorow, "cut off or curtail relational possibilities for parenting in boys, and keep them open and extend them in girls" (91).

To demonstrate this, Chodorow pointed to the gender differences observable in the "preoedipal period" of development. Freud and his interpreters in the various analytic traditions all agreed that the pre-Oedipal period, the period of undifferentiated mother-infant attachment, lasted longer in girls than in boys. While in girls the attachment lingered as a prolonged exclusive involvement of the child with the mother, often into the fourth and fifth year of childhood, in boys, this pre-Oedipal attachment became rapidly transformed into an Oedipal attachment, a possessive and competitive relationship that included rivalry with the father. Chodorow expressed this difference thus:

> The content of a girl's attachment to her mother differs from a boy's precisely in that it is not at this time oedipal (sexualized, focused on possession, which means focused on someone clearly different and opposite). The preoedipal attachment of daughter to mother continues to be concerned with early mother-infant relational issues. It

> sustains the mother-infant exclusivity and the intensity, ambivalence, and boundary confusion of the child still preoccupied with issues of dependence and individuation. By contrast, the boy's "active attachment" to his mother expresses his sense of difference from and masculine oppositeness to her. . . . (97)

The source of this difference, said Chodorow, was the asymmetry caused by the fact that both girls and boys were usually raised by mothers.[3] It grew, more specifically, out of the fact that mothers perceived and treated their girl-children as continuous with themselves, while they perceived and treated their boy-children as separate from and other than themselves. Chodorow drew on the clinical cases cited by the object-relations theorists to show that, in the pre-Oedipal period, in the case of girl children, mothers tended to prolong the period of originally necessary symbiosis, of psychological unity with the infant, the sense of the infant as coextensive with the self. With boy children, mothers tended to end the symbiotic period early and to emphasize the "otherness," the separateness of the infant.

Given this difference, girls developed a different personality structure from boys. In the Oedipal period, when girls turned their libidinal interest to their fathers, it was in a much less complete and overwhelming fashion than the libidinal attachment of boys to their mothers. Chodorow suggested, with Gayle Rubin, that the Freudian interpretation of female development missed the point. Freud had hypothesized that girls turned to their fathers out of penis envy. That is, discovering that the mother lacked a penis, and that they themselves suffered from this same defect, they turned away from the mother, with hostility, to the father, who was possessed of one, and whom they hoped to possess sexually. Thus in the Freudian account, the Oedipal development of boys and girls was symmetrical.[4] In this way, women generally became heterosexual in their choice of a love object, that is, they let go of their initial attachment to the mother.

Chodorow rejected this interpretation. With Alice Balint and other object-relations theorists, she held that for most women, the primary attachment remained to the mother. Indeed, girls turned to their fathers as a way of escaping from the maternal attachment, and of establishing autonomy and a separate identity. In addition, penis envy, as a phenomenon in young girls, was better explained by the discovery that, despite their genital similarity to the mother, daughters did not receive love from her with the appropriate intensity. Mothers seemed to prefer the father (or the brother) to them. Thus girls turned to fathers out of pique and rejection, out of disappointed love for the mother.

At this point in Chodorow's account, she assumed that the infant daughter could sense that her mother's love for her brother was more intense than, and of a different quality from, the mother's love for her. Chodorow wrote that the daughter realized that "her mother *prefers* people like her father (and brother) who have penises" (125). The love that a mother expressed for a son—a "differentiated, anaclitic love relation"—was experienced by the daughter as a more valuable kind of love than that she got from the mother, which was love for "part of a narcissistically defined self" (121–22). But why was the mother's sexualized love of the other, the boy-child, necessarily more intense that her pre-Oedipal, undifferentiated love of the self, the girl-child? Why did the daughter experience the love she received as second-rate? The lesser value accorded by the mother to herself as a woman and to her daughter for the same reason was here suggested, but not made explicit. The development of a heterosexual attachment in women, the "change of object" from mother to father, then, remained partial and incomplete. "The turn to the father . . ." Chodorow wrote,

> expresses hostility to her mother; it results from an attempt to win her mother's love; it is a reaction to powerlessness vis-à-vis maternal omnipotence and to primary identification. Every step of the way, as the analysts describe it, a girl develops her relationship to her father while looking back at her mother—to see if her mother is envious, to make sure she is in fact separate, to see if she can in this way win her mother, to see if she is really independent. Her turn to her father is both an attack on her mother and an expression of love for her. (126)

The divergent experiences of boys and girls in the pre-Oedipal period produced major differences in the personality structure of the genders. Girls emerged with a greater degree than boys of what Chodorow called "relational potential" (166–67). They retained a greater capacity for empathy with others, and they experienced themselves as less sharply separated from other persons, and from the "object-world" in general. In addition, they retained the capacity to "regress" to a less individuated state, and to experience themselves as connected to others, a capacity crucial to the mothering function. Girls did not experience this sense of relatedness and connection as threatening to their sense of self and identity. In contrast, boys, in whom separateness and difference, rather than sameness and continuity, had been stressed by the mother, experienced themselves as more sharply separate from other people and things, and found regression to pre-Oedipal "relational modes" more threatening to the sense of self. "From the retention of preoedipal attachments to their mother," wrote Chodorow,

> growing girls come to define and experience themselves as continuous with others; their experience of self contains more flexible or permeable ego boundaries. Boys come to define themselves as more separate and distinct, with a greater sense of rigid ego boundaries and differentiation. The basic feminine sense of self is connected to the world, the basic masculine sense of self is separate. (169)

In addition, the heterosexual attachment of most women to men was less exclusive and unilateral than the heterosexual attachment of most men to women. In turning to their fathers as objects of sexual desire in the Oedipal period, women retained a profound attachment to their mothers from the pre-Oedipal period. Their experience of sexuality in the prelatent period was thus of a triangular, rather than of a dyadic relationship. Women had a more complex psychic structure than men. Their sexual attachments constituted a triangle of infant-mother-father, with the primary connection remaining between daughter and mother, and the connection to the father remaining secondary.

These differences, Chodorow held, impelled women to become mothers in later life. Their greater capacity for self-in-relationship, and their original experience of the Oedipal triangle ensured that women, rather than men, reared children. The significance of the triangle was that, in later life, women were impelled to recreate their infantile experience by having an infant of their own. They sought to reproduce the Oedipal triangle of infant-mother-father with its points realigned as mother-infant-father (although Chodorow did not make this explicit). During childhood the axis of mother-daughter closeness dominated while the daughter-father connection was less intense. In adulthood, this psychic structure impelled women to recreate the primal triangle. The mother-infant dyad recaptured the primary intensity from the side of the adult who was once the child. (191–204)

This formulation raised a number of questions. First, what about the case in which the mother gave birth to a son, rather than to a daughter? How did the triangle get reconstituted? Second, Chodorow appeared to be arguing that it was women, rather than men, who had a propensity for triangles. If so, then this did not square with the folk wisdom which said that it was men, rather than women, who resisted monogamy and sought relationships with several women, while women preferred a stable relationship with one man. Was there a relationship between the primal triangle of woman-infant-man and the eternal triangle of man-woman-other woman? The issue was not addressed (although, to be fair, Chodorow was primarily discussing female psychology).[5]

Finally, and most crucially, if it was the woman-to-woman (daughter-mother) relationship that was primary to women, then lesbianism, not motherhood, would be the choice of most women. Chodorow was elusive on this point. On the one hand, she acknowledged the view expressed by Gayle Rubin that heterosexuality was socially constructed in women. It was the (arbitrary) heterosexuality of the mother, her sexual preference for male over female, that so wounded the daughter. But elsewhere Chodorow pulled back from this view and begged the question.

> [D]eep affective relationships to women are hard to come by on a routine, daily, ongoing basis for many women. Lesbian relationships do tend to recreate mother-daughter emotions and connections, but *most women are heterosexual.* This heterosexual preference and taboos against homosexuality, in addition to objective economic dependence on men, make the option of primary sexual bonds with other women unlikely—although more prevalent in recent years. (200; my italics)

It was precisely the fact that "most women are heterosexual" that needed to be explained rather than posited. In Chodorow's explanatory model, mothering was caused by the channeling of women's primary attachment to the mother into the bearing and raising of children. If this were the case, then the reproduction of mothering had to be seen as the method of persuading most women to remain heterosexual. They had children rather than becoming lesbians.[6]

In any case, in Chodorow's view, the creation of gender differences within the family had fateful consequences for women. The fact that women and not men mothered was caused primarily by the creation of the psychological differences she described, in which women "grow up with the relational capacities and needs, and psychological definition of self-in-relationship, which commits them to mothering" (209). Women's mothering was the primary cause of the sexual division of labor, and of the continued domination of women by men. "[H]istorically and cross-culturally," Chodorow wrote, "we cannot separate the sexual division of labor from sexual inequality. The sexual division of labor and women's responsibility for child care are linked to and generate male dominance" (214).

Chodorow's interpretation dovetailed with that of Firestone, Ortner, and Rosaldo. While she gave women's domestic responsibilities a psychosexual, rather than either a biological or an economic basis, she saw them as the fundamental reason for the oppression of women, which she judged to be universal.[7] On the significance of mothering for the perpetuation of male dominance, Chodorow differed from Dinnerstein, who focused on the unappeased anger of both men and women over their infantile experience of capricious female power as a cause of their continuing acquiescence in the control of women by men. In contrast, Chodorow emphasized the unconscious need of women to reproduce their infantile experience when adults. In a sense, then, Dinnerstein saw female mothering as a source of rage, while Chodorow saw it as a seductive locus of connectedness and intimacy. But both agreed on the solution for the future. The chain of causation must be broken, Chodorow argued, by men learning to be "equal" parents. This change would help to break down the present division of personality by gender. Men could learn the essential qualities of "self-in-relationship," while women could usefully learn to increase their sense of autonomy without losing their nurturant skills.[8] Chodorow looked to a society in which men and women mothered, and in which sexual inequality would disappear through a transformation of the "social organization of gender" (219).

10

The Critique of Masculinity

A woman-centered perspective inevitably shed new light on masculinity and maleness. To make women central was to divert the mainstream of Western culture, in which, according to Simone de Beauvoir, woman was the Other, that is, different, alien, and abnormal. If women's experience was taken as the norm, then men and maleness became the Other, as Gerda Lerner noted.[1] In the patriarchal tradition, "male" was equivalent to "human," while "female" was both deviant and inferior. If this pattern were reversed, then men and maleness would become objects of analysis, in order to explain their degree of deviancy from the female.

In her examination of gender identity, Nancy Chodorow focused initially on female psychological development.[2] But this investigation offered some interesting suggestions as well about the psychological development of males. Chodorow pursued these ideas further, in an examination of male and female attitudes toward gender difference.[3] On the basis of her reinterpretation of object-relations theory, Chodorow argued that gender identity in women and men developed along different paths. This was the case almost by definition, because of the asymmetry of conventional childrearing arrangements. Gender identity for both sexes developed vis-à-vis a female person, the mother. In particular, this asymmetry was relevant for the development of men.

Male gender identity, Chodorow held, was conflictual and difficult in a way that female gender identity was not. According to object-relations theorists, everyone's original experience of infancy was a sense of unity, empathy, oneness, and identity with the mother. In a process of "separation-individuation," all children learned the fundamental fact that "I" am "not-you." Chodorow argued that girls had little difficulty with the development of their female "core gender identity." This grew out of, and was built upon, a "primary sense of oneness and identification" with the mother (14). Chodorow did not deny the difficulties undergone by female children in accepting the "feminine" role in later life. But she argued that these difficulties began at a later stage of development, when girl children began to assimilate what it meant to be female in a male-dominated culture.[4]

Boys, on the other hand, encountered a more complex task. They originally experienced the same sense of unity and oneness with their mothers as did their sisters. But they then had to undergo a radical denial of sameness with the mother. They needed to develop as "not-females," and specifically, as "not the mother." Because of this contradiction, there was built into the sense of maleness a residual feeling of femaleness, of identity with the mother, which had to be denied or repressed:

> [B]ecause of a primary oneness and identification with his mother, a primary femaleness, a boy's and a man's core gender identity itself—the seemingly unproblematic cognitive sense of being male— is an issue. A boy must learn his gender identity as being not-female, or not-mother. (13)

Their relatively fragile sense of gender identity led men, in Chodorow's view, to focus on the significance of gender differences, and to seek to intensify them, in order to keep the boundaries clear and distinct between what is feminine and what masculine. She pointed to research showing that in families, it was generally the father, more than the mother, who "sex-type[d]" children and insisted upon gender-appropriate behavior from them (13). At the same time, because men exercised "cultural hegemony," they were in a position to elevate maleness into the definition of human normality. They defined femaleness and females as secondary or abnormal, rather than as the primary source of the "generically human," which it was, at the psychic level, for both males and females. Thus, Chodorow argued, men compensated for a relatively fragile sense of masculinity by ensuring that, in the "real world," power stayed in the hands of males. The residual "femaleness" of their psychic identity could be thus in some sense kept at bay (14–5).

Chodorow's argument here was circular, in the following sense. Men must define themselves as not-women, because they have been raised by women, but are not, and must not, become women themselves. Why? Because men are not women, and to be a woman is to be not a man. But being not a man is only a failing, or a danger, in a world where women are devalued. In other words, the argument presupposes what it attempts to explain, that men are in danger of feeling themselves to be really women, in a situation in which the meanings of maleness and femaleness are already rigidly established, and in which the one is superior to the other. Here, as elsewhere in Chodorow's work, the origins of women's devalued status were not addressed, except in terms of the traditional meaning of female as mother.

A second weakness in the argument was that Chodorow was implying that male dominance over women was the result of a private experience of a man's inability to "dominate" or to "control" the female within his individual male psyche. That is, men in the public realm who exert power over women are acting out a private personal struggle over male gender identity, by subduing real, live women, rather than encountering and confronting the sense of female identification that lies within themselves. This was fair enough. But in this analysis, the economic, social, and political structures that underlay the subordination of women were apparently reduced to buttresses of the private struggles of individual men. Thus the power of men as a collectivity over women was not addressed.

Nonetheless Chodorow's analysis of male gender development was a fruitful source for understanding certain aspects of masculinity in Western culture. It gave a plausible psychological basis for the male experience of women as "other." The fact that men learned to define themselves as not-women had further consequences. In a convergent analysis, Evelyn Fox Keller argued that there was a fundamental congruence between maleness, as culturally defined, and the scientific world view that dominated modern Western thought.[5]

Keller posed the general question as to why, in common discourse, most people associated "science" with maleness and masculinity. This connection, she argued, went far beyond the fact that, until recent times, most scientists had been male (a fact largely unchanged as of this writing). It was, she said, a commonplace of Western culture to associate "maleness" with science, and with the concept of scientific inquiry in general. This automatic association—which was a difficult fact of everyday life for women scientists—grew out of another, connected, common association, that of science with "objectivity."[6]

Modern Western science, Keller argued, was "genderized," that is, it was overwhelmingly associated in a cultural sense with "maleness" and "masculinity." This association extended not only to the concepts of "science" and "scientific" themselves, but to the way in which the activity of scientific investigation was supposed to be carried out. "The relation specified between knower and known," Keller wrote, "is one of distance and separation. It is that between a subject and object radically divided, which is to say no worldly relation. Simply put, nature is objectified"

(414–15). Culturally, this mode of investigation was identified as a masculine mode:

> [T]he characterization of both the scientific mind and its modes of access to knowledge as masculine is indeed significant. Masculine here connotes, as it so often does, autonomy, separation, and distance. It connotes a radical rejection of any commingling of subject and object, which are . . . quite consistently identified as male and female. (415)

What was the basis of this definition of scientific knowledge? Keller argued that it grew out of a cultural tradition in which "nature" was seen as female, and the knower of nature was seen as male, a metaphor that could be traced back to Francis Bacon (if not earlier). But she also connected the definition to a psychological arena, namely, to the development of autonomy in the pre-Oedipal period of childhood. Along with Nancy Chodrow, Keller cited the work of D. W. Winnicott. As the child developed the sense of a separate "I," he/she did so as against, or at least, with reference to, an "other" who was female, namely, the mother. Keller argued that boys developed an especially acute sense of autonomy, of disidentification with the object-mother, in part because of the cultural pressures against retaining any connections with that which was seen as "feminine":

> The cultural definitions of masculine as what can never appear feminine, and of autonomy as what can never be relaxed, conspire to reinforce the child's earliest associations of female with the pleasures and dangers of merging, and male with both the comfort and the loneliness of separateness. The boy's internal anxiety about both self and gender is here echoed by the cultural anxiety; together they can lead to postures of exaggerated and rigidified autonomy and masculinity which can—indeed which may be designed to—defend against that anxiety and the longing which generates it. (426)

How did this general set of psychocultural facts affect the practice of science? Keller suggested that there was a form of self-selection taking place. Individuals in whom this form of masculine anxiety about autonomy and separation was strongest were drawn to that cultural activity in which these qualities were celebrated as the highest form of human knowledge. In other words, a certain view of science as the shrine of objectivity attracted a certain kind of (male) personality type, who gravitated toward scientific activity. In turn the profession reinforced that concept of science among its practitioners, which attracted a certain personality type, and so forth, in a kind of cultural vicious circle. "The persistence of the characterization of science as masculine," Keller wrote, "as objectivist, as autonomous of psychological as well as of social and political forces would then be encouraged, through such selection, by the kinds of emotional satisfaction it provides" (427–28).

In Keller's view, the simple-minded association of science with masculinity was a distortion (indeed, her argument implied, a distortion of both terms of the equation), which was rapidly becoming outdated as a version of science as currently practiced. For example, contemporary physicists had moved beyond the old concept of the radical separation of the observer from the observed, in part because of developments within physics itself since the beginning of the twentieth century. Physicists, Keller wrote, increasingly were interested in "a process description of reality—a move inspired by, perhaps even necessitated by, quantum mechanics. In these descriptions object reality acquires a dynamic character, akin to the more fluid concept of autonomy emerging from psychoanalysis." (431–32).

Keller argued that the self-selecting process she described affected the practice of research at a number of levels. It led to the conflation of "objectivity" with the need to master and dominate, rather than with a wish to understand. This influenced the style of research carried out by most scientists, who sought to master their material, rather than, in the manner of some dissident scientists such as George Wald, to carry on "a quiet conversation with Nature."[7] It even affected the choice of paradigms. Keller cited the work of Barbara McClintock on the operation of DNA, work largely rejected by the scientific community, because she saw the structure as interactive with the organism it inhabited, rather than as dominating and controlling it in a hierarchical manner.[8]

The dissolution of the mythological connection between (male) gender and science would benefit both the practice of science itself, and social attitudes toward maleness and femaleness, imbuing both with greater flexibility and room to maneuver. "The disengagement of our thinking about science," she wrote, "from our notions of what is masculine could lead to a freeing of both from some of the rigidities to which they have been bound, with profound ramifications for both" (431).

A feminist critique of masculinity, then, led to a questioning of the very basis of Western scientific culture. On this point, Keller, Chodorow, and Dinnerstein echoed the sentiments of Theodore Roszak and others who, in the 1960s, had questioned the apotheosis of scientific objectivity. Because of the prestige of science, the stance of radical separation from the object-world had become glorified as the only reliable source of knowledge. As Roszak commented, "[o]bjectivity as a state of being fills the very air we breathe in a scientific culture; it grips us subliminally in all we say, feel, and do. The mentality of the ideal scientist becomes the very soul of the society."[9]

That the scientific world view had its dangers was not a new idea. But what a feminist perspective contributed was the realization this stance was linked to male psychology and male dominance. Jessica Benjamin termed the stance "rational violence." As she wrote,

> male rationality and individuality are culturally hegemonic. . . . Further, . . . male rationality and violence are linked within institutions that appear to be sexless and genderless, but which exhibit the same tendencies to control and objectify the other out of existence that we find in the erotic form of domination. That is, the male posture in our culture is embodied in exceedingly powerful and dangerous forms of destructiveness and objectification.[10]

In this perspective, culturally defined maleness was very far indeed from the normative role ascribed to it by Simone de Beauvoir. On the contrary, a woman-centered analysis presented maleness and masculinity as a deformation of the human, and as a source of ultimate danger to the continuity of life.

III Beyond the Impasse of Difference

Prologue

Woman-centered analysis moved feminist theory to a new focus and a new set of issues. In the early years of the second wave, emphasis was placed on the elimination of female difference as a prerequisite for women's liberation. In the late 1970s, the emphasis shifted dramatically. Female difference was not only worth preserving, it was to be celebrated.

Consciousness-raising and lesbian feminist theory pointed the way to a woman-centered perspective, in which female experience was the stuff of analysis. The "woman-identified woman" saw female difference as a source of strength. Charlotte Bunch and Adrienne Rich argued for the dissection of compulsory heterosexuality as an oppressive social institution. Jean Baker Miller rejected androgyny and argued that women's psychology, not men's, was the model for truly human behavior. Rich initiated a feminist reassessment of motherhood, in which the physiological and psychological capacities of women were revalued. Dorothy Dinnerstein and Nancy Chodorow looked at mothering in its psychological and cultural aspects. If, unlike Rich, they retained the concept of mothering as a primary source of female oppression, they added to this the issue of male dominance as a product of women's enforced monopoly on childrearing. Dinnerstein, Chodorow, and Evelyn Fox Keller connected the exaggerated autonomy and separateness of male psychology to the excesses of the scientific world view. Male difference itself was coming under the feminist microscope.

Part III examines the further development of the woman-centered analysis to a point of paradox, in which the difference of women, deplored as a source of subordination by de Beauvoir, reappeared as a renewal of essentialism, a feminist version of the eternal female. Chapter 11 analyzes the work of Mary Daly on the world system of patriarchy, and its implications for political strategy. Chapter 12 assesses the work of Susan Griffin and Andrea Dworkin on pornography as the ideology of male domination. Chapter 13 reviews some elements of feminist analysis that have remained constant, despite the pendulum swing from androgyny to difference. Finally, chapter 14 suggests the need for some rethinking, to incorporate the insights of the woman-centered analysis into a newly radical vision (in the political sense) for the future.

II

Spinning, Sparking, and the Innocence of Women

> We cannot be satisfied with turning in place,
> with dancing all alone in our circle, while *they
> are there,* walling us in, barring the roads to
> liberty.
>
> Nicole-Claude Mathieu[1]

Mary Daly's *Gyn/Ecology* was a landmark in woman-centered analysis, marking the boundary, the point where the pendulum of difference swung to its outer limit.[2] Characterized by its author as a restatement of the radical feminist position, the book called upon women to reject the reformism and co-optation of the women's movement, and to embark upon a further journey toward liberation. Daly was well-known to feminist scholars for previous publications, in which she explored the implications of feminism for Christians and particularly for Catholics.[3] But *Gyn/Ecology* marked a futher stage on Daly's journey beyond Christianity. An astonishing synthesis of poetry, history, philosophy, literary criticism, and diatribe, this work drew a map for the radical feminist voyage. The "journey of women becoming, that is, radical feminism" (1), was described in three "Passages" or stages of the journey. The book as a whole evoked a process of "exorcism," the movement of the woman-identified woman from the "Male Maze" of patriarchy to the "Otherworld," the "Ecstasy" of feminist creation.

A complex and difficult work, *Gyn/Ecology* demanded from the reader a detailed attention to language, and to the wordplay and word-invention Daly used to recapture the power of language for women. In its medical usage, the word *"gynecology"* meant "that department of medical science which treats of the functions and diseases peculiar to women; also *loosely*

the science of womankind" (10, citing the *Oxford English Dictionary*). But
Daly wrote that she was

> using the term *Gyn/Ecology* very loosely, that is freely, to describe
> the science, that is the process of know-ing, of "loose" women who
> choose to be subjects and not mere objects of enquiry. Gyn/Ecology is
> by and about women a-mazing all the male-authored "sciences of
> womankind," weaving world tapestries *of our own kind.* (10)

Daly began the journey with an account of the power of patriarchy over
women. Her definition of patriarchy was sweeping, encompassing all other
ideologies, religious or secular:

> *Patriarchy is itself the prevailing religion of the entire planet.* . . . . All of
> the so-called religions legitimating patriarchy are mere sects sub-
> sumed under its vast umbrella/canopy. They are essentially similar,
> despite the variations. All—from buddhism and hinduism to islam,
> judaism, christianity, to secular derivatives such as freudianism, jun-
> gianism, marxism, and maoism—are infrastructures of the edifice of
> patriarchy. (39)

The fundamental secret of patriarchy was that it was parasitical upon
women, their lives, and their energies. Daly portrayed men as drawing all
of their strength and power from women. In a suggestive passage, she
argued that male opposition to abortion stemmed from a profound identification with the unborn fetus. Men sensed "as their own condition the role
of controller, possessor, inhabitor of women. Draining female energy, they
feel 'fetal'" (59).

Daly named the male requirement of female energy *"necrophilia,"* not,
she wrote, "in the sense of love for actual corpses, but of love for those
victimized into a state of living death" (59). Under patriarchy, Daly argued,
women were frozen into a state of "robotitude," that is, "the reduction of
life in the state of servitude to mechanical motion" like the women in *The
Stepford Wives.* [4] The state of robotitude was induced in women by a
system of myths which were devised by men, but which women had
allowed themselves to believe. To break out of robotitude, women had to
begin "breaking the casts into which we have been molded and breaking
away from the cast/caste condemned to act out the roles prescribed by
masculinist myth. Re-considering the imposed choices of the past means
acknowledging that a spell has been cast upon us . . ." (55).

The original spell of patriarchal myth, in Daly's account, was Christianity. The Christian myth dismembered the original Goddess religion,

incorporating some of its elements into a new mythology stripped of any female power. The Trinity, the cross, the Chalice of the Mass, the virgin birth of Jesus, and the rebirth of Jesus in the resurrection, all drew on and transformed elements of the Goddess religion as retained in Greek mythology. But in the Christian version, female symbols were turned into male: thus the rebirth of the Son of God repeated the myth of Demeter and Persephone. But "[t]here is no female presence involved in this Monogender Male Automotherhood" (87).[5]

Daly argued that the central message of Christianity was sadomasochism. Torture, and particularly, the torture of women, were extensions of the sadomasochism inherent in the Christian myth. She did not hold that Christianity had invented sadomasochism. However, it served to legitimize it worldwide: "Sadomasochism is the style and basic content of patriarchy's structures, including those antecedent to and outside christianity. Rather, christianity, with its torture cross symbolism, has been one expression of this basic pattern." But because of the influence of Western civilization on "[v]irtually all of modern patriarchal society," the "ever more deceptively refined/coarsened/extended tentacles of the torture cross syndrome pervade the planet" (96).

In the second Passage, Daly described in chilling detail what she called the "sado-rituals," those customs that embodied the murder of the Goddess, the "Self-affirming being of women" (111). Daly examined these crimes against women one by one: Indian *suttee,* the burning of the widow on her husband's funeral pyre; Chinese footbinding as an erotic ritual, with its crippling effects; African genital mutilation, that is, clitoridectomy and infibulation performed on young girls; the witch burnings of early modern Europe; and American gynecological and psychotherapeutic practices, such as unnecessary hysterectomies and mastectomies, estrogen replacement therapy, and the pill.[6] In recounting these atrocities, Daly drew attention to the work of male scholars, which, through neutral language and conceptualizations, had the effect of legitimizing the behavior described, rather than exposing its cruelty. As Daly wrote, "The scholars of patriarchy . . . embrace and perpetuate the same Higher Order as the ritual performers/destroyers they are studying. . . . [P]atriarchal scholarship is an extension and continuation of sado-ritual . . ." (112).

In winding their way through the first two Passages, women had to come to terms with the reality of woman-hating, past and present, and to recognize the degree to which women were despised by the culture they inhabited. In the third Passage, Daly suggested, women could begin a process of exorcism. Ridding themselves of robotitude, they began a "dis-spelling of . . . mind/spirit/body pollution" from the sado-rituals and the "meta-rituals such as 'scholarship'" which erased "our Selves." "This knowing/acting/Self-centering Process," Daly wrote, "is itself the creating of a new, woman-identified environment. It is the becoming of Gyn/Ecology" (315). The new environment, in Daly's sense, was not so much physical as it was psychological, a "Hagocentric psychic space" (341), reached by the process of "cleansing/depolluting of the Self by the Self" (339). All means to this end—comfortable clothing; self-confident and relaxed styles of movement; learning self-defense—were ways of shaking off the messages of the male-dominated environment, even when one was trapped within it. Women were "finding ways of 'breaking set'—of focusing upon different patterns of meaning than those explicitly expressed and accepted by the cognitive majority" (341).

Daly was, in fact, describing a process of consciousness-raising, the experience of discovering the repressed and difficult knowledge of one's oppression as a woman. This discovery, however, contained within it the seeds of a new, woman-identified consciousness. This consciousness looked backward as well as forward in time, remembering the "sources of the Self's original movement" (315). Did Daly refer to childhood memories, to a moment from the pre-Oedipal period of female sovereignty, before the advent of the law of the father? Or did the Self look back to some ancestral, female time when the Goddess reigned? In either case, the voyage through the third Passage was psychological. The "time/space" created by following Daly through her narration, and by coming to terms with the realities it presented to the reader, was cognitive. Exorcism of the demons of male culture, and their replacement by woman-identification, was a task each woman had to do for herself, within her own mind.[7]

By means of this Self-centering, women learned how to spark, that is, to bond with other women. Unlike male bonding, which was based on merging and self-annihilation, as in "warrior-comradeship," female bonding was based in the affirmation of the individual self. Both friendship and erotic love among women strengthened individual selfhood. "Women loving women do not seek to lose our identity, but to express it, dis-cover it, create it. . . . The sparking of ideas and the flaming of physical passion emerge from the same source" (373).

Daly's metaphor of women sparking together evoked the fires that burned witches at the stake. In her vision, the sparking of the new Amazons would lead to a blaze that avenged the witches, and that celebrated the rising up of women.

> In our rising together, Hags affirm the true identity of our
> foremothers who were burned as witches during the alleged "renais-
> sance." We affirm the reality hidden by the "wicked stepmother"
> image—the reality of the women of Wicce, whose fire still burns in
> every Haggard heart. (384)

The fire thus built would force the enemies of women to see, by its light,
the history of their violence, a "history of holocausts, . . . the multitudes of
women sacrificed as burnt offerings . . ." (384).

In the final moment of the Third Passage, women learned to be "Spinsters," to spin and weave their way into "another frame of reference" (423).
Spinning was a complex image for "living 'on the boundary'" (394) or for
"Gyn/Ecological movement" (389), the mode of "be-ing" that women had to
invent for themselves. The voyage of the Spinster was a spiraling journey to
the "center of knowing," "following the spiral net converging toward the
mystic center of creation" (401).

Marking the end-point of the journey was the "Dissembly of Exorcism,"
in which the Spinsters invoked and then dismissed all of the demons of the
patriarchy. One by one the speakers at the Dissembly offered help, "Aids for
Amazons: rest-cures for the haggard ones; religion and psychotherapy for
the psychic ones; hormones for the healthy ones; affirmative action for the
Self-affirming ones; equal rights for the superior ones . . . ; courses in
re-search and re-covery of women's history for the wise ones" (419). These
and other offerings were all hooted out of existence by the Spinsters. The
costumes of the demons unraveled into nothingness, and their power was
shown to be ephemeral.

The meaning of the tale, Daly concluded, was that it taught women their
strength: "We use the visitation of demons to come more deeply into touch
with our powers/virtues" (423). While the demons were not banished
forever, and would continue to "re-materialize," the scene was intended to
empower women. Reminded of their strength, they would continue on the
Voyage toward "the Background," the "listening deep" (424).

Despite its poetic and metaphorical style, Daly's *Gyn/Ecology* made a
number of clear theoretical statements, each with important political
implications for feminism. First, it identified women as wholly good, and
men as wholly evil. Ross Kraemer has argued that Daly's analysis could be
seen as a revival of the views of the Christian Gnostics, whose theology
was the basis of the medieval heresy of Manicheanism. In this religious
vision, the world is divided into two great powers, light and darkness,
which are in a monumental struggle for rule of the universe and for the

possession of the human soul. In Daly's neo-Manichean system, women embodied the force of light and men the force of darkness.[8]

In her account of the sado-rituals, where women played an active role, Daly excused them on the ground that they were not responsible for their own actions. In clitoridectomy and infibulation, it was (and is) the women who performed these operations on young girls, usually under unsanitary conditions and without the use of anesthetic.[9] Girls without these mutilations were considered unmarriageable, as the purpose was male sexual pleasure in a narrow female vaginal opening, and the reduction of female pleasure and therefore independence. As it was men who required the operations, women's participation in performing them was not what it seemed. "The apparently 'active' role of the women, themselves mutilated," Daly wrote, "is in fact a passive, instrumental role. It hides the real castrators of women. Mentally castrated, these women participate in the destruction of their own kind—of womankind—and in the destruction of strength and bonding among women" (163–64). That women perpetuated the custom did not mean that they had started it: "The idea that such procedures, or any part of them, could be woman-originated is only thinkable in the mind-set of phallocracy, for it is, in fact, unthinkable" (165). That is, it is unthinkable in Daly's framework, that of the overriding power of patriarchal structures. Daly acknowledged the physical involvement of women in the mutilation of other women, but not their cultural responsibility.

Curiously, although Daly presented patriarchy as based on sadomasochism, she nowhere defined this term, in contrast to her careful explanation of other terms throughout *Gyn/Ecology*. With this omission, she evaded the critical issue of masochism, the second part of the term that, in common usage, implies the willing complicity of the victim. In saying this, I do not mean to argue for a simple model of women's complicity in their own victimization. But in my view, the role of women in the perpetuation of misogynistic cultures remains an open question. Daly's version reduced this complicated issue to a form of magic. When women act in evil ways— when they act as "token torturers"—it is because they are under a spell cast by the male sex. Once freed of this spell, women are entirely a force for good. They are biophiliac, creative, sources of energy, and loving. This view of women, and of the fundamental difference between women and men, was problematic, particularly as Daly nowhere addressed the origins of this difference. Instead, she portrayed women as fundamentally innocent, the powerless victims of male cruelty and violence throughout the long history of civilization since the lost paradise of the Goddess.

Second, in her emphasis on spiritual change, Daly made light of the practical political difficulties encountered by the women's movement. To her, feminism was not a matter of winning sufficient numbers of women to the banner. "[F]eminists often begin the Journey," she wrote, "with the misconception that we require large numbers in order to have a realistic hope of victory. This mistake is rooted in a serious underestimation of the force/fire of female bonding." Because female sisterhood was such a powerful force, women, unlike men, did not need "large numbers of self-sacrificing comrades . . . [T]he force of female bonding does not require multitudes" (379). Understanding this, Daly concluded, "Amazons can stop worrying about the false problem of numbers" (380).[10]

Nor did she place a great importance on questions of strategy. On the much-vexed question of separatism, for example, Daly argued for a psychological interpretation. The political tactic of lesbian separatism meant choosing to put energy into creating a separate community of lesbian feminists, rather than working together with heterosexual feminists to reform "mainstream" society. But Daly, using her own speculative etymology, interpreted *separate* to mean "paring away from the Self all that is alienating and confining." The "basic task of paring away the layers of false selves," she wrote, was "Crone-logically prior" to all discussions of political separatism. This process, "paring away, burning away the false selves encasing the Self, is the core of all authentic separations and thus is normative for all personal/political decisions about acts/forms of separatism" (381). Daly's point appeared to be that all decisions about separatism as a political strategy were to be preceded by a thorough process of personal individuation, although this is not entirely clear. (What is the meaning of the word "normative" in the passage just cited?) A similar tone pervades Daly's discussion of "the physical spaces of which we dream" (342). Daly envisaged the creation of new physical spaces, very different from the women's centers created thus far, which she criticized for not going "beyond very mild measures such as 'vocational counselling.'. . ." The "Hags who find and make" the new spaces would build them "in the Otherworld journey" (342). The physical spaces would grow directly out of the psychic spaces in the minds of the Journeyers. But how, where, and what form they were to take was not clarified. In both cases, Daly moved easily from one level of meaning to another, gliding between the psychological and the material, as though the one either connoted or contained the other, or, alternatively, as though the one could create the other automatically.

Third, Daly dismissed many achievements of the women's movement.

She was particularly contemptuous of women who made their way into the system, as doctors, lawyers, or other professionals. "[S]uch women," she argued, were "allowed into pieces of patriarchal territory as a *show of female presence*. They . . . represent the female 'half of the human species' in male terrain" (334). In Daly's inversion of Jerzy Kosinski's image, all women were supposed to be "painted birds."[11] Those feminists who took off their paint became freaks, and were ostracized by the community. But the condition of being painted, of being a feminized artifact, of being, therefore, a token, was compounded by these women: each of them was a "token token," "drawn from the ranks of the token *women*—those most tokenized, cosmeticized, most identified with male purposes. This quasi-chemical combination equals 'Athena'." Worst of all, the Athena—that is, Daddy's girl, sprung full-blown from the head of Zeus, male-identified and acknowledging no connection with her female parentage—was likely to "call herself a 'feminist.' We are then confronted with the presence of a triply compounded product of patriarchal ingenuity: a 'token feminist'" (335). Such a woman functioned to mask male power, and thus to mystify her sisters further:

> [T]he doubly/triply tokenized woman, the multiply Painted Bird, functions in the antiprocess of double-crossing her sisters, polluting them with poisonous paint, making them less and less real in their own eyes. . . . For unknowingly, she is herself a carrier of the paint disease, an intensifier of the common condition of women under patriarchy. (336)

In this indictment, Daly named no names, but by implication placed all "successful" women into one undifferentiated mass. Daly's analysis eliminated any criteria for distinguishing between someone who, like Eleanor Holmes Norton, won an important political appointment as a feminist and a strong advocate of minority rights, and someone like Margaret Thatcher who exercised power in a traditional manner and dismissed any connection between herself and the women's movement.[12] All women who achieved positions of visibility and influence in patriarchal institutions were dismissed *ipso facto* as painted birds. In the process, some feminist victories got labeled as defeats.

Daly argued that reforms won by the women's movement were merely tokens. Affirmative action, abortion rights, equal rights—all of these struggles were used by patriarchy as a way of sapping female energy. Only partial victories were permitted, which could always be withdrawn when the women fighting for them had run out of steam. Daly's impatience with the lack of radicalism of feminist reforms was understandable. Her call for a more radical form of feminism, however, seemed to point in a very different direction, toward a "Journey" that was psychic and inward-looking, rather than toward more fundamental social change. In addition, her contempt for these reforms failed to give credit to the women's movement itself for bringing them about. In her analysis, antidiscrimination laws, Women's Studies programs, rape crisis centers, women's caucuses in professional organizations and unions, in short, all of the political achievements of the organized women's movement were reduced to gifts of the patriarchy, rather than concessions won in struggle.

Daly's journey, then, turned away from a confrontation with patriarchy. Eschewing any attempt to win over sufficient numbers of women to bring about effective and lasting change in the political arena, Daly addressed herself to those "Amazons" with sufficient education, leisure, and depth of feminist understanding to come on the journey with her. Daly carried a woman-centered analysis to its logical conclusion. Women were everything men said they were: witches, crones, hags, and spinsters. In appropriating these terms, Daly sought to revalue them as terms of pride for a new women's culture. But in accepting this attribution of women's qualities, she also implicitly accepted the concomitant dichotomization: rationality, linearity, logic, and science were all male. Daly rejected the possibility of a transformation of patriarchal structures, urging women instead to embark upon an inner journey of discovery. Embracing female difference thus appeared to imply withdrawal from political struggle, and the development of an entirely separate and self-contained women's culture.[13]

12

Sexual Politics Revisited:
Pornography and Sadomasochism

Like rape, pornography was placed on the feminist agenda in the first instance by a grassroots campaign. But the ensuing theoretical debate was fed, in part, by issues arising from the internal logic of a woman-centered analysis. There could scarcely be a more urgent and powerful link between theory and practice, between the personal and the political: by the early 1980s, a hot debate was raging between those opposing pornography as antiwoman, and those defending sadomasochism as a legitimate expression of female desire. The whole question of sexuality as a feminist issue was reopened for examination, with an intensity that recalled the early days of consciousness-raising.[1]

The focus on pornography emerged in 1976, with the formation in San Francisco of a group called Women Against Violence in Pornography and Media. Public attention was drawn to the issue with the campaign to have a Warner Brothers billboard for the Rolling Stones removed from Sunset Strip in Los Angeles. The billboard read: "I'm black and blue from the Rolling Stones and I love it," and was illustrated with a picture of a woman bound in chains and covered with bruises. The campaign was successful, and the advertisement was withdrawn. In 1978, WAVPM organized a national conference, "Feminist Perspectives on Pornography," in San Francisco, culminating in a "take back the night" march through the red-light district. By 1979, the campaign had spread east to New York, with the founding of Women Against Pornography. This group organized a march and a conference in 1980, and led tours through the 42nd Street sex shops. They also developed a slide-show of brutal pornographic images from publications like *Hustler* and *Playboy*. Similar groups formed in other cities in the United States and elsewhere.[2]

The burden of the campaign was that pornography embodied a dangerous "ideology of cultural sadism" directed against women. In recent years, the impact of pornographic imagery had increased in two ways. First, it had vastly grown in circulation, expanding from its somewhat limited traditional audience to a mass market.

> From "snuff" films and miserable magazines in pornographic stores to *Hustler,* to phonograph album covers and advertisements, to *Vogue,* pornography has come to occupy its own niche in the communications and entertainment media and to acquire a quasi-institutional character. . . . Its acceptance by the mass media . . . means a cultural endorsement of its message.[3]

Second, the imagery employed appeared to be escalating in the degree of violence depicted. Images of a woman being fed head-first into a meat-grinder, or of a woman bound and gagged, or with a pistol thrusting in and out of her mouth, effectively fused sexual excitement with the infliction of pain and injury on women.[4] This escalation in the availability and acceptance of pornography, and in the depiction of the torture and destruction of women, carried a cultural message of "sexual fascism." It was an all-out assault, an encouragement to "rape, woman-battering, and other crimes of violence against women." As Robin Morgan argued, "[p]ornography is the theory, and rape is the practice."[5]

The campaign against pornography provoked unease in some quarters. The way had been paved for the contemporary expansion by some important court cases over publications like James Joyce's *Ulysses* and the writings of Henry Miller earlier in the century. Were some feminists now making common cause with the New Right, and favoring a return to censorship?[6] In their discussions of the issue, Susan Griffin and Andrea Dworkin argued that, on the contrary, pornography itself was a form of censorship, silencing the authentic voice of women.[7]

Griffin held that pornography expressed a fundamental theme of Western Christian tradition, namely, hatred of the flesh. Like the church fathers against whom he thought he was rebelling, the Marquis de Sade, prototype of all pornographers, accepted the equation between "female" and carnality. Women were associated with the body, with the evocation of desire. This connection, the "idea that the sight of a woman's body calls a man back to his own animal nature," reverberated throughout Christian culture, all the way back to the story of Eve.[8]

What Griffin termed "the pornographic imagination" was not directed, in the first instance, against real women. Rather, it was aimed at what women's bodies evoked in the male imagination: "The pornographer, like the church father, hates and denies a part of himself. He rejects his knowledge of the physical world and . . . of his own body. . . . But he cannot reject this knowledge entirely. It comes back to him . . . through desire" (20). The images of women in pornography were symbols for the "denied parts" of the pornographer (39).

Men feared women's images, as a source of the loss of control over themselves and their own desire. The only way to counter this was to control women, to treat them as objects, and to have the capacity to destroy the object. The sadism of pornography lay in its objectification of another's body, and in the humiliation of that body. But the symbolic meaning of such sadomasochistic relationships in pornographic literature was the struggle of one person, one being, divided against itself.

> [T]he real identity of who we call "the man" in pornography, and of who we call the "woman," or of those pornographic couples, . . . the parent and the child, the teacher and the student (. . . or the master and the slave), [a]ll these couples represent one being divided into a mind and a body. . . . [I]t is that part of the mind which belongs to culture pitted against the body. (54–55)

Because feelings, sexual desire, refused to die, the pornographer had to attempt to kill that part of himself over and over again. Griffin saw pornography, therefore, as a form of ritual, an enacted drama, in which the flesh of the female had to be desecrated. The intention, she wrote, was to kill the heart, that is, feelings, to sever the connection between mind and body once and for all.

In this context, the symbolic language of pornography dictated that the liberty of men required the right to control women. The much vaunted "freedom of speech" of the pornographer, Griffin argued, meant the right to symbolically control, torture, and murder women. Above all, it meant the right to silence women, and the voice of women, that is, of eros. The image of women in pornography, she wrote, was "an identity of nothingness," symbolized by the protagonist in *The Story of O*[9] (232). But it was not only in pornographic literature that women were silenced. Griffin argued that pornographic culture spilled over into everyday life.

To argue that pornography did not influence behavior, Griffin wrote, was to place it in a different category from every other aspect of culture as it was commonly understood. Because of the delusional nature of the pornographic imagination, the position that pornography provided a form of catharsis that prevented real-life violence against women did not make sense. On the contrary, pornographic representations of violence reflected and reinforced the projection within the male psyche of violent feelings onto women. This psychological mechanism masked the origins of those feelings within the self, and encouraged the acting out of the feelings upon others. She cited the case of Lawrence Singleton, a seaman who raped and sodomized a fifteen-year-old girl, and then cut off her hands, saying "Now you are free": "[T]o be liberated from a part of himself, a man—believing his own desire lives in the body of another—mutilates that body" (101).

The influence of the pornographic imagination on women was to teach them silence and self-annihilation as a cultural norm. "Not only is our silence the perfect complement to pornographic fantasy," Griffin wrote, "the screen on which the image of ourselves as nothing can be projected; our silence is also a part of the annihilation which pornography wishes for us" (232). As women absorbed the lessons of the pornographic mind, which, she argued, was "a mind in which we all participate" (2), they learned to identify with meaninglessness, with nothingness, and there-fore, began to lose the desire for life itself: "Like O, as we impersonate the pornographic idea of women, we betray ourselves, and someone within us, who is condemned to silence, begins to die" (232).

Far from embodying the erotic, as its defenders protested, pornography silenced both eros and women, seen as the embodiment of eros. Griffin argued that the pornographic imagination represented the precise oppo-site of the truly erotic. She identified truly erotic feeling with childhood, a precultural state, in which one retained the knowledge of the body. In lovemaking, she argued, one returned to this "state of innocence," a time before "culture" had taught forgetfulness of the body: "We grope with our mouths toward the body of another being, whom we trust, who takes us in her arms. . . . We are back in a natural world before culture tried to erase our experience of nature" (254).

Griffin's analysis of pornography built upon the foundations of a previous work, in which she traced the history of the pervasive metaphor of Western science as a means of control of and domination over nature, perceived as female.[10] Pornography thus expressed the psychosexual need of Western masculinity, not only to control the "female," identified with nature and eros, but to annihilate it, both within the male self, and within its embodiments in images of women, and women themselves. Her argument depended upon the opposition of culture to nature, and on the identification of these as, respectively, male and female. At the outset she drew attention to the fact that this distinction was itself an artifact of culture, a Western conceit. Indeed, she traced this association to a perva-sive division of labor in Western culture, that artificially assigned language, culture, and authority to men, and nature, sexuality, and feeling to women. Even Freud, in her view, despite his attempt to liberate sexuality from repression, had fallen victim to this trap, seeing "culture" and "nature," in the form of sexuality, as inevitably opposed to one another.

In presenting infancy as a moment of pure "eros," preceding the advent of culture, however, Griffin fell into this trap herself. As Sherry Ortner and others argued, the identification of female and the domestic sphere with nature as opposed to culture was one of the prime sources of women's oppression.[11] Griffin appeared to agree, at some level, that real women, or at least women in their role as nurturers, did embody feelings and eros, and did inhabit, therefore, a world located in some way outside of culture and language. In her terms, then, the peculiar logic of the pornographic imagination was not inaccurate in its assessment of the essential female.[12] Despite this ambiguity in the terms of her argument, Griffin made a powerful case against the view that pornography represented a force for freedom and liberation.

Like Griffin, Andrea Dworkin placed pornography into a broader cultural context. In her interpretation, pornography was a genre that celebrated and justified male power. In this theoretical framework, the major component of male identity was sexual violence, and the purpose of pornography was to channel all of this violence against women, and away from other men. The claim of men to "humanism," Dworkin wrote, was belied by their behavior: they were "rapists, batterers, plunderers, killers. . . ."[13] But because "[o]ne-to-one sexual combat between fathers and sons would rend the fabric of patriarchy," fathers made sure that their sons' sexual aggression remained focused upon women (59).[14]

How did boy children, who started out like all children sensitive to the world and to other human beings, acquire the characteristics of male violence? Dworkin rejected Dorothy Dinnerstein's proposition that men went through life resenting the original power of their mothers over them in infancy. Men wielded real power over women, and the boy child perceived this early in life. To protect themselves from this power, boys made an alliance with their fathers. Sensing the powerlessness of their mothers, boys learned to shake off any feelings of empathy with them, and to identify, instead, with the power of their fathers: "Boys become men to escape being victims by definition" (51).

In the late twentieth century, male nihilism and its products had brought humanity to the brink of extinction. Dworkin blamed male sexual obsession for all the brutality and violence recorded in recent history. Yet, she argued, men held fast to their "unchanging faith" in masculinity, refusing to see it clearly as a "double-edged commitment to suicide and genocide" (68). Pornography expressed the "tenets" of this faith: it was the "holy corpus of men who would rather die than change" (68–69). It revealed the true nature of male desire, which was inextricably bound up with victimizing, hurting, and exploiting others.

The experience of the concentration camps in World War II, Dworkin held, had been assimilated into the erotic sensibility of the late twentieth century: "in creating a female degraded beyond human recognition, the Nazis set a new standard of masculinity" (145). Dworkin compared all women to the Jews and other victims of the Nazi concentration camps. They were "metaphysical victims," destined for slaughter. The force used against this kind of victim, she argued, was disguised by an ideology that made its use seem both inevitable and unremarkable. In this system of thought, the victim was "responsible for the violence used against her" (148). The presentation of women in pornographic imagery as willing victims codified this vision of women as desiring male violence against them, and therefore, as causing it. Dworkin showed the congruence between these fantasy icons of female existence, and the writing on female sexuality by those "experts" like Havelock Ellis, Robert Stoller, and Theodore Reik who posited a fundamental, "natural" female masochism. Pornographic narratives presented women as actively soliciting the use of force and violence against them. "In this context, rape and battery cannot exist as violations of female will because they are viewed as expressions of female will" (164). Dworkin held that the "truth" about women, as purveyed in pornography, was believed by "otherwise thoughtful men," men of "sensibility and intelligence and cultural achievement," who had incorporated pornographic values into the mainstream of culture—"art, religion, law, literature, philosophy, and now psychology, films, and so forth" (166). Because women were silenced, and had no "voice in the cultural dialogue," the belief was held by men that "sexual violence is desired by the normal female, needed by her, suggested or demanded by her" (166). Dworkin cited *The Story of the Eye,* by Georges Bataille, published in 1928, as the kind of intellectual work that carried the prestige of high culture as certified by writers such as Sartre, Foucault, and Susan Sontag. This work embodied a vision of sexual pleasure as linked to sadism, bloodshed, and ultimately the death of the female victim. In Bataille's later commentary on this work, Dworkin wrote, the force used in violating the women in this text was cleverly obscured by

> romanticizing death. Force is inconsequential when the cosmic forces
> move through men in sex. It is plodding and pedestrian to demand that
> one pay attention to it. What matters is the poetry that is the violence
> leading to death that is the ecstasy. The language stylizes the violence
> and denies its fundamental meaning to women, who do in fact end up
> dead because men believe what Bataille believes and makes pretty:
> that death is the dirty secret of sex. (176)

Dworkin argued (somewhat confusingly) that in the current American
context, both left and right embraced pornography. Yet pornography
conventionally embodied racist assumptions, and celebrated the humiliation and torture of black women. The "prime purpose and consequence" of
pornography, she wrote, was "the sexualization of race." The "racist
system" of the United States had as its foundation "its black whores, its
bottom, the carnal underclass" (217). The celebration of pornographers
such as Larry Flynt as heroic American dissenters by "distinguished leftist
literati" (208) was thus a betrayal of their own values. "How . . . does one
fight racism and jerk off to it at the same time? The Left cannot have its
whores and its politics too" (217). Women would know they were free,
Dworkin concluded, only when pornography had ceased to exist. Until
then, all women were the women depicted in pornography, "used by the
same power, subject to the same valuation . . ." (224).

There were some theoretical differences between the interpretations of
pornography offered by Griffin and Dworkin. Dworkin's use of language
was extravagant (and occasionally racist), as was her claim that all recent
"violence" stemmed from male sexuality. Her ahistorical vision obscured
significant ideological and political differences, and glossed over the inroads made into culture by the new chorus of feminist voices. In Dworkin's
view, the chief engine of history appeared to be male sexual violence,
possibly rooted in biology. Griffin's account was more sensitive to history
and, more than Dworkin, she acknowledged the pervasive influence of
pornographic thought on women as well as on men. But her view of
causation was equally suspect. The "pornographic imagination" was an
idealistic concept to which she attributed remarkable powers to affect
material reality. Thus, for example, Griffin ascribed the "shabby . . .
dilapidation and seediness" of districts selling pornography to the "ugli-
ness" of its contents.[15]

Both analyses, however, proceeded from some common assumptions,
drawn from a woman-centered perspective. They extended the critique of
masculinity begun by Chodorow and Keller: male psychosexual development incorporated a need to differentiate the self from the other, and to

dominate the other.[16] Both authors presented pornography as the expression of purely male sexual fantasy. Although Griffin conceded that women participated in this fantasy, she argued that they did so at their peril. Similarly, Dworkin attributed feelings of sexual violence only to men, and to their aspirations to control women and other men. The implication was that woman-to-woman sexuality was of another quality altogether. Indeed, Griffin's writing elsewhere about women's lovemaking evoked a natural inheritance of beauty and harmony, expressing "what is still wild in us" but escaping from the destructive violence of man-made culture.[17] Thus the analysis of pornography indicated that sadomasochism, that is, interpersonal psychic and/or physical violence as a source of sexual pleasure, was a male phenomenon. Male sexual violence was the ultimate expression of masculinity. The polarization of male and female behavior, and indeed, of male and female "natures" so much deplored in the early writing of the second wave, here reappeared as allegedly fundamental to sexual appetite and sexuality itself.

In a reaction to the campaign against pornography, some feminist writers argued that the enthusiasm for this stance was closing off debate about women's real sexual feelings. Paula Webster argued that the campaign created a new feminist orthodoxy, in which "erotica," which was approved, meant "stimulation appropriate to a feminist consciousness," while pornography, "defined as exclusively male," meant the fusing of sex and violence, which was definitely not approved. "The implications of this neat dichotomization and sex-typing of desire reflect, unchanged, the Victorian ideology of innate differences in the nature of male and female libido and fantasy."[18] Similarly, Pat Califia, a member of the California-based Samois group,[19] blamed the women's movement for a new puritanism. Feminism was turning into "a moralistic force," which could "contribute to the self-loathing and misery experienced by sexual minorities."[20] Califia argued that the campaign against pornography was part of a new censoriousness in feminism, which passed judgment on people's individual sexual practices and fantasies, and which admitted only some forms of sexuality to the feminist canon of orthodoxy. In making the case for consensual lesbian S/M (sadomasochistic practices followed by lesbian partners as the expression of dominance-submission fantasies), Califia argued that those feminists who were horrified by these practices were confusing the creative use of fantasy in mutual sexual exploration with interpersonal physical violence. "Banning S/M porn," she wrote, is "the equivalent of making fantasy a criminal act. Violence against women will not be reduced by increasing sexual repression."[21]

Underlying this discussion was a controversy about women's "true" nature, and the correct direction for feminist politics. Were women and men members of the same species, polarized into "masculine" and "feminine" behaviors by the operations of the social construction of gender? Or were they constituted as entirely different by virtue of their sexual biology? The arguments of Dworkin, Griffin, and others seemed to echo a prefeminist view of an innate female and male nature, each somehow preordained and embodied in their modes of sexual appetite. In contrast, the lesbian-feminist S/M position seemed closer to the view of Chodorow and others that women were different from men as the result of culture rather than nature. It acknowledged that women, too, participated in sadomasochistic feelings in relation to sexuality, that they, too, experienced sexuality as linked to dominance and hierarchy.

A related question was, what path should women take in the direction of their own liberation? Within feminism, some argued that women should learn to behave more like men, and learn to compete equally with them, entering the structures they had designed on equal terms with men. Others argued that women should go their own way, developing the qualities acquired in oppression as the foundation of a new women's culture. This set of issues, too, was echoed in the debate over female sexuality. The "romantic" view of lesbian sexuality argued for a "pure" form of sex, divorced from any issues of power.[22] In contrast, the defenders of lesbian S/M were in effect arguing for the exploration of a previously male style of sexual expression: women were to have the freedom to objectify one another. They argued that women did experience lust, and did need to "act out" their desires for dominance and submission in sex. The antipornographers in effect denied that female sexuality, in its "pure" form, contained the appetite for power, and for destruction of the object, that they attributed to male sexuality.

It is arguable that the discussion of lesbian S/M took the debate a step forward, in acknowledging the link between female sexuality and power. But neither the antipornographers nor the pro-S/M writers approximated a new vision of feminist sexuality. Like gender identity, sexuality and sexual appetite were also socially constructed, subject to analysis and to change. A full exploration of sexuality in feminist terms thus remained on the agenda for the future.[23]

13

Changes and Continuities: The Roots of Metaphysical Feminism

The movement from the critique of sex roles to the development of a woman-centered perspective represented a fundamental shift of emphasis. Nonetheless there were important continuities between the two phases. These common assumptions, persistent habits of thought, left the way open for the exaggeration of the woman-centered perspective to a point of theoretical impasse. The three elements of continuity examined here are: (1) a divorce from the left and from Marxism; (2) a focus on psychology at the expense of economics; and (3) a false universalism in the analysis of gender.

"Goodbye to All That": The Divorce from the Left

The first element of continuity in radical feminist writing was a current of hostility to the political left and to Marxism. The theme of an angry or a weary rejection of Marxism and socialism appears in the work of many contemporary radical feminist writers. Adrienne Rich, for example, writes: "Much of what is narrowly termed 'politics' seems to rest on a longing for certainty, even at the cost of honesty, for an analysis which, once given, need not be reexamined. *Such is the deadendedness—for women—of Marxism in our time.*"[1] And, elsewhere in the same collection:

> For many of us, the word "revolution" itself has become not only a dead relic of Leftism, but a key to the deadendedness of male politics: the "revolution" of a wheel which returns in the end to the same place; the "revolving door" of a politics which has "liberated" women only to use them, and only within the limits of male tolerance.[2]

Similarly, Leah Fritz dismisses the possibility of any further connection between feminism and the political left. And Mary Daly simply lumps Marxism with Maoism, Christianity, and Islam, as subcategories of the "prevailing religion of the planet," namely, patriarchy.[3]

The rejection of Marxism can be traced, in part, to the origins of radical feminism in the 1960s: the radical wing of the new feminist movement grew out of, and in some sense in direct opposition to, the male New Left. These early practitioners of the second wave first served their apprenticeship in the ranks of the civil rights movement. As the "Movement" gathered steam in the second half of the 1960s, and developed into its various branches—black, student, antiwar, and counterculture—these women found themselves in the middle of a contradiction. Politicized and radicalized by their experience as organizers, fighting for the cause of equality and justice on behalf of blacks, Vietnamese, and other victims of oppression, they were at the same time treated, within the ranks of the New Left itself, as inferiors, servants, and sexual objects, who were exploited and oppressed themselves.[4] The attempts of some of these women to gain a voice in the leadership of the Movement, and to get a hearing for their growing sense of themselves as members of a "second-class" social category fell upon deaf ears. The much-quoted remark of Stokely Carmichael, exponent of the Black Power movement, was emblematic of the reaction to this unsuccessful effort: "The only position for women in SNCC [the Student Non-Violent Coordinating Committee] is prone."[5] Robin Morgan has recounted the episode in which radical feminists took over the left publication, *Rat*, in a coup which encapsulated the anger, frustration, and impatience of the new feminists with their erstwhile (male) comrades, who seemed incapable of hearing, and grasping, the implications of the theoretical insights of feminism, despite their grandiose claims to be revolutionaries.[6] In their declarations of independence from the New Left, then, the newly formed radical feminist groups rejected the New Left on both theoretical and practical grounds. They argued that the New Left was hypocritical: while claiming to be fighting for the elimination of oppression, its members nonetheless had neither analyzed nor acknowledged their own role as oppressors of the women who had been fighting at their side.

In calling themselves "radical feminists," the early theorists distinguished themselves from two other groups, namely, liberal feminists, and the men of the New Left. Shulamith Firestone characterized the "mainstream," liberal, or bourgeois branch of the women's movement as conservative. "This camp . . .," she wrote,

> is perhaps still best exemplified by its pioneer (and thus more hard-core feminist than is generally believed) NOW, the National Organization of Women, begun in 1965 by Betty Friedan after her reverberating publication of *The Feminine Mystique*. Often called the NAACP of

the women's movement . . . NOW concentrates on the more superficial symptoms of sexism—legal inequities, employment discrimination, and the like.[7]

In contrast, the radical branch of the women's movement claimed to have a program of change more sweeping and fundamental than anything envisaged by Friedan and her colleagues. But it also claimed to be more radical than the male left. As Firestone wrote, "The contemporary radical feminist position . . . sees feminist issues not only as *women's* first priority, but as central to any larger revolutionary analysis. It refuses to accept the existing leftist analysis is not because it is too radical, but because *it is not radical enough*. . . ."[8]

In appropriating the term "radical," the theorists of the second wave referred to its etymological meaning of "root." The oppression of women was at the root of all other oppressions, racial, economic, or political. As Robin Morgan wrote, "sexism is the root oppression, the one which, until and unless we *up*root it, will continue to put forth the branches of racism, class hatred, ageism, competition, ecological disaster, and economic exploitation."[9] Thus to eliminate women's oppression would create a new form of revolutionary change, going well beyond any previously known forms of political or cultural transformation. In its original usage, then, the "radical" in radical feminism referred to a more fundamentally revolutionary stance than that of the New Left. As Morgan declared, "Women are the real Left."[10]

As radical feminist theory expanded its scope in the years after 1970, it became clear that this mode of analysis represented a fundamental challenge to Marxism. It raised an array of issues in relation to women's condition that, despite Engels's acknowledgment of the "world-historical defeat of women," had been ignored or trivialized in the Marxist theoretical tradition.[11] Indeed, the questions addressed by feminists seemed increasingly difficult to place anywhere along the traditional political spectrum from left to right.[12] Precisely because they concerned the erstwhile "private" domain to which women had been consigned, women's issues began to appear, to some, as finding a place that was entirely off the map of male politics. The analysis of patriarchy, of rape, lesbianism, gender identity, pornography, and the like, seemed to require a different set of axes from those defining the traditional political grid.

This point of view was espoused, for example, by members of the Women Against Pornography campaign. Laura Lederer argued that a feminist perspective on pornography was neither liberal nor conservative, neither left nor right, but a third way.

> Until recently, there have been only two sides to the pornography
> issue: the conservative approach, which argues that pornography is
> immoral because it exposes the human body; and the liberal approach,
> which presents pornography as just one more aspect of our ever-
> expanding human sexuality. This book presents a third and feminist
> perspective: That pornography is the ideology of a culture which
> promotes and condones rape, woman-battering, and other crimes of
> violence against women. [13]

The fact that the goals of the New Right appeared to converge with those
of the campaign against pornography was not to be given any particular
weight. Diana Russell argued that it had been a mistake for feminists to shy
away from the issue, simply because this was something on which they and
right-wing forces agreed. "[T]he anti-pornography forces have almost
always been conservative, homophobic, antisex, and pro the traditional
family. . . . They are often against abortion, the Equal Rights Amendment, and the Women's Liberation Movement. We have been so put off by
the politics of these people, that our knee-jerk response is that we must be
for whatever they are *against*."[14]

While some sought to place the politics of feminism outside of the
traditional spectrum, others, most notably self-proclaimed socialist
feminists, began to attempt a rapprochement between feminism and the
left. They saw the need for reconciling the two modes of analysis that
placed patriarchy, on the one hand, and capitalism, on the other, as the twin
oppressors of women. While cognizant of the intellectual and political
difficulties of such an enterprise, these writers argued that only an analysis
that accommodated both class and gender could both account for the
oppression of women in its full complexity, and lay the groundwork for
ending it. This strand of feminist analysis placed feminist issues such as
reproductive self-determination in the context of an overall political struggle for a feminist democratic socialism, a new hybrid never before grown in
the garden of world politics. [15]

The attempts to conciliate the "unhappy marriage" of Marxism and
feminism remained tentative, and perhaps raised more questions than they
answered. But this was obviously a crucial area of inquiry. It seemed evident
that a feminist analysis that failed to take account of the effects of class, and of
the impact of the needs of a late monopoly capitalist economy on the position
of women domestically and internationally, would be less than adequate as a
tool either of analysis or of prediction. In addition, the concept that feminist
issues could somehow define themselves as outside of, or separate from,

the rest of the political spectrum seemed increasingly naive as that spectrum moved sharply to the right during the early 1980s. Ellen Willis noted that the feminist "preoccupation with pornography" converged with the "'pro-family' fundamentalism" of the New Right: was this, then, merely an attempt to "extend the movement's critique of sexism," or was it also "evidence that feminists have been affected by the conservative climate and are unconsciously moving with the cultural tide"?[16] If some feminists thought they could still carve themselves a space neither to the right nor to the left, this was not the view of the New Right, which clearly defined women's claims to self-determination as a dangerous part of the "secular humanism" they set out to defeat once and for all.[17]

It seemed, though, that the formative experience of the mid-1960s might have left lasting scars. Robin Morgan's bitterness toward the male editors of *Rat,* whose names have lapsed into relative obscurity, is still palpable on the page.[18] The anger of personal experience seemed to have been translated into a rejection of all aspects of Marxism, and in particular of any possible connections between the socialist tradition and that of feminism. If in fact part of this strand in radical feminism could be traced to a residue of anger at the events of the late 1960s, and at the violent male chauvinism of the New Left, and if this anger was still informing some feminist analysis at the opening of the 1980s, surely this was a misapplication of the principle that the "personal is the political." I do not mean to appear unsympathetic to the experiences of those who, like Leah Fritz, Robin Morgan, and others, came to feminism via a searing history of conflict with the New Left. It is certainly reasonable to argue, as Leah Fritz does, that the "male" style of SDS politics eventually doomed their revolutionary project to failure.[19] But a broader view of the history of feminist theory suggests important connections with the history of socialism. To extrapolate from an experience of failed communication and alliance in the conjuncture of the mid-1960s to an outright rejection of all Marxist categories of thought, and of all socialist experience and practice, would seem both methodologically unsound and foolhardy.

"The Personal is Political": Psychology as the Locus of Power

A second element of continuity in radical feminist theory was an emphasis on psychology as the major locus of power. As Heidi Hartmann noted, "The great thrust of radical feminist writing has been directed to the documentation of the slogan 'the personal is political.' . . . [I]ts focus on psychology is consistent."[20] Much has been written about the angry reaction to the New Left as a point of origin for radical feminist theory.[21] Not enough has been said, however, about the theoretical points of connection between the two. The split that took place politically was not replicated intellectually. In particular, the feminist concept of "the personal is the political" had important connections to the reexamination of power undertaken by elements of the (male) New Left. Like those streams of analysis from which it flowed, radical feminist theory retained an emphasis on the psychological, often at the expense of the underlying economic and social factors helping to shape it.

The reexamination of power and of power relations was a central focus of New Left theoretical and organizing work. Many "gurus" of the New Left were writers who addressed the psychological side effects of capitalism and colonialism—R. D. Laing, Herbert Marcuse, Frantz Fanon, and Wilhelm Reich, among others—and who, in this context, addressed issues of interpersonal domination. Those themes were taken up by subgroups within the Movement. Thus Laing's examination of interpersonal politics in the family was the basis of the work of groups such as the Radical Therapist. The student movement addressed itself to the issue of power in the classroom, and the interaction between students and teacher. As the civil rights movement developed, it introduced the concept of "Black Power." Relations between black and white were analyzed, no longer in liberal terms of winning equality under the law, but in terms of interpersonal power and domination.[22]

All of these strands of analysis were attempts to demystify the conventional, semiofficial discussions of political life in the United States. As depicted in textbooks of history and political science, the issue of power was addressed only in terms of the official "game" of lobbying and electoral politics. The real distribution of power and influence in the country was not seen as a legitimate area of inquiry. (Witness the treatment received by C. Wright Mills on the publication of *The Power Elite,* and his pessimism and isolation from the rest of intellectual life in the 1950s.[23]) To be sure, there was a Marxist tradition that located the analysis of power in the economic organization of society, and in particular, in the ownership of the means of production (although this tradition had effectively been silenced in American academic and political life during the 1950s). But the New Left distinguished itself from the Old, in part, by its focus upon those elements of power that lay in the realm of cultural assumptions and of psychological attitudes, or, in other words, in systems of belief, or ideologies. In the manner of Gramsci and Althusser, the New Left and the members of the counterculture sought to explain the continued power of capitalism by examining the hegemony of cultural attitudes, and the exercise of interpersonal power in all arenas of life, in the family, the school, university, church, the media, and elsewhere.

There were ample precedents for seeing that "the personal is political" when this slogan was coined by Carol Hanisch in 1970.[24] But radical feminist theory exposed the inadequacy of all previous work on power, in failing to analyze the domination of women as a central form and (possibly) a model for all other structures of interpersonal domination. This new analysis depicted the relation between men and women as one of domination and subordination, with the ideology of love serving to mask the realities of power.[25] The emphasis on power, and on the relative power-lessness of women as a sex class, was a major theme of the early women's liberation literature.[26] Thus the theorists of radical feminism were influenced, despite themselves, by the theorists of the New Left. But the intention of New Left theorists was to link issues of interpersonal power to the larger social and economic structures in which this power operated. In the development of radical feminist theory, this linkage was not always attended to.

The focus on gender as a locus of power relations set the terms of debate for much theoretical writing of the 1970s. The great strength of radical feminism lay in its brilliant dissection of the mythology surrounding gender. But to the extent that gender difference dominated the discussion, a tradition of feminist theoretical writing on psychological, rather than on political, economic, or social issues, became central and influential in the United States, even among writers like Chodorow who counted themselves as socialist feminists.[27] In some recent texts, this attachment to the psychological as causal of women's oppression was carried to an extreme: for example, Robin Morgan's slogan, "Pornography is the theory, rape the practice," implying that the psychology of male power, expressed in cultural artifacts, gave rise in and of itself to the physical domination of women.[28] In such a construct, the economic powerlessness of women got short shrift indeed.

The emphasis on psychology, and on power in interpersonal situations such as marriage, may have given many women the impression that in order to transform their situation, it sufficed to change the way they thought about the world. To say this is in no way to minimize the importance of consciousness-raising. On the contrary, I would argue that this process must be ongoing, undertaken anew by each generation of new arrivals to the country of feminism. But it needs to be stressed that the psychological interacts with the economic, the social, and the political. A feminist analysis that locates power only in individual psychology is both naive and damaging.

"All Women . . .": False Universalism

The third element of continuity between the two phases of radical feminism was a false universalism that generalized about the experience of women, ignoring the specificities of race, class, and culture. A feminist perspective assumed that all women in the world, whatever their race, religion, class, or sexual preference, had something fundamentally in common. Some versions of feminism took this assumption a step further: they insisted that what women had in common, by virtue of their membership in the group of women, outweighed all of their other differences, or (to put this another way) that the similarity of their situation as female was more fundamental than their economic and cultural differences. The second step in this argument is what I term "false" universalism. To some extent, this habit of thought grew inevitably from the need to establish gender as a legitimate intellectual category. But too often it gave rise to analysis that, in spite of its narrow base of white, middle-class experience, purported to speak about and on behalf of all women, black or white, poor or rich.

Much ink was spilled in the late 1960s and early 1970s in the attempt to define women as a social group. Shulamith Firestone spoke of women as a "sex class," but Juliet Mitchell held that none of the terms applied to other oppressed groups were quite appropriate to women: properly speaking they were neither a class, nor a caste. To cope with the difficulty, Gayle Rubin coined the term "sex/gender system." The categories of male and female interacted in a complex way with other social categories like class and race, but they never overlapped completely with these other categories. They were in and of themselves constitutive elements of any social order. Whatever expression one used, the fundamental propositions were the same: gender was a significant category of social analysis, and the experience of femaleness—of being socially designated a woman—was a comparable source of oppression the world over.[29]

One source of the "universalist" emphasis was the institution of consciousness-raising. The technique sought to establish among members of a given group the extent to which individual experiences, which members might have seen as personal and even idiosyncratic, could in fact be fitted together into a pattern that reflected a structure of oppression.[30]

The impact was to enable the participants to deemphasize their differences, and to focus on the experiences they had in common. The generalizing that took place in these groups could, of course, only describe the experience of the women who participated. By and large, these were college-educated white women. The networks through which CR groups were created deliberately followed lines of friendship and acquaintance (this was a recommendation from at least one set of guidelines on how to form a group). Generalizations about the condition of women necessarily reflected these networks, and therefore, their limitations.[31] The tendency of some radical feminist texts, however, was to ignore the narrowness of this base of information, and to speak globally. It was common to make generalizations about oppression that included, either explicitly or implicitly, all of the women in the world. Writers as different as Jean Baker Miller and Susan Brownmiller shared the rhetorical habit of referring, without modification or disclaimer, to "all women."[32]

False universalism in feminist analysis was particularly damaging in relation to the issue of race. Black women and other women of color pointed to the insensitivity of white feminists in assuming that their experience could speak for that of all women, or, alternatively, in using the experience of blacks as a metaphor for that of (white) women, without noticing the unconscious racism of their language and assumptions.[33] In addition, white feminist writing often misinterpreted the experience of black women in the United States, in ways that fundamentally undermined the credibility of their analysis. Thus Alison Edwards accused Susan Brownmiller of outright racism, in failing to grasp the crucial differences between the experience of black and white women, and in particular, the enormous differential of power, measured by both income and range of options, that separated black from white women. Brownmiller's view of the crime of rape showed a failure of sensitivity to the issue of violent crime in relation to racism in the American context. In her accounts of the use of rape to frame black men, Brownmiller did not present these events in the context of a racist system of criminal justice. She thus lined up a feminist perspective with the forces of white "law and order."[34] Angela Davis pointed out that most white feminist analysis of rape omitted the historical background to the "myth" of the black rapist. This myth, she wrote, was developed as a political weapon during the period of Reconstruction, when the lynching of black men became a basic weapon in preserving the economic and political subordination of black people after their emancipation from slavery. In this context, the history of rape written by Brownmiller and others fed into racist mythology, rather than placing the struggle against sexism alongside of, and directly allied to, the struggle against racism.[35]

The net effect of this false universalism was to align feminist theory with a form of neo-colonialism or neo-imperialism. Audre Lorde took Mary Daly to task for mentioning the experience of women of color only in the context of their victimization, and not as a source of wisdom. As a result, Lorde wrote, Daly's account was just another example of the "work of women of color being ghettoized by a white woman dealing only out of a patriarchal western-european frame of reference."[36] Without a sensitivity to the experience of nonwhite women, it was futile for white feminists to imagine that they were in the process of creating a new analytical framework. As Judit Moschkovich, a Latina-Jewish woman, wrote, "When Anglo-American women speak of developing a new feminist or women's culture, they are still working and thinking within an Anglo-American cultural framework. This new culture would still be just as racist and ethnocentric as patriarchal American culture."[37]

The concept of "all women," then, was a double-edged sword. On the one hand, it seemed to denote a powerful new vision, cutting across all of the boundaries of nationality, race, and religion. It declared that women all over the world were part of an oppressed group, even more universal than the international proletariat of Marxism. On the other hand, the universalism of this vision ignored the differences among women, and the political weight of those differences. As Edwards wrote, "[i]n this framework, Happy Rockefeller has more in common with a black woman in an auto plant than has a male black autoworker."[38]

"Metaphysical" Feminism

The three elements of continuity—a divorce from the left, a focus on psychology, and a false universalism—were present in much of feminist theoretical writing during the 1970s. But they came together in an exaggerated form in the version of feminism characterized by Judith Clavir (following Robin Morgan) as "metaphysical" feminism. In this world view,

> one woman's experience is all women's experience, because all women have a bond which is eternal, biological, and historical. Women's culture with its rituals, poetry, and magic is an expression of their very body chemistry; and it is this chemistry with its limitless energy that patriarchs of all classes, nations, and eras of history try to dominate and control. This biology and this oppression bonds [sic] together all women who have ever lived.

Opposed to the collectivity of women was "an entity they call 'the patriarchy' which becomes in its own right an eternal and unchanging actor on the world stage. 'The patriarchy' acts but cannot be acted upon."[39]

The original claim of radical feminism was to "go further" than liberal feminism. Liberal or bourgeois feminism seemed to limit itself to reformism, seeking to improve the status of women within the "system," but not fundamentally contesting either its operations or its legitimacy. The full equality of women could be accommodated within the framework of monopoly capitalism. In contrast, radical feminism meant changes that went so "far" as to contest the system at its foundation. Because these changes could not be accommodated, the program of radical feminism was one of fundamental, revolutionary challenge. As radical feminist theory developed, however, the emphasis upon psychology and the refusal of alliance with forces on the left meant a retreat from confrontation. In the world view described by Clavir, radical feminism had moved very far from the principles espoused by Millett and Firestone. In the language of Daly and Morgan, "going too far" appeared to mean, not a challenge to the status quo, but an inner, psychological voyage. Without a grounding in the realities of race, class, and history, the radical feminist voyage became a metaphysical or spiritual journey, rather than a political one.[40]

"Metaphysical" feminism was, in fact, the woman-centered perspective carried to an extreme. Paradoxically, though, the net effect of this "woman-centered" vision was not to place women at the center of culture and society, but to recapitulate, and in some sense to accept, the formulation of woman as Other, the very category of being against which Simone de Beauvoir had originally rebelled. Philosophically, the view of woman as an eternal "essence" represented a retreat from the fundamentally liberating concept of woman as agent, actor, and subject, rather than object.[41] And politically, at least in some versions, it meant a retreat from struggle, in a period when all of the issues raised by the second wave, from rape to equal pay, remained unresolved, in a period of deepening economic depression.

14

Conclusion:
Restoring the Radical to
Radical Feminism

In the evolution of feminist theory from Shulamith Firestone to Mary Daly, the word "radical" shifted in meaning. In its use among the feminists who broke with the New Left in the late 1960s, "radical" meant a commitment to a kind of social change even more fundamental than that espoused by the revolutionaries of SDS. In the definition offered by Mary Daly, however, "radical" meant metaphysical, that is, it referred to an inner voyage, and a retreat from political struggle, a withdrawal from the attempt to enter the structures of patriarchy on any terms.[1]

What explained this shift in meaning? I have argued that it stemmed, in some measure, from some of the assumptions of radical feminism as it was first outlined, and from the internal logic of those assumptions.[2] But I believe that it was also, in part, an expression of impatience and disillusionment with the path taken by the women's movement. In particular, it was a reaction to what appeared to be the reformism, the piecemeal character, of feminist achievement in the public sphere.

The vision of radical transformation that was embodied in the work of Millett and Firestone bore little resemblance to the actual impact of the women's movement on society. As incorporated into the capitalist democracies, feminism came to mean a narrowly defined form of social change, most notably, the recruitment of women into some of the areas of power and privilege from which they had been previously excluded. Thus, in the United States, the 1970s saw the admission of women into elite colleges like Yale and Princeton, the expansion of women's enrollment in male-dominated professional schools of law, medicine, and engineering, and the entry of women into the middle reaches of corporate management and public administration. They saw, too, the passage of legislation to ensure equal opportunity in matters of education, credit, and employment, and the establishment of procedures, via courts and commissions, securing the entry of women and minorities into white male-dominated areas of employment such as mining and construction. The appointment of the first woman justice to the Supreme Court in 1981 also followed this pattern. The kind of social transformation envisaged by Shulamith Firestone—the "feminist revolution" she called for—did not take place. The structures oppressing women, especially the nuclear family, were not dismantled. Rather, the changes that took place appeared to accommodate and co-opt feminist demands, in the familiar pattern of American liberalism, without making any basic changes in the structures of political, economic, or social life.

In the 1980s, all the gains of feminism—however limited and reformist they might appear to be—were coming under threat from the New Right. In her reconsideration of feminism, Betty Friedan placed some of the blame for the backlash on the excesses of the early radical feminists.[3] According to Friedan, what she termed the rhetoric of sexual politics had diverted the energies of the women's movement. By attacking heterosexual sexuality and the family, radical feminists had alienated ordinary women, and thus facilitated the rise of the conservative reaction. "If only we had won the Equal Rights Amendment in those heady first seven years—" Friedan wrote,

> as we should and could have, if we hadn't been diverted by sexual politics or co-opted by "masculine" political power—it would not be so easy for right-wing Senators to dismantle affirmative-action programs against sex discrimination in education and employment, as they announced they intended to do, less than a week after the 1980 Reagan landslide election. (203)

From a political and a historical point of view, Friedan's interpretation was, I believe, profoundly erroneous. Far from being the cause of the backlash, the radical views of those espousing sexual politics at the beginning of the second wave made it possible for the less sweeping reforms of liberal or bourgeois feminism to make some headway. In this, the recent period of feminism recalled earlier experience: writing about the first wave, Willie Lee Rose noted that "[it] may . . . have been true of this period of reform, as it has been true of our own, that the existence of a more radical and ideological left made the work of those engaged in practical efforts for concrete and immediate improvements easier than it might otherwise have been."[4] Precisely because women were raising such a wide range of issues, across such a broad spectrum of sexual, social, economic, and political demands, certain of the less threatening of these were able to find their way into legislative and judicial decisions benefitting women.

Ironically, Friedan's judgment about the recent evolution of the women's movement converged with that of some of those feminists in the tradition of sexual politics that she disavowed with such energy. In recounting her reaction to an encounter with the women training as officers at West Point, Friedan drew back in dismay. Self-consciously evoking the language of the 1960s, she asked:

> Was that really what it was all about, our great revolutionary women's movement—advancing women to death-dealing power in the military-industrial complex? . . . had feminism simply delivered women into the militaristic, materialistic bowels of late capitalist American imperialism? . . . Must the women's movement for equality come into ultimate conflict with the profound values of life that, for me as for others, have always been associated with women? (164–65)

In effect, Friedan was writing a woman-centered analysis. She was criticizing the women's movement for having created the possibility for women to climb the corporate ladder toward ever increasing power, with ever diminishing regard for and involvement with the traditionally female concerns of intimacy and nurturance. Like Mary Daly, Friedan was critical of the effect of feminist "success" in producing women who were merely clones of their male counterparts. Like Adrienne Rich, Friedan implicitly rejected the androgynous model. The original hypothesis about sex-role stereotyping was, it seemed, all too accurate. Men and women were not that different fundamentally from one another. Women could learn to be aggressive, to compete, and to exploit the labor of others with impunity.

In despair over these developments, Daly redefined "radical," as noted, calling on women to reject tokenism, turn their backs on patriarchy and attempts to reform it, and to embark on the journey to the Otherworld. Friedan, for her part, counseled the abandonment of radical positions on sexual politics, on issues such as abortion, rape, and lesbianism. Instead, she said, women should return to an emphasis on the values of community and the interpersonal ties of intimacy. "Family," she wrote, was "not just a buzz word for reaction. . . ." It was

> the symbol of that last area where one has any hope of individual control over one's destiny, of meeting one's most basic human needs, of nourishing that core of personhood threatened now by vast imper-

sonal institutions and uncontrollable corporate and government bureaucracies and the bewildering, accelerating pace of change. (229)

In a curious way, the analyses of Mary Daly and of Betty Friedan converged. After fifteen years of debate over gender difference, disillusionment with the pace and the direction of the changes wrought by the second wave led both writers—one the self-proclaimed mother of liberal feminism, the other, a high priestess of lesbian separatism—to similar conclusions. The structures of male power were unchangeable, despite the access to them won by women. The salvation of women (indeed, in Friedan's version, of both women and men) lay in the creation of another, private realm, where the values associated with women could be safely nurtured. Daly and Friedan, in different ways, had created parallel versions of a retreat to the separate sphere of women. A "haven in a heartless world," indeed![5]

The implicit pessimism of the positions expressed by Daly and Friedan, and their disillusionment with the impact of the renewed feminism of the 1970s, was shortsighted. I have suggested that, in its project of ending the subordination of women, feminism drew upon three streams of political and social theory: political rights, as defined in eighteenth- and nineteenth-century liberalism; economic rights, as defined in nineteenth- and twentieth-century socialist theory; and sexual rights, as defined in twentieth-century theories of sexual liberation. Further, for women, liberation meant reproductive self-determination as well, a category omitted by a male-defined political tradition. These requirements complicated and subverted traditional definitions of male politics. Women were enmeshed in structures of power both private and public.[6] In addition, from a historical point of view, women were seeking to acquire many of these rights— won by men for themselves over more than two centuries—within the space of a single decade and a half.[7] Even in the advanced industrial states, women were far from having achieved this. The defeat of the Equal Rights Amendment in 1982 underlined this reality: women in the United States had failed, as yet, to complete their bourgeois revolution, let alone the feminist revolution envisaged by some more ambitious theorists of the second wave.

To say this was not to argue for the abandonment of the feminist project. On the contrary, it was to place it in historical perspective. In addition, given the enormity of the task, it was to argue for an appreciation, on the part of feminist theorists, of the considerable gains won by the women's movement. The debate over gender difference initiated by the second wave began a process of change that, however limited in scope compared to its potential, nonetheless appeared to be irreversible. Despite reverses over the right to funded, unrestricted abortion, and over the Equal Rights Amendment, and despite an apparent increase in male violence toward women, Ann Ferguson and Nancy Folbre argued that

> these setbacks do not mean that feminist efforts are being completely neutralized. The increase in male violence may represent a frustrated response to the weakening of forms of male control which were once considered legitimate. The possibility remains that some future political or economic changes will enable men to reestablish traditional levels of control over women's reproductive decisions. It is difficult, however, to imagine what shape such changes might take short of outright fascism.[8]

Rather than dismissing the achievements of the revived women's movement as reformist or as forms of co-optation, feminist theory needed to take account of them, to analyze them critically and in detail, and to assess their implications for further change. As Linda Gordon and Ellen Dubois pointed out, "[i]t is vital to strategy-building to know when we are winning and when losing, and where. Failing to claim and take pride in our victories leads to the false conclusion that nothing has changed."[9]

If the pessimism of Daly and Friedan stemmed, in part, from a historically ill-informed impatience with reform, it was related, as well, to the development of the reactionary view of gender difference associated with metaphysical feminism.[10] To recapitulate: if the account presented here is accurate, then there has been a dialectical movement in feminist thought since 1970 on this issue. From an attempt to minimize differences between men and women, feminist theory moved to a celebration of female difference, and a woman-centered perspective. The critique of patriarchy led initially to an argument for androgyny, for the amalgamation of "male" and "female" traits into a new, monogendered personality. The feminist attack on sex roles was taken up by social scientists and the media, and the analysis of power in sexual politics became diffused. Instead, the emphasis moved to what was wrong with women, and how they required resocialization in order to compete on an equal basis with men.

In the reaction against androgyny and its co-optation, some feminists called for a perspective that valued women's experience and traditional values, rather than one that required women to imitate the worst features of male behavior. As the woman-centered perspective developed, however, in some versions of it the concept of the social construction of gender was replaced by a claim to the intrinsic moral superiority of women. In a new codification of sex differences, women were seen as pure by definition, and men as corrupt. If all culture and political power were male, then political struggle by feminists lost its meaning: the male structures of power were by definition hopelessly impermeable to womanly or female values.

To hold, as Daly, Dworkin, and others did, that a feminist perspective fundamentally opposed sadomasochism, or to say that female culture was opposed to, and an alternative to a death-loving male culture, seemed valid enough statements. But to go one step further, and to make these cultural and political clusters equivalent to, coextensive with, biological femaleness and maleness respectively, was to reenter the world of biological determinism, of "anatomy is destiny." It was, in addition, to make a fundamentally pessimistic statement about the possibility of both personal and social change in women and men. Arguing for the intrinsic superiority of the female was abandoning the original revolutionary insight of Millett, Firestone, and others, that gender differences were socially constructed, and that they were susceptible, therefore, to transformation.

There was, however, an alternative direction for feminist theory. This was to incorporate the insights of a woman-centered analysis, without jettisoning the basic understanding of the social construction of gender, into a renewed commitment to the struggle for fundamental social change. It is outside of the framework of the present study to elaborate in any detail upon the content of such a newly radical feminist theory. But I have already indicated some of its necessary constituent elements. First among these would be a retreat from false universalism, and a sensitivity to the diversity of women's experiences and needs. This process was already underway; as Ann Snitow noted, "[t]here is a growing understanding among feminists that the recognition of gender as a significant political category in no way bypasses the crucial differences among women; of class, race, and sexual preference."[11] Among anthropologists, sweeping generalizations about the universal and presumably identical oppression of women in all cultures were being contested. In a reconsideration of the public/domestic split as a universal feature of human societies, Michelle Rosaldo cautioned against the oversimplified use of her original concept. "I now believe," she wrote, "that gender is not a unitary fact determined everywhere by the same sorts of concerns, but, instead, the complex product of a variety of social forces. The most serious objections to my 1974 account have demonstrated . . . that 'women's status' is itself not one but many things. . . ."[12]

In a parallel development, women from non-Western countries were beginning to indicate their requirements for autonomy in regard to their own feminist undertakings, and to call on feminists from Western countries to respect this need, even in reference to highly emotive questions such as the genital mutilation of young girls. Thus the Association of African Women for Research and Development, based in Dakar, Senegal, reproached some Western feminists for a failure to see the issue in a broader framework.

> [F]ighting against genital mutilation without placing it in the context of ignorance, obscurantism, exploitation, poverty, etc., . . . , without questioning the structures and social relations which perpetuate this situation, is like "refusing to see the sun in the middle of the day". . . . especially since Westerners necessarily profit from the exploitation of the peoples and women of Africa, whether directly or indirectly.

Western feminists, they wrote, needed to acknowledge the fact that this issue could only be resolved with the "conscious participation of African women," and needed to avoid "ill-timed interference, maternalism, ethnocentrism, and misuse of power."[13]

Similarly, within the United States, women of color were beginning to articulate their own experience, and to point to some of the historical and cultural differences that made for a distinctive approach to the meaning of feminism in their own lives. They were indicating, as well, the need of the "white sector of the feminist movement" for an accurate account of the intersection of racism with sexism. Thus the naive, and sometimes racist, generalizations of the second wave about the automatic commonalities of all women were beginning to be superseded by the sounds of a dialogue among many voices, black, white, and brown. As Gloria Joseph and Jill Lewis wrote, "in that we speak as Black, as White, as Black woman, as White woman, we are not a homogenized unit. . . . We speak from our own histories and cultures. But we also speak *to each other*. . . ."[14]

Second, feminist theory would need to reconsider its emphasis on psychological issues, and specifically, the tradition established by Millett and Firestone of linking the powerlessness of women to their socialization into the female role. Unlike its counterparts in Great Britain and elsewhere, much feminist theory in the United States during the 1970s did not focus upon the sexual division of labor, as it functioned in the workplace as well as the home, but instead analyzed the powerlessness of women chiefly in psychological terms.[15] Obviously, it was not a question of eliminating one perspective or the other, but rather, of seeing the two levels as dialectically interrelated, and of investigating that interaction: how did the material situation of women affect their psychology, and vice versa? On the one hand, the crisis women faced in the 1980s was fundamentally economic in nature: lack of jobs, of child care, of resources for welfare, education, and training, as well as lack of access to affordable abortions, combined with forced sterilization. On the other hand, the radical feminist analysis of sex roles remained of crucial relevance. The strength of conditioning into those roles continued to be a major factor in keeping most women from contesting their assignment to certain kinds of low-paid work, including unpaid domestic work, despite the inroads of feminist analysis into public consciousness.[16]

Such an approach was of particular importance in the discussion of sexual issues such as sexual preference, and pornography, which otherwise tended to be debated as though sexuality could be separated from the body, with all of its other appetites, and from the social relations within which it found expression. This required an awareness of the uses of sexuality by capitalism, its packaging as a commodity, and its co-optation (for example, via the new marketing of homosexuality).[17] As Ferguson and Folbre wrote:

> Sexual freedom is important because women need to define themselves as *sexual subjects,* not sexual objects. We have to find ways to combat the commoditization of sexuality which oppresses women (e.g. the fight against pornography which associates sexual pleasure with violence against women) without falling into a puritanism which discredits the right to sexual pleasure as an end in itself.[18]

But it also required an awareness of the relation between sexual expression and material comfort: the leisure for sexual experimentation was a scarce and expensive commodity, as well.

Finally, a new radical feminist theory would see the women's movement as connected, both theoretically and practically, to other struggles for social justice. Such a theoretical position would place women's needs and women's goals at the center of a progressive political program. As Ferguson and Folbre point out, a woman-centered perspective directly challenged the values of the newly militant political right:

> Women are nurturers: we keep the systems we work in (the family, service jobs in wage labor) together by nurturing. The social relations of our nurturance work account on the one hand for our oppression (sacrificing our own interests for those of men and children), and on

the other hand for our potential strength as bearers of a radical
culture: we support an ethic of sharing, cooperation, and collective
involvement that stands in clear opposition to an ethic based on
individualism, competition, and private profit.[19]

What Adrienne Rich called "a politics of *asking women's questions*"[20] would
help to lay the groundwork for a revived campaign for the goals of
feminism, in a period when the most elementary rights of women (and
others)—to education, health, jobs, childcare—were under attack. It
would also pave the way for working coalitions and alliances between a
strong and autonomous women's movement, and other groups with related goals: members of progressive caucuses within labor unions, the
antinuclear movement, pro-environment groups, groups fighting racism,
groups fighting for gay liberation, democratic socialists and others inside
and outside of electoral politics. All such organizations and individuals could
eventually be infused with a feminist vision, and a feminist set of issues and
priorities.

Such a path for feminist practice is, of course, paved with difficulties. It
would be foolish to minimize the obstacles to creating and maintaining
these connections: an effective alliance between the women's movement
and the male-dominated left, in *groupuscules,* minority parties, or
mainstream institutions such as the Democratic Party in the United States
or the Labor Party in Australia, is arguably the work of more than one
lifetime. In addition, it would be unjust to place the responsibility for
building such alliances solely on the shoulders of feminists. But I believe
that this path is mandated by the logic of the analysis of gender difference.
From the history of feminist thought since 1970, one can glean three
options for women. First, there is the option of agreeing to compete in the
male-defined world of politics on its own terms, in the manner of a
Margaret Thatcher. Second, there is the option of withdrawing from that
world, out of pessimism as to its essentially patriarchal nature, creating
instead an otherworld of female retreat. This presupposes that one can
afford the real estate, and that one is willing to gamble that the world itself
will continue to escape nuclear destruction.

Finally, there is the option of entering the world and attempting to
change it, in the image of the woman-centered values at the core of
feminism. I believe that only this last option offers any hope. From a
practical point of view, it requires alliances with those sharing some of
these political goals. From a theoretical point of view, it means associating
feminism with the liberating traditions of Western thought, from Locke and
Rousseau to Marx and Engels, tending in the direction of greater equality,

shared decision-making, and justice. But it means, too, transforming these traditions, by imbuing them with the woman-centered values of nurturance and intimacy, as necessary and legitimate goals of political life. If achieve-ing such a set of transformations appears a Herculean (or Amazonian) task, one can nonetheless take heart for the struggle from the strength and resourcefulness shown by women in their quest for liberation up to now. However utopian the vision, realizing it is, in my view, the chief work of feminist theory and practice for the foreseeable future.

Notes and References

Introduction

1. Linda Gordon, "The Struggle for Reproductive Freedom: Three Stages of Feminism," in *Capitalist Patriarchy and the Case for Socialist Feminism*, ed. Zillah R. Eisenstein (New York: Monthly Review Press, 1979), p. 107n.

2. In *The New Feminist Movement* (New York: Russell Sage Foundation, 1974), Maren Lockwood Carden dates the "second wave" from about 1966 (p. 66), when the first demonstrations and mimeographed broadsheets began to appear. The term was coined by Martha Weinman Lear, "The Second Feminist Wave," *New York Times Magazine,* 10 March 1968. See the article by the late (and sorely missed) Joan Kelly, "Early Feminist Theory and the *Querelle des Femmes,* 1400–1789," *Signs: Journal of Women in Culture and Society* 8, no. 1 (Autumn 1982):4–28. For a convenient overview of feminist thought since the eighteenth century, see Alice S. Rossi, ed., *The Feminist Papers: From Adams to de Beauvoir* (New York: Columbia University Press, 1973).

3. Iris Young, "Socialist Feminism and the Limits of Dual Systems Theory," *Socialist Review,* nos. 50–51 (March–June 1980), pp. 170–71.

4. The present work is part of a cohort of books published in the last few years undertaking a common task of assessment. See Michèle Barrett, *Women's Oppression Today: Problems in Marxist Feminist Analysis* (London: Verso Editions and NLB, 1980); Zillah R. Eisenstein, *The Radical Future of Liberal Feminism* (New York: Longman, 1981); Z. Eisenstein, *Capitalist Patriarchy;* Annette Kuhn and AnnMarie Wolpe, eds., *Feminism and Materialism: Women and Modes of Production* (London: Routledge and Kegan Paul, 1978); Lydia Sargent, ed., *Women and Revolution: A Discussion of the Unhappy Marriage of Marxism and Feminism* (Boston: South End Press, 1981). See also Clare Burton, "From the Family to Social Reproduction: The Development of Feminist Theory" (Ph.D. diss. Macquarie University, Sydney, 1979). There are also a number of useful essay collections: see Charlotte Bunch, Jane Flax, Alexa Freeman, Nancy Hartsock, and Mary-Helen Manther, eds., *Building Feminist Theory: Essays from Quest, a Feminist Quarterly* (New York: Longman, 1981), and Sheila Ruth, ed., *Issues in Feminism: A First Course in Women's Studies* (Boston: Houghton Mifflin, 1980),

among others. As far as I know, however, my book is the first full-length study to consider the development of feminist theory in its own terms, rather than in conjunction either with Marxist or liberal social theory.

5. Elaine Showalter is preparing an anthology of feminist utopias from the 17th to the 20th century (Elaine Showalter, personal communication, March 1983). Two well-known utopias in the tradition of Thomas More are Charlotte Perkins Gilman's recently resurrected *Herland,* ed. Ann J. Lane (New York: Pantheon Books, 1979), and Monique Wittig, *Les Guérillères* (Paris: Les Editions de Minuit, 1969); trans. David Levay (New York: Viking, 1971). But I refer here to the utopian quality of nonfiction feminist writing. Cf. Elaine Marks and Isabelle de Courtrivon, eds., *New French Feminisms: An Anthology* (Amherst: University of Massachusetts Press, 1980): "the *utopias* toward which all feminisms tend" (p. xiii) and "Utopias. This section communicates the vision of the new worlds to which feminist thought and action are dedicated" (p. 231).

6. In this regard, a report on Hanna Holborn Gray's first twenty months of service as president of the University of Chicago was revealing. "[T]he first woman president of a major private research university," readers were reassuringly informed, ". . . is essentially no different from the men who head other such institutions" (Gene Maeroff, "Female President Settles in Comfortably at University of Chicago," *New York Times,* 16 March 1980).

7. On this point, see Sheila M. Rothman, *Woman's Proper Place: A History of Changing Ideals and Practices, 1870 to the Present* (New York: Basic Books, 1978), pp. 61 ff.; Nancy Chodorow, "Gender, Relation, and Difference in Psychoanalytic Perspective," in *The Future of Difference,* ed. Hester Eisenstein and Alice Jardine (Boston: G. K. Hall, 1980), p. 3; Jane Addams, 1897, quoted in Jurate Kazickas and Lynn Sherr, *The Woman's Calendar for 1980* (New York: Universe Books, 1979), back pages: "I am not one of these who believe—broadly speaking—that women are better than men. We have not wrecked railroads, nor corrupted Legislatures, nor done many unholy things that men have done; but then we must remember that we have not had the chance."

8. On Juliet Mitchell, see below, chapter 2.

9. Z. Eisenstein, *Radical Future,* passim.

10. Ibid.

11. Anatole France, *Le Lys Rouge* (1894), chapter 7. A form of proto-feminism was an element of utopian socialism among Fourierists, Saint-Simonians, and others. On the relations between feminism and Marxism, see Batya Weinbaum, *The Curious Courtship of Women's Liberation and Socialism* (Boston: South End Press, 1978), and works cited in note 4, above. See also below, chapter 13.

12. See, on this point, Juliet Mitchell, *Psychoanalysis and Feminism* (New York: Pantheon Books, 1974).

13. An example of this attitude is the decision of the *Des femmes* group in Paris to abandon the use of the word "feminism" altogether, on the ground that it is "one more 'ism,' that is, a reformist, opportunistic, capitalist ideology" (Christiane

Makward, "To Be or Not to Be . . . a Feminist Speaker," in *Future of Difference,* ed. Eisenstein and Jardine, p. 99. See also Jessie Bernard, "Foreword," in *Feminist Movement,* by Carden, p. x, who argues that feminists have been successful because they are performing a basic function of forcing society to accommodate to changes that have already occurred in the labor force and elsewhere. God, she writes, "has chosen mettlesome feminists to modernize our creaking societal structures, especially the sex-role structure."

14. Members of the current women's movement have unfortunately begun in recent years to retreat from radical stances, thereby giving credence to this critique of feminism from the left. One example is the reluctance of the Women Against Pornography campaign to endorse either abortion rights or the rights of lesbians and gay men in connection with their conference and march in 1980, for fear of alienating some of their support in the Catholic Church and elsewhere. Another was the reluctance of organizers for the Equal Rights Amendment in N.O.W. to support abortion rights, for fear of alienating the legislators whose backing they sought (see Letta Taylor, "Abortion Battle Continues Nationwide," *Guardian,* 23 July 1980, p. 4).

15. A facile and insensitive comparison between the experience of "women" and "blacks" in the United States was virtually a cliché of feminist writing in the 1970s. Bell Hooks (Gloria Watkins) correctly castigates white feminists for impressing "upon the American public their sense that the word 'woman' meant white women by drawing endless analogies between 'women' and 'blacks.'" Bell Hooks, *Ain't I A Woman: Black Women and Feminism* (Boston: South End Press, 1981), p. 139. On the retreat from universalism, see below, chapter 14.

16. See Herbert Gintis, "Communication and Politics: Marxism and the 'Problem' of Liberal Democracy," *Socialist Review,* nos. 50–51 (March–June 1980), pp. 195–96.

17. Alix Kates Shulman, "Dancing in the Revolution: Emma Goldman's Feminism," *Socialist Review,* no. 62 (March–April 1982), pp. 32–33.

18. Ibid., p. 33.

19. See Sarah Stage's review article, "Women's History and 'Woman's Sphere': Major Works of the 1970s", *Socialist Review,* nos. 50–51 (March–June 1980), pp. 245–53. I am indebted to Catharine R. Stimpson for the suggestion that this body of feminist scholarship contributed to the evolution of feminist thought described here (personal communication, December 1979).

20. See Monique Wittig, "One is Not Born a Woman," *Feminist Issues* 1, no. 2 (Winter 1981):47–54.

21. Chodorow, "Gender, Relation, and Difference," p. 3.

22. See Lenore Manderson, "Self, Couple, and Community: Recent Writings on Lesbian Women," *Hecate: A Women's Interdisciplinary Journal* (Brisbane) 6, no. 1 (1980):75 ff.

23. On the history of the second wave, see Barbara Sinclair Deckard, *The Women's Movement: Political, Socioeconomic, and Psychological Issues* (New York:

Harper & Row, 1979); Sara Evans, *Personal Politics: The Roots of Women's Liberation in the Civil Rights Movement and the New Left* (New York: Vintage Books, 1979); Carden, *Feminist Movement;* Jo Freeman, *The Politics of Women's Liberation: A Case Study of an Emerging Social Movement and Its Relation to the Policy Process* (New York: David McKay, 1975); on the women's movement in Great Britain, see Anna Coote and Beatrix Campbell, *Sweet Freedom: The Struggle for Women's Liberation* (London: Picador, 1982).

24. Many Women's Studies researchers are working on this project; see, for example, Katherine O'Sullivan See, "Feminism and Political Philosophy," *Feminist Studies* 8, no. 1 (Spring 1982):179–94, reviewing Z. Eisenstein, *Radical Future,* and Susan Moller Okin, *Women in Western Political Thought* (Princeton: Princeton University Press, 1979).

25. See for example Gayle Graham Yates, *What Women Want: The Ideas of the Movement* (Cambridge: Harvard University Press, 1975), characterizing the women's movement as having three ideological divisions (which form sections of the book): "feminist," "women's liberationist," and "androgynous."

26. Thus Alix Shulman lists bourgeois, socialist, conservative, radical, lesbian-separatist, the feminism of women's culture "(called in France 'neo-femininity'), the woman's studies movement, the woman's health movement, the reproductive rights movement, and many more" (Shulman, "Dancing in the Revolution," p. 33).

27. Simone de Beauvoir, *The Second Sex,* trans. H. M. Parshley (New York: Alfred A. Knopf, 1953)—originally published as *Le Deuxième Sexe* (Paris: Gallimard, 1949); Betty Friedan, *The Feminine Mystique* (New York: Dell Publishing, 1963); Germaine Greer, *The Female Eunuch* (1971; reprint ed., New York: Bantam Books, 1972).

Part I: Prologue

1. de Beauvoir, *Second Sex,* pp. xviii–xix.

2. Catharine R. Stimpson has pointed to the influence of de Beauvoir particularly on Millett, "who would simply never have written as she did if it had not been for *The Second Sex.*" (Personal communication, July 1982).

3. Joan Didion, "The Women's Movement" (1972), in *The White Album* (New York: Simon and Schuster, 1979), p. 117.

4. The argument of parts I–II of this book elaborates on the analysis I outlined in my introduction, in *Future of Difference,* ed. Eisenstein and Jardine, pp. i–xxiv.

Chapter 1

1. Kate Millett, *Sexual Politics* (1970; reprint ed., New York: Avon Books, 1971).

2. The term was not, of course, invented by feminists, although it was used by feminist writers such as Virginia Woolf before the "second wave," as Veronica Beechey has noted; see Beechey, "On Patriarchy," *Feminist Review,* no. 3 (1979),

pp. 66–82. For other discussions of the use of the word by feminists, see Barrett, *Women's Oppression*, pp. 10–19, and Z. Eisenstein, *Radical Future*, pp. 18–30.

3. Adrienne Rich, *Of Woman Born: Motherhood as Experience and Institution* (New York: W. W. Norton, 1976), pp. 57–58. For discussion of this book, see chapter 7, below. The universalism of patriarchy has become a major focus of feminist debate; see chapter 13, below.

4. Millett, *Sexual Politics,* p. 25. Hereafter page numbers to this and other books are cited in the text.

5. While Millett mentioned rape in passing, the emphasis on it and wife battering as forms of male coercion emerged later. See chapter 3, below.

6. Millett, *Sexual Politics,* pp. 26 ff.

7. See Friedan, *Feminine Mystique,* pp. 95 ff. Millett's other villains include literary figures such as D. H. Lawrence, Henry Miller, and Norman Mailer. I refer the reader to the literary and historical analysis that makes up the bulk of her text, which is too rich and complex for summary here.

8. Chodorow, "Gender, Relation, and Difference," p. 12.

9. In insisting on the cultural origins of sex differences Millett and others built not only on the work of Margaret Mead, but on that of the preceding, now largely obscure, generation of feminist researchers, as Rosalind Rosenberg has shown; see *Beyond Separate Spheres: Intellectual Roots of Modern Feminism* (New Haven: Yale University Press, 1982), passim. See also Michelle Z. Rosaldo, "Woman, Culture, and Society: A Theoretical Overview," in *Woman, Culture, and Society,* ed. Rosaldo and Louise Lamphere (Stanford: Stanford University Press, 1974), p. 18, and Suzanne J. Kessler and Wendy McKenna, *Gender: An Ethnomethodological Approach* (New York: John Wiley & Sons, 1978), pp. 23–4, citing Mead and Millett. The controversy over Derek Freeman's critique of Mead's work in Samoa (*Margaret Mead and Samoa: The Making and Unmaking of An Anthropological Myth* [Cambridge, Mass.: Harvard University Press and Canberra: Australian National University Press, 1983]) does not invalidate the broader conclusions of her writings; see Robert F. Murphy, Alexander Alland, Jr., and Elliott P. Skinner, "An Abortive Attack on 'Coming of Age,'" letter to the *New York Times,* 6 February 1983.

10. From table drawn up by Orville G. Brim, Jr., using the work of Talcott Parsons, R. F. Bales, and others as a theoretical basis; see Millett, *Sexual Politics,* pp. 228–30. This point was expanded upon by feminist psychologists later on; see below, chapter 6.

11. Elizabeth Janeway, *Man's World, Woman's Place: A Study in Social Mythology* (New York: Dell Publishing Co., 1971).

12. After more than a decade of the women's movement, this split has reappeared as one experienced internally by working mothers. See Diane Ehrensaft, "When Women and Men Mother," *Socialist Review,* no. 49 (January–February 1980), p. 55; "[w]ithin her own psyche the sharing mother has a hard time integrating a work identity with being a mother: 'When you go out to work, the job

is something you *do*. But the work of a housewife and mother is not just something you do, it's something you *are*.'"

13. On this point, see also Friedan, *Feminine Mystique,* passim.

14. On Parsons, see also Veronica Beechey, "Women and Production: a Critical Analysis of Some Sociological Theories of Women's Work," in *Feminism and Materialism,* ed. Kuhn and Wolpe, pp. 158 ff. An honorable exception in the sex roles literature was Mirra Komarovsky, whose writing dissented from the conventional wisdom. See Komarovsky, "Functional Analysis of Sex Roles," *American Sociological Review* 15, no. 4 (August 1950):508–15, cited by Millett; "Cultural Contradictions and Sex Roles," *American Journal of Sociology* 52 (1946):184–89; and Komarovsky, *Women in the Modern World: Their Education and Their Dilemmas* (Boston: Little Brown, 1953).

15. Millett, *Sexual Politics,* pp. 1–22, 237–361.

16. Carol Hanisch, "The Personal is Political," in *The Radical Therapist,* ed. Jerome Agel (New York: Ballantine Books, 1971), pp. 152–57; reprinted from *Notes from the Second Year: Women's Liberation, Major Writings of the Radical Feminists,* ed. Shulamith Firestone and Anne Koedt (New York: Radical Feminists, 1970). See below, chapter 4.

17. Anne Koedt, "The Myth of the Vaginal Orgasm," in *Radical Feminism,* ed. Anne Koedt, Ellen Levine and Anita Rapone (New York: Quadrangle/New York Times Book Co., 1973), pp. 198–207.

18. Millett, *Sexual Politics,* pp. 115 ff.

19. Ibid., pp. 336 ff.

20. Cited in Janeway, *Man's World,* p. 306.

21. Shulamith Firestone, *The Dialectic of Sex: The Case for Feminist Revolution* (New York: Bantam Books, 1970), p. 126. See below, chapter 2.

22. Ibid., pp. 131–32.

Chapter 2

1. Firestone, *Dialectic of Sex,* pp. 1–12.

2. Cf. Lourdes Beneria and Gita Sen, "Accumulation, Reproduction, and Women's Role in Economic Development: Boserup Revisited," *Signs* 7, no. 2 (1981):290, n. 32; on the ambiguities in the use of the term "reproduction," see Felicity Edholm, Olivia Harris, and Kate Young, "Conceptualizing Women," *Critique of Anthropology* 3, nos. 9–10 (1977):101–30. See also chapter 7, below. Obviously the link between economic base and cultural and social superstructure in Marxist theory is also a much vexed question. But Firestone's materialism seemed to gloss over the transition from biology to culture much too glibly. For an account of the debate among socialist feminists over Firestone's biological materialism, see Barrett, *Women's Oppression,* pp. 11 ff.; and Lise Vogel, "Marxism and Feminism: Unhappy Marriage, Trial Separation, or Something Else?" *Women and Revolution,* ed. Sargent, pp. 206 ff.

3. Juliet Mitchell, *Woman's Estate* (1971; reprint ed., New York: Vintage Books, 1973).

4. See Ruth Milkman, "Organizing the Sexual Division of Labor: Historical Perspectives on 'Women's Work' and the American Labor Movement," *Socialist Review,* no. 49 (January–February 1980), p. 100; "while the proportion of adult women in the paid labor force had grown from 18 per cent in 1890 to 26 per cent in 1940, it skyrocketed to 35 per cent in 1955 and then to over 50 per cent today." For the European developments, see Theresa McBride, "The Long Road Home: Women's Work and Industrialization," in *Becoming Visible: Women in European History,* ed. Renate Bridenthal and Claudia Koonz (Boston: Houghton Mifflin, 1977), pp. 280–95. The combination of protective legislation and exclusion from male-dominated trade unions in the reduction of women in the paid workforce has been a focus of discussion among feminist scholars as an instance of the collaboration between capitalism and patriarchy; on this point see Heidi Hartmann, "Capitalism, Patriarchy, and Job Segregation by Sex," in *Women and the Workplace: The Implications of Occupational Segregation,* ed. Martha Blaxall and Barbara Reagan (Chicago: University of Chicago Press, 1976), pp. 137–169.

5. Rosaldo, "A Theoretical Overview," pp. 17–42. See chapter 13, below, for an account of Rosaldo's modification of this position, shortly before her death in a tragic accident in 1981.

6. Sherry Ortner, "Is Female to Male as Nature is to Culture?" in *Woman, Culture and Society,* ed. Rosaldo and Lamphere, pp. 67–87.

7. For an alternative interpretation by an anthropologist see Karen Sacks, "Engels Revisited: Women, the Organization of Production, and Private Property," in *Women, Culture and Society,* ed. Rosaldo and Lamphere, pp. 207–22. For an account of the development of socialist feminist theory on the "mode of reproduction" and the sexual division of labor, see Vogel, "Marxism and Feminism," pp. 195–217.

Chapter 3

1. Susan Brownmiller, *Against Our Will: Men, Women, and Rape* (New York: Simon and Schuster, 1975), p. 209.

2. Brownmiller, *Against Our Will,* p. 12; she argued that in *The Sexual Revolution* (1945), Reich had briefly entertained "the vision of a 'masculine ideology of rape,'" but failed to develop the concept into a full "political analysis of rape."

3. See, inter alia, Lionel Tiger and Robin Fox, *The Imperial Animal* (New York: Delta, 1971). See "Male Dominance Revisited," *Time Magazine,* 22 September 1980, for an account of a recent contribution to this tradition (review of Robin Fox, *The Red Lamp of Incest* [New York: Dutton, 1980]).

4. Brownmiller, *Against Our Will,* pp. 180 ff.

5. Susan Griffin, "Rape: The All-American Crime," *Ramparts* 10 (September 1971):26–35; reprinted in *Women: A Feminist Perspective,* ed. Jo Freeman (Palo

Alto, Calif.: Mayfield Publishing, 1975), pp. 24–39, and in Susan Griffin, *Rape: The Power of Consciousness* (San Francisco: Harper and Row, 1979), pp. 3–22. On Susan Griffin's later work, see below, chapter 12.

6. Salso Andra Medea and Kathleen Thompson, *Against Rape* (New York: Farrar, Straus and Giroux, 1974).

7. *Rape Culture* (Cambridge Documentary Films, Inc., 1975). There is a direct connection between the terms of this analysis and those of the campaign against pornography, to which Brownmiller turned her attention in the late 1970s. See chapter 12, below.

8. Her involvement in some of this organizing activity in 1970 and 1971 drew Brownmiller into writing the book, as she noted in the acknowledgments.

9. The right of a woman to sue her husband for rape has now been recognized in law in the state of Oregon, and over half the states have made some changes in their rape laws, most of these in reference to removing the requirement of evidence of a victim's previous sexual history. See Deckard, *Women's Movement,* p. 435. At this writing there have also been reforms in the rape laws of Canada, Italy, and New South Wales (Australia).

10. See chapter 13, below.

11. Marge Piercy, *Vida* (New York: Summit Books, 1979), p. 201; see pp. 200 ff. for the entire exchange.

12. See Carol Ehrlich, "The Unhappy Marriage of Marxism and Feminism: Can It Be Saved?" in *Women and Revolution,* ed. Sargent, pp. 127 ff., on rape as a form of male control over women cross-culturally.

Chapter 4

1. Millett, *Sexual Politics,* quoted in Mitchell, *Woman's Estate,* p. 65.

2. Term used by Carden, *Feminist Movement,* p. 33.

3. Alix Kates Shulman, "Sex and Power: Sexual Bases of Radical Feminism," *Signs* 5, no. 4 (Summer 1980):594. Jo Freeman states that "(t)his technique evolved independently of, but is similar to, the Chinese revolutionary practice of 'speaking bitterness.'" She cites William Hinton, *Fanshen* (New York: Vintage Books, 1966). See Freeman, *Women's Liberation,* p. 118, n. 24. Note, however, that Shulman's is an eyewitness account.

4. The technique was described in Kathie Sarachild, "A Program for Feminist Consciousnessraising," *Notes from the Second Year,* cited in Shulman, "Sex and Power," p. 594; Pamela Allen, *Free Space: A Perspective on the Small Group in Women's Liberation* (New York: Times Change Press, 1970); and Vivian Gornick, "Consciousness," in *Essays in Feminisim* (New York: Harper & Row, 1978), pp. 47–68, reprinted from the *New York Times Magazine,* January 1971, among other publications.

5. de Beauvoir, *Second Sex,* p. 301.

6. Mitchell, *Woman's Estate,* p. 61.

7. See Freeman, *Women's Liberation*, pp. 116 ff.; Carden, *Feminist Movement*, pp. 33 ff. Shulman, "Sex and Power," passim, discusses the fundamental critique of sexual relationships as the locus of male domination as derived by the early CR groups, and the importance of retaining "our awareness of the political dimension of sexual relations, with its powerful potential for change," in the current period of right-wing repression (p. 604).

8. Cf. Shulman, "Sex and Power," as quoted earlier, p. 118. See Arlyn Diamond and Lee R. Edwards, eds., *The Authority of Experience: Essays in Feminist Criticism* (Amherst: University of Massachusetts Press, 1977). In relying upon the authority of experience, women were reversing a longstanding tradition of relying upon (or being expected to rely upon) the advice of male experts. See Barbara Ehrenreich and Deirdre English, *For Her Own Good: 150 Years of The Experts' Advice to Women* (New York: Anchor Press/Doubleday, 1978).

9. Cf. Shulman, "Sex and Power," pp. 594ff.

10. The "authority of experience" here is mine.

11. Allen, *Free Space*, pp. 17–27.

12. The "chip system" is described by Lydia Sargent, "New Left Women and Men: The Honeymoon is Over," in *Women and Revolution*, ed. Sargent, p. xviii, n.

13. See Nancy Hartsock, "Feminist Theory and the Development of Revolutionary Strategy," in *Capitalist Patriarchy*, ed. Z. Eisenstein, esp. pp. 68–70.

Part II: Prologue

1. Mitchell, *Woman's Estate*, p. 99.

2. Catharine R. Stimpson, personal communication, July 1982.

3. See Mary Jane Sherfey, "A Theory of Female Sexuality," (1966) in *Sisterhood is Powerful*, ed. Robin Morgan (New York: Vintage Books, 1970), p. 226.

4. See Gerda Lerner, *The Majority Finds Its Past: Placing Women in History* (New York: Oxford University Press, 1979), p. xxxi. I am indebted to Gerda Lerner for the term "woman-centered analysis," which I have extended in this account to refer not only to scholarship on women (especially in women's history), but to the focus of feminist theory.

Chapter 5

1. On the invisibility of lesbians in culture, see Blanche Wiesen Cook, "'Women Alone Stir My Imagination': Lesbianism and the Cultural Tradition," *Signs* 4, no. 4 (Summer 1979):718–39. In her ironic summary of her own experience of the 1950s: "Denied access to an accurate historical record, we knew only that our foresisters wore neckties, and committed suicide all over the last pages of the novel. With little to read and practically nothing to wear, we occupied an alien and threatening environment" (p. 720).

2. On the "gay/straight split" of the early 1970s, see Freeman, *Politics of Women's Liberation,* pp. 134ff., and Sidney Abbott and Barbara Love, *Sappho Was a Right-On Woman: A Liberated View of Lesbianism* (New York: Stein and Day, 1972), pp. 109 ff.

3. Jill Johnston, *Lesbian Nation: The Feminist Solution* (New York: Simon and Schuster, 1974), p. 278.

4. From statements read at a press conference, 17 December 1971, in response to an article on women's liberation in *Time* magazine maligning Kate Millett for being bisexual, and dismissing "all liberationists as Lesbians" (quotes from statement by Aileen Hernandez, then national president of N.O.W., and Kate Millett, cited in *Sappho Was a Right-On Woman,* ed. Abbott and Love; see pp. 121, 124).

5. Ti-Grace Atkinson, "Lesbianism and Feminism: Justice for Women as Unnatural," in *Amazon Odyssey* (New York: Links Books, 1974), pp. 131–34.

6. Radicalesbians, "The Woman-Identified Woman" (1970), in *Radical Feminism,* ed. Koedt et al., pp. 240–45. The authors of this text were March Hoffman (Artemis March), Ellen Bedoz, Cynthia Funk, Rita Mae Brown, Lois Hart, and "Barbara XX, with other Radicalesbians" (from mimeographed copy, 1 May 1970); quote from pp. 241–42.

7. Ibid., p. 240.

8. Charlotte Bunch, "Not for Lesbians Only" (1975), in *Building Feminist Theory,* ed. Bunch et al., p. 68.

9. Adrienne Rich, "Compulsory Heterosexuality and Lesbian Existence," *Signs* 5, no. 4 (Summer 1980):631–660. Rich's article is examined here; despite the chronological leap, as it develops the idea of heterosexuality as a social institution introduced by Charlotte Bunch, Lucia Valeska, and others in the early 1970s. But it was published, in part, as a critical response to some more recent feminist theoretical publications, specifically those by Jean Baker Miller, Nancy Chodorow, and Dorothy Dinnerstein. See below, chapters 6, 8–9, for accounts of these texts. See also Lucia Valeska, "The Future of Female Separatism" (1975), in *Building Feminist Theory,* ed. Bunch et al., pp. 20–31, and Nancy Myron and Charlotte Bunch, eds., *Lesbianism and the Women's Movement* (Baltimore: Diana Press, 1975).

10. Rich, "Compulsory Heterosexuality." p. 648.

11. For an interesting reaction to Rich's article, see Martha E. Thompson, "Comment on Rich's 'Compulsory Heterosexuality and Lesbian Existence,'" *Signs* 6, no. 4 (Summer 1981):790–94. See also Ann Ferguson, Jacquelyn N. Zita, and Kathryn Pyne Addelson, "On 'Compulsory Heterosexuality and Lesbian Existence': Defining the Issues," in Nannerl O. Keohane, Michelle Z. Rosaldo, and Barbara C. Gelpi, eds., *Feminist Theory: A Critique of Ideology* (Chicago: University of Chicago Press, 1982), pp. 147–88.

12. On consciousness-raising, see above, chapter 4.

Chapter 6

1. Phyllis Chesler, *Women and Madness* (Garden City, N.Y.: Doubleday, 1972).

2. See Naomi Weisstein, "'*Kinder, Kuche, Kirche*' As Scientific Law: Psychology Constructs the Female," in *Sisterhood is Powerful*, ed. Morgan, p. 219, and above, chapter 1.

3. Chesler, *Women and Madness*, pp. 67 ff., citing study by Inge K. Broverman et al., "Sex Role Stereotypes and Clinical Judgments of Mental Health," *Journal of Consulting and Clinical Psychology* (1970).

4. Chesler, *Women and Madness*, pp. 56–57 and passim.

5. Carolyn G. Heilbrun, *Toward a Recognition of Androgyny* (New York: Alfred A. Knopf, 1973), pp. x–xi.

6. Sandra L. Bem, "Probing the Promise of Androgyny," in *Beyond Sex-Role Stereotypes: Readings Toward a Psychology of Androgyny*, ed. Alexandra G. Kaplan and Joan P. Bean (Boston: Little, Brown, 1976), pp. 51 ff.

7. Carolyn G. Heilbrun, "Androgyny and the Psychology of Sex Differences," in *Future of Difference*, ed. Eisenstein and Jardine, p. 256.

8. Ibid., citing Bem, "Promise of Androgyny," p. 261.

9. Ibid., pp. 261–62.

10. Marlo Thomas et al., *Free to Be . . . You and Me* (New York: McGraw-Hill, 1974) and television special, 11 March 1974, ABC-Television; Lois Gould, "X: A Fabulous Child's Story," *Ms.*, December 1972, pp. 74–77 (reprinted, New York: Daughters Publishing Co., 1978; and rev. ed., New York: Stonesong Press, 1980).

11. Rich, *Of Woman Born*, p. 76 n. Carolyn Heilbrun has expressed bewilderment over the retreat of Rich and other feminists from an earlier acceptance of androgyny as a feminist ideal (see Heilbrun, "Androgyny and Psychology of Sex Differences," pp. 258 ff.). The difference lies in the point I am arguing here, namely, the realization that androgyny implies an integration of women into the social and political status quo.

12. Janice Raymond, *The Transsexual Empire: The Making of the She-Male* (Boston: Beacon Press, 1979), p. 160.

13. Catharine R. Stimpson, "The Androgyne and the Homosexual," *Women's Studies* 2 (1974):237–38, quoted in Rich, *Of Woman Born*, p. 77n.

14. Bem, "Promise of Androgyny," p. 52, from table 1, "The Masculine, Feminine, and Neutral Items on the BSRI." The androgynous personality appeared to be designed for positions in management, rather than on the assembly line, where it would appear, traditionally "female" traits such as passivity and lack of initiative might come in handy.

15. Ibid.

16. Raymond, *Transsexual Empire*, p. 161.

17. Jean Baker Miller, *Toward a New Psychology of Women* (Boston: Beacon Press, 1976), p. 79.

18. Ibid, passim.

19. Miller referred here specifically to women's skill at and knowledge of affiliation with others, in creating and maintaining a complex network of relationships.

20. Cf. Hester Eisenstein and Susan Riemer Sacks, "Women in Search of Autonomy: An Action Design," *Social Change* 5, no. 2 (1975):4–6, and Susan Riemer Sacks and Hester Eisenstein, "Feminism and Psychological Autonomy: A Study in Decision Making," *Personnel and Guidance Journal* 57 (April 1979):419–23, for a similar account of the need to redefine autonomy for women. The argument is that, for women in a small group, affiliation and autonomy are in a dialectical relation, each serving to enhance the other.

Chapter 7

1. Rich, *Of Woman Born,* discussed in this chapter; Dorothy Dinnerstein, *The Mermaid and the Minotaur: Sexual Arrangements and Human Malaise* (New York: Harper and Row, 1977), discussed in chapter 8; Nancy B. Chodorow, *The Reproduction of Mothering: Psychoanalysis and the Sociology of Gender* (Berkeley: University of California Press, 1978), discussed in chapter 9. See also Jane Lazarre, *The Mother Knot* (New York: McGraw-Hill, 1976); the much-criticized but interesting Nancy Friday, *My Mother/My Self* (New York: Delacorte Press, 1977); and Jane Flax, "The Conflict Between Nurturance and Autonomy in Mother-Daughter Relationships and Within Feminism," *Feminist Studies* 4, no. 2 (June 1978):171–189; the entire issue of this journal is devoted to "a feminist theory of motherhood." See also Sara Ruddick, "Maternal Thinking," *Feminist Studies* 6, no. 2 (Summer 1980):342–67.

2. Alix Kates Shulman, conversation, October 1979.

3. Firestone, *Dialectic of Sex,* p. 238; see above, chapter 2.

4. See Linda Gordon, *Woman's Body, Woman's Right: A Social History of Birth Control in America* (New York: Grossman Publishers, 1976), passim. See also Ellen Willis, "Sisters Under the Skin? Confronting Race and Sex," *Village Voice Literary Supplement,* no. 8 (June 1982), p. 12: "Abortion is first of all the key issue of the new right's antifeminist campign, the ground on which a larger battle over the very idea of women's liberation is being fought."

5. In this, these women participated in the patriarchal conspiracy of blaming the less powerful for their own oppression. I am indebted for this observation to Karen Machover. On this point, see also Rich, *Of Woman Born,* chapter 9, "Motherhood and Daughterhood."

6. See Alice Rossi, "A Biosocial Perspective on Parenting," *Daedalus: Journal of the American Academy of Arts and Sciences* 106, no. 2 (Spring 1977):1–31; and Harriet Engel Gross et al., "Considering 'A Biosocial Perspective on Parenting,' *Signs* 4, no. 4 (Summer 1979):695–717.

7. Rich, *Of Woman Born,* p. 13.

8. See above, chapter 1.

9. See Rich, *Of Woman Born,* pp. 84–127. Other works on the feminist implications of the Great Goddess tradition are Elizabeth Fisher, *Woman's Creation: Sexual Evolution and the Shaping of Society* (Garden City, N.Y.: Anchor Press/Doubleday, 1979), and Merlin Stone, *When God Was a Woman* (New York: Harcourt Brace Jovanovich, 1978; originally published as *The Paradise Papers* [London, Virago, 1976]). Rich sidestepped the issue of women's actual political and/or cultural power in the pre-Judaeo-Christian period by speaking in terms of symbolic evocations of female power, whether created "by women's or men's hands" (p. 93).

10. Adrienne Rich, remarks at the Columbia University Seminar on Women and Society, 1976.

11. On the critique of patriarchy as an ahistorical concept, see chapter 1, n. 2, and chapter 13, below.

12. As Rich wrote, "the term 'non-father' does not exist in any realm of social categories" (p. 11).

Chapter 8

1. Dinnerstein, *Mermaid and Minotaur,* p. 26.

2. Janeway, *Man's World,* p. 53. Elizabeth Janeway's *Powers of the Weak* (New York: Alfred A. Knopf, 1980) is in part an elaboration of this idea.

3. Dinnerstein drew upon the Freudian and Gestalt traditions of psychoanalysis for her theoretical position. In this, she departed from the feminist tradition established in the writing of Millett and Firestone of rejecting Freudian and post-Freudian concepts as inimical to women. Chodorow and others have continued on this path, seeking to incorporate some elements of the psychoanalytic tradition into a feminist analysis. See chapter 9, below. On the debate as a whole, see Mitchell, *Psychoanalysis and Feminism,* passim.

4. See Rich, *Of Woman Born,* chapter 9, pp. 218–55.

5. See above, chapter 6.

Chapter 9

1. Chodorow, *Reproduction of Mothering,* pp. 11–30. See esp. pp. 18 ff., in which Chodorow challenges the view of Alice Rossi that there is some "biosocial" basis for female mothering. See also above, chapter 7, n. 6. For earlier versions of Chodorow's fundamental arguments see Chodorow, "Family Structure and Feminine Personality," in *Women, Culture, and Society,* ed. Rosaldo and Lamphere, pp. 43–66, and Chodorow, "Mothering, Male Dominance, and Capitalism," in *Capitalist Patriarchy,* ed. Z. Eisenstein, pp. 83–106. See also Judith Lorber et al., "On *The Reproduction of Mothering:* A Methodological Debate," *Signs* 6, no. 3 (Spring 1981): 482–514, which includes a reply from Chodorow.

2. As with Freud and the neo-Freudians, object-relations theorists drew their accounts of normal development from clinical experience with the abnormal or mentally ill, as Chodorow pointed out.

3. Chodorow's argument concerned the reproduction of mothering, the fact that while mothers bore and reared children of both sexes, only one of those sexes—the female—went on to bear and rear children of both sexes. Chodorow accepted the hypothesis that this was originally the case for sound reasons of species survival. What she sought to explain was its continuation in a historical period when this was arguably no longer the case.

4. Chodorow pointed out that in Freud's hypothesis women never did learn to desire first their fathers, and then other men, for the sake of sexual experience in and of itself, but only for the sake of acquiring possession of a penis, via "having" the father's or, by substitution, having a baby (= penis) with the father.

5. Cf. Dinnerstein on this point, p. 82 above.

6. Chodorow cites Rubin, "Traffic in Women." I am indebted to Rosemary Pringle for the elaboration of this point (conversation, 10 October 1980). See also Rich, "Compulsory Heterosexuality," pp. 635–37, and discussion of this article, above, chapter 5. At issue here is whether heterosexuality in human society has a "natural" basis, or whether it is socially produced. Chodorow is ambiguous throughout as to whether there is a biologically based heterosexual drive that governs the sexual preference of most women. Rubin's view that heterosexuality is entirely the product of enforcement by a kinship system has been criticized by Felicity Edholm et al. "The implication of her argument is that primates, too, and even non-primates, have 'kinship systems' which enjoin strict heterosexuality, unless she is positing a model of human sexuality in which only the pre-Oedipal infant with its polymorphous drives can be considered 'natural'" ("Conceptualizing Women," p. 121).

7. See above, chapter 2. On this point, Chodorow is vulnerable to the charge laid by Edholm et al. at the door of feminist theorists, of using "concepts of apparently universal applicability . . . often with scant regard for historical or cultural specificity." In particular, Chodorow assumes universal characteristics for gender identity. But Edholm et al. write: "The way gender categories are constructed in culture has the effect of rendering them non-comparable . . ." ("Conceptualizing Women," p. 102).

8. Although addressing a different issue, Carol Gilligan's analysis of female moral development converges in part with that of Chodorow and of Jean Baker Miller, both of whom she cites. In particular, Gilligan relies on Chodorow's view of female gender identity, which is established via embeddedness in relationship, as opposed to male gender identity, stemming from separation and autonomy. Gilligan relates this difference to a perception of morality as connected with responsibilities to others, while male perceptions (as documented by Lawrence Kohlberg and others) relate primarily to the balancing of rights. Gilligan seeks to have women's pattern of moral development "added on" to that of men's, in order to create a more representative picture of human development. But unlike Chodorow, who sees male psychological development ultimately as related to male dominance over women (see below, chapter 10), Gilligan speaks (p. 174) of a "marriage" between male and female styles of moral development; in this sense her thesis is closer to

the androgyny school of feminist psychology than to a woman-centered perspective. I am indebted to Barbara Haber for pointing out the similarities between Gilligan's work and that of Chodorow, and to Susan Riemer Sacks for an assessment of Gilligan's work (personal communication, February, 1983). See Carol Gilligan, *In A Different Voice: Psychological Theory and Women's Development* (Cambridge: Harvard University Press, 1982); see also Gilligan, "In a Different Voice: Women's Conceptions of Self and of Morality," in Eisenstein and Jardine, eds., *Future of Difference*, pp. 274–317.

Chapter 10

1. Lerner, *Majority Finds Its Past*, p. xxxi.

2. See above, chapter 9.

3. Chodorow, "Gender, Relation, and Difference."

4. Core gender identity is believed to be established in the first two years. Chodorow writes that conflicts surrounding female identity in a male-defined culture arise "later in development," although she does not specify what age (see p. 14). In saying this, Chodorow contradicted her own argument about the triangular nature of female sexual attachments. If girls turned away from their mothers to their fathers out of anger at their mothers' rejection of them as less valuable than their brothers or fathers, then daughters encountered the social devaluation of women at the very beginning of their emotional lives, not at some later phase of entry into social life outside of the family. For an alternative view of the difficulties of female psychological development, see Jane Flax, "Mother-Daughter Relationships: Psychodynamics, Politics, and Philosophy," in *Future of Difference*, ed. Eisenstein and Jardine, pp. 20–40, and Flax, "Nurturance and Autonomy."

5. Evelyn Fox Keller, "Gender and Science," *Psychoanalysis and Contemporary Thought* 1 (1978):409–33.

6. Elsewhere Keller documented her experience of the attitude that women cannot, by definition, be scientists, and of the devastating impact this had on her graduate training at Harvard, and her career choices (eventually moving out of physics and into molecular biology); see Evelyn Fox Keller, "The Anomaly of a Woman in Physics," in *Working It Out: 23 Women Writers, Artists, Scientists, and Scholars Talk About Their Lives and Work*, ed. Sara Ruddick and Pamela Daniels (New York: Pantheon Books, 1977), pp. 77–91.

7. Cited in Evelyn Fox Keller, "Feminism and Science," *Signs* 7, no. 3 (Spring 1982):599.

8. Ibid., pp. 600–601.

9. Theodore Roszak, *The Making of a Counter Culture* (New York: Doubleday, 1969), p. 216. On the prestige of scientific objectivity in the training of historians in the 1960s, see my paper, "Is 'Objectivity' a Code-Word for Male Domination?" presented at The Second Sex—Thirty Years Later conference, New York Institute for the Humanities, 28 September 1979. Evelyn Fox Keller dissociates herself from the "nihilist retreat" of some feminists from the scientific

project altogether, arguing instead that scientific research can and should be separated from its genderized impulse to domination; see Keller, "Feminism and Science," pp. 589–602.

10. Jessica Benjamin, "The Bonds of Love: Rational Violence and Erotic Domination," in *Future of Difference*, ed. Eisenstein and Jardine, p. 63.

Chapter 11

1. Nicole-Claude Mathieu, in Editors of *Questions Féministes*, "Variations on Some Common Themes," *Feminist Issues* 1, no. 1 (Summer 1980):16.

2. Mary Daly, *Gyn/Ecology: The Metaethics of Radical Feminism* (Boston: Beacon Press, 1978).

3. Mary Daly, *The Church and The Second Sex* (New York: Harper and Row, 1968; reissued 1975 with "A New Feminist Post-Christian Introduction by the Author"); Daly, *Beyond God the Father: Toward a Philosophy of Women's Liberation* (Boston: Beacon Press, 1973).

4. Daly coined "robotitude" on the model of Françoise d'Eubonne's usage of *féminitude*, to connote "the state of servitude of women in a phallocratic world" (Daly, *Gyn/Ecology*, p. 53). The word is used in a different sense by Nicole-Claude Mathieu to characterize "cultural feminism"; similar to *négritude*, it celebrates female difference as valuable, but fails to see it as culturally and politically produced. This criticism applies to Daly's work. (See Editors, *Questions Féministes*, "Some Common Themes," p. 16.)

5. The suppression and incorporation of elements from the Great Goddess religion within Christianity is also documented in Stone, *When God Was a Woman*. While Daly and Stone present the elimination of the Goddess religion as part of a general devaluation of women in culture, Daly begs the question of whether that tradition enshrined any meaningful role for women in social and political life. On this point see above, chapter 7, n. 9. On the elimination of the female principle from the Trinity, see Elaine H. Pagels, "What Became of God the Mother? Conflicting Images of God in Early Christianity," *Signs* 2, no. 2 (Winter 1976):293–303.

6. This section of the book covers some of the same ground as Andrea Dworkin, *Womanhating* (New York: E. P. Dutton, 1974). See also Diana Russell and Nicole Van de Ven, eds., *Proceedings of the International Tribunal on Crimes Against Women* (Millbrae, Calif.: Les Femmes, 1976).

7. I write this on the assumption that the colloquy between Daly and her reader is one-to-one, although the voice of the passage analyzed is "we." That is, usually, one reads alone. Of course Daly's book could be read and discussed in groups; but in contrast to CR, Daly's "Self-Centering Process" appears to be a solitary activity. See above, chapter 4.

8. Ross E. Kraemer, review of Daly, *Gyn/Ecology*, in *Signs* 5, no. 3 (Winter 1979):354–56.

9. See Fran P. Hosken, *The Hosken Report: Genital/Sexual Mutilation of Females* (Lexington, Mass.: WIN News, 1979).

10. In a footnote to this remarkable statement, Daly adds that "the issue of

numbers is not false/unreal in every specific situation, especially in cases of physical violence," but goes on to note that even in such cases, "the psychic combination of women's energies can significantly increase our power" (p. 380n.).

11. Daly uses the image from Jerzy Kosinski, *The Painted Bird,* in which the protagonist paints a bird, who then becomes unrecognizable to the others of its species; they react by torturing and killing it. Daly quotes Thomas Szasz who calls the Painted Bird a "perfect symbol of the Other, the Stranger, The Scapegoat" (quoted from p. 333).

12. Respectively, the black lawyer and former head of the Equal Employment Opportunities Commission under the Carter administration, and the Tory prime minister of England at this writing. In an intermediary category would be Sandra Day O'Connor, who was appointed to the Supreme Court by Ronald Reagan under pressure from the women's movement, but who does not identify herself as a feminist.

13. In a radio interview, Daly warned readers of *Gyn/Ecology* against interpreting it as a political program, and reserved the right to reject parts of it in her future writing, including the forthcoming *Pure Lust,* the second volume of a proposed trilogy ("The Coming Out Show," Australian Broadcasting Company, September 5 1981).

Chapter 12

1. See Laura Lederer, ed., *Take Back the Night: Women on Pornography* (New York: Wm. Morrow, 1980); Susan Griffin, *Pornography and Silence: Culture's Revenge Against Nature* (New York: Harper and Row, 1981); Andrea Dworkin, *Pornography: Men Possessing Women* (New York: Perigee/G. P. Putnam's, 1981). See also "Sex Issue," *Heresies: A Feminist Publication on Art & Politics,* no. 12 (1981); *Women: Sex and Sexuality,* ed. Catharine R. Stimpson and Ethel Spector Person, *Signs* 5, no. 4 (Summer 1980; reprint ed., Chicago: University of Chicago Press, 1980), and Hannah Alderfer, Meryl Altman, Kate Ellis, Beth Jaker, Marybeth Nelson, Esther Newton, Ann Snitow, and Carole S. Vance, eds., "Diary of a Conference on Sexuality," from *The Scholar and The Feminist IX: Toward a Politics of Sexuality,* Barnard College Women's Center, New York, April 1982. See also Martha Vicinus, "Sexuality and Power: A Review of Current Work in the History of Sexuality," *Feminist Studies* 8, no. 1 (Spring 1982):134–56.

2. Lederer, *Take Back the Night,* pp. 15, 23; Coote and Campbell, *Sweet Freedom,* pp. 203 ff.

3. Kathleen Barry, "Beyond Pornography: From Defensive Politics to Creating a Vision," p. 308; Helen E. Longino, "Pornography, Oppression, and Freedom: A Closer Look," pp. 47–48; both in Lederer, *Take Back the Night.*

4. See *Not a Love Story* (film), Canadian Film Board, 1981.

5. Lederer, "*Playboy* Isn't Playing: An Interview With Judith Bat-Ada," p. 127; Lederer, "Introduction," pp. 19–20; Robin Morgan, "Theory and Practice: Pornography and Rape," pp. 139–40; all in Lederer, *Take Back the Night.*

6. See Ellen Willis, "Nature's Revenge," *New York Times Book Review,* 12 July

1981, p. 9 ff., reviewing books cited in n. 1 by Griffin and Dworkin.

7. See n. 1, above.

8. Griffin, *Pornography and Silence*, p. 31.

9. Pauline Réage, *Story of O*, trans. S. D'Estree (New York: Grove Press, 1965; originally published 1954). Réage is thought to be the pseudonym of a male author. For an analysis of this work as a paradigm of sadomasochistic erotic relations, see Benjamin, "Bonds of Love," pp. 51 ff.

10. Susan Griffin, *Woman and Nature: The Roaring Inside Her* (New York: Harper & Row, 1978).

11. See above, chapter 2.

12. Griffin's vision of infancy has an echo of the pre-Oedipal state as analyzed by French Lacanian feminists such as Julia Kristeva; see Carolyn G. Burke, "Rethinking the Maternal," in *Future of Difference*, ed. Eisenstein and Jardine, pp. 107 ff. But there is no moment of infantile experience, I would argue, that is "outside" of culture. Even while in the womb, the infant hears language. Griffin's identification of female with nature is even more strongly expressed in *Woman and Nature*.

13. Dworkin, *Pornography*, p. 48.

14. This was the explanation for the taboo upon male homosexuality, in Dworkin's view.

15. For Dworkin's (unconscious) racism, see, for example, her uncritical acceptance of the stereotyped generalization that "Hispanic communities in the United States" are characterized by "the cult of machismo . . . lived to its fullest: gang warfare . . ." (p. 158), in contrast presumably to all other ethnic communities. The quote on the dilapidating effects of pornography is from Griffin, *Pornography and Silence*, pp. 118–19.

16. See above, chapter 10.

17. Griffin, *Woman and Nature*, pp. 217 ff.

18. Paula Webster, "Pornography and Pleasure," *Heresies*, no. 12 (1981), p. 49.

19. See Members of Samois, (eds.), *Coming to Power: Writings and Graphics on Lesbian S/M* (San Francisco: Samois, 1981); see also Susan Ardill and Nora Neumark, "Putting Sex Back Into Lesbianism: Is the Way to a Woman's Heart Through Her Sadomasochism?" *Gay Information* 11 (Spring 1982):4–11.

20. Pat Califia, "Feminism and Sadomasochism," *Heresies*, no. 12 (1981), p. 30.

21. Ibid., p. 34.

22. See Deirdre English, Amber Hollibaugh, and Gayle Rubin, "Talking Sex: A Conversation on Sexuality and Feminism," *Socialist Review*, no. 58 (July–August 1981), pp. 43–62. See especially Gayle Rubin's sarcastic definition of "legitimate sex" as "not focused on orgasm, it's very gentle and it takes place in the context of a long-term, caring relationship. It's the missionary position of the women's movement" (p. 50).

23. On this point, see Amber Hollibaugh and Cherríe Moraga, "What We're Rollin Around in Bed With—Sexual Silences in Feminism: A Conversation toward Ending Them," *Heresies*, no. 12 (1981), 58–62; the article suggests that women

return to CR groups to work on an adequate feminist sexual theory that begins to "*politically* deal with sexuality in a broad-based, cross-cultural way," including perspectives on racial and class differences (p. 62).

Chapter 13

1. Adrienne Rich, *On Lies, Secrets, and Silence: Selected Prose, 1966–1978* (New York: W. W. Norton, 1979), p. 193; my italics.

2. Ibid., p. 248.

3. See Leah Fritz, *Dreamers and Dealers: An Intimate Appraisal of the Women's Movement* (Boston: Beacon Press, 1979), pp. 112–67; on Daly, see above, chapter 11.

4. See Evans, *Personal Politics,* esp. pp. 156–92. Evans makes the point that in its trajectory from civil rights to women's liberation, the second wave recapitulated the history of the first: "[t]wice in the history of the United States the struggle for racial equality has been midwife to a feminist movement . . . [i]n the abolition movement of the 1830s and again in the civil rights movement of the 1960s . . ." (p.24).

5. Quoted in Evans, *Personal Politics,* p. 87.

6. See Robin Morgan, *Going Too Far: The Personal Chronicle of a Feminist* (New York: Random House, 1977), pp. 115–30; the piece published on that occasion, and reprinted here, "Goodbye to All That" (1970), was Morgan's angry manifesto of her departure from the New Left. For another account of the estrangement between the New Left and the new radical feminists, see Lydia Sargent, "New Left Men and Women: The Honeymoon is Over," in *Women and Revolution,* pp. xi–xxii.

7. Firestone, *Dialectic of Sex,* p. 32.

8. Ibid., p. 37.

9. Morgan, *Going Too Far,* p. 9. Morgan's "chronicle" is a useful source, in that she has collected her writings from the decade 1967 to 1977, with a commentary written in 1977, from which this quote is taken.

10. Ibid., p. 130 (from "Goodbye to All That").

11. I am leaving aside here the separate, but related issue, of the treatment of women by socialist regimes in the twentieth century. On this point see Weinbaum, *Curious Courtship,* esp. pp. 135 ff., and Maxine Molyneux, "Socialist Societies Old and New: Progress Toward Women's Emancipation?" *Monthly Review* 34, no. 3 (July–August 1982):56–100.

12. In the conventional drawing, dear to the heart of political scientists:

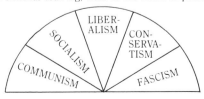

13. Lederer, introduction to *Take Back the Night,* pp. 19–20. On the Women Against Pornography campaign, see above, chapter 12.

14. Diana E. H. Russell, "Pornography and the Women's Liberation Movement," in *Take Back the Night,* ed. Lederer, p. 301.

15. On this point, see "The Doubled Vision of Feminist Theory," by Joan Kelly, in *Feminist Studies* 5, no. 1 (1979):216–27. See, inter alia, most of the essays in Sargent, *Women and Revolution;* Z. Eisenstein, *Capitalist Patriarchy;* Gordon, *Woman's Body, Woman's Right;* Rosalind Petchesky, *Reproductive Freedom: The Social and Political Dimensions of Birth Control* (New York: Longman, forthcoming) for examples of this kind of analysis.

16. Willis, "Nature's Revenge," p. 9; she concluded that it was both.

17. See Frances Fitzgerald, "The Triumphs of the New Right," *New York Review of Books,* 19 November 1981, pp. 19 ff.

18. See Morgan, *Going Too Far,* p. 122.

19. See Fritz, *Dreamers and Dealers,* pp. 112 ff.

20. Heidi Hartmann, "The Unhappy Marriage of Marxism and Feminism: Towards a More Progressive Union," in *Women and Revolution,* ed. Sargent, p. 13.

21. See preceding section, this chapter.

22. See Jerome Agel, ed., *The Radical Therapist* (New York: Ballantine Books, 1971); Michael Rossman, *On Learning and Social Change: Transcending the Totalitarian Classroom* (New York: Vintage Books, 1972). On the development of the Black Power concept, see Manning Marable, "Black Nationalism in the 1970s: Through the Prism of Race and Class," *Socialist Review,* nos. 50–51, (March–June 1980), pp. 57–108.

23. See Carl Oglesby, "The Idea of the New Left," in *The New Left Reader,* ed. Carl Oglesby (New York: Grove Press, 1969), pp. 6 ff.

24. See Carol Hanisch, "The Personal is Political," in *Radical Therapist,* ed. Agel, pp. 152–57.

25. See above, chapters 1–2.

26. See for example the titles of two major anthologies, Vivian Gornick and Barabara K. Moran, eds., *Woman in Sexist Society: Studies in Power and Powerlessness* (1971; reprint ed., New York: Signet Books, 1972) and Robin Morgan, ed., *Sisterhood is Powerful: An Anthology of Writings from the Women's Liberation Movement* (New York: Vintage Books, 1970).

27. See above, passim.

28. Robin Morgan, "Theory and Practice: Pornography and Rape," in Lederer, *Take Back the Night,* p. 139.

29. See above, chapter 2; Mitchell, *Woman's Estate,* pp. 99 ff.; Rubin, "Traffic in Women." Neither Mitchell nor Rubin were false universalizers, in that they both sought to suggest the great variety of ways in which sexuality could be socially organized.

30. See above, chapter 4, and H. Eisenstein, introduction to *Future of Difference,* ed. Eisenstein and Jardine.

31. See Carden, *Feminist Movement,* pp. 19 ff.; Freeman, *Women's Liberation,*

pp. 17 ff.; on forming a CR group among one's friends, see Vivian Gornick, "Consciousness" (1971), in *Essays in Feminism* (New York: Harper and Row, 1978), pp. 47–68. Cf. also Blanche McCrary Boyd, "Growing Up Racist," *Village Voice,* 5–11 August 1981.

32. See Miller, *New Psychology of Women,* p. x; Brownmiller, *Against Our Will,* p. 65.

33. See Hooks, *Ain't I a Woman,* pp. 137 ff.

34. Alison Edwards, *Rape, Racism, and the White Women's Movement: An Answer to Susan Brownmiller* (Chicago: Sojourner Truth Organization, n.d.), pp. 1–21.

35. Angela Y. Davis, *Women, Race and Class* (New York: Random House, 1981), pp. 178 ff.

36. Audre Lorde, "An Open Letter to Mary Daly," in *This Bridge Called My Back: Writings by Radical Women of Color,* ed. Cherríe Moraga and Gloria Anzaldúa (Watertown, Mass.:Persephone Press, 1981), pp. 95–96.

37. Judit Moschkovich, "'—But I Know You, American Woman,'" in *This Bridge Called My Back,* ed. Moraga and Anzaldúa, p. 83.

38. Edwards, *Rape, Racism,* p. 4 (referring to Susan Brownmiller's analysis "that women's shared oppression by men outweighs all potential for alliances along other lines . . .").

39. Judith Clavir, "Choosing Either/Or: A Critique of Metaphysical Feminism," *Feminist Studies,* 5, no. 2 (Summer 1979):404–5, reviewing Morgan, *Going Too Far.* For Morgan's own definition, see *Going Too Far,* pp. 290 ff.

40. To be fair, Morgan herself rejects the notion that her definition of "metaphysical" feminism means that she is retreating from political struggle, insisting instead on her right to move in both spheres. For a more recent formulation, see Robin Morgan, "A Quantum Leap in Feminist Theory," *Ms.,* December 1982, pp. 101 ff., excerpted from *The Anatomy of Freedom: Feminism, Physics, and Global Politics* (New York: Doubleday/Anchor, 1982). Morgan's book appeared too late to be considered fully in this study. I note, however, that her view still conforms to the false universalism I have criticized in this chapter. See, for example, her characterization of women's oppression: "Women share this suffering across the barriers of age, race, class, nationality, culture, sexual preference, and ethnic background: a Hong Kong prostitute and a Grosse Pointe matron are battered because both are women; . . . a Kenyan adolescent is physically clitoridectomized and a Swiss nurse is psychologically clitoridectomized because both are female human beings" (101). I note also, however, that in the failure of alliance with the political left during the 1970s, not only feminists were at fault.

41. See Editors, *Questions Féministes,* "Some Common Themes," p. 20.

Chapter 14

1. See above, chapter 11.

2. See above, chapter 13.

3. Betty Friedan, *The Second Stage* (New York: Summit Books, 1981).

4. Willie Lee Rose, "Reforming Women," *New York Review of Books,* 7 October 1982, p. 49.

5. See Christopher Lasch, *Haven in a Heartless World: The Family Besieged* (New York: Basic Books, 1979). My reference is ironic (need I explain?), given Lasch's well-known ambivalence toward feminism.

6. See on this point Z. Eisenstein, *Radical Future,* passim.

7. If one accepts the argument that the chief gains for women of the first wave of feminism were the right to vote, the right of married women to property, and the right of women to education, then all of the other demands of the contemporary women's movement—from the right to physical safety from rape to the right to equal pay for work of equal value—remain on the feminist agenda. Cf. Z. Eisenstein, *Radical Future,* p. 230.

8. Ann Ferguson and Nancy Folbre, "The Unhappy Marriage of Patriarchy and Capitalism," in *Women and Revolution,* ed. Sargent, p. 327–28. The Supreme Court was to rule in 1983 on numerous state and local regulations requiring parental consent, hospitalization, and other limitations on access to abortion; see "Abortion: The Issue that Won't Go Away," *Newsweek,* 31 January 1983, p. 82.

9. Linda Gordon and Ellen Dubois, "Seeking Ecstasy on the Battlefield: Danger and Pleasure in Nineteenth Century Feminist Sexual Thought," paper delivered at The Scholar and The Feminist IX, Barnard College Women's Center Conference, New York, April 24, 1982, p. 15. For an example of such analysis, see Z. Eisenstein, *Radical Future,* pp. 229 ff., looking at the implications of legal reform for radicalizing liberal feminists.

10. See above, chapter 13.

11. Ann Barr Snitow, "The Front Line: Notes on Sex in Novels by Women, 1969–1979," *Signs* 5, no. 4 (Summer 1980):708.

12. Michelle Z. Rosaldo, "The Use and Abuse of Anthropology: Reflections on Feminism and Cross-Cultural Understanding," *Signs* 5, no. 3 (Spring 1980):401. On the public/domestic split, see above, chapter 2.

13. "Genital Mutilation: A Statement by the Association of African Women for Research and Development (AAWORD)," *Resources for Feminist Research* 9, no. 1 (March 1980):8–9.

14. Cherríe Moraga, "Preface," in *This Bridge Called My Back,* ed. Moraga and Anzaldúa, p. xiii; Gloria I. Joseph and Jill Lewis, *Common Differences: Conflicts in Black and White Perspectives* (Garden City, N.Y.: Anchor Books, 1981), p. 13. On the critique of white feminists for racism, see above, chapter 13.

15. For example, in the work of writers such as Ann Oakley, *Woman's Work: The Housewife, Past and Present* (New York: Vintage, 1974), and Sheila Rowbotham, *Woman's Consciousness, Man's World* (London: Penguin Books, 1973).

16. This is the approach espoused and practiced by Natalie J. Sokoloff, *Between Money and Love: The Dialectics of Women's Home and Market Work* (New York: Praeger, 1980).

17. Dennis Altman makes the point that "the relaxation of sexual restraints" can act, not to contest, but to "strengthen the existing system," and argues that the

new market for gay bars is "the contemporary equivalent of bread and circuses." See Dennis Altman, *The Homosexualization of America, The Americanization of The Homosexual* (New York: St. Martin's Press, 1982), p. 94.

18. Ferguson and Folbre, "Patriarchy and Capitalism," p. 331.

19. Ibid., p. 329.

20. Adrienne Rich, "Foreword: On History, Illiteracy, Passivity, Violence, and Women's Culture," in *Lies, Secrets, and Silence,* p. 17. The full citation reads: "It is . . . crucial that we understand lesbian/feminism in the deepest, most radical sense as that love for ourselves and other women, that commitment to the freedom of all of us, which transcends the category of 'sexual preference' and the issue of civil rights, to become a politics of *asking women's questions,* demanding a world in which the integrity of all women—not a chosen few—shall be honored and validated in every aspect of culture."

Bibliography

This listing comprises periodicals, books, and articles cited, as well as those consulted in the preparation of this book or influential in shaping it. The bibliography is by no means an exhaustive list of publications on contemporary feminist thought. An asterisk (*) indicates those works containing useful guides to further reading and research.

Under "Books and Articles," some periodicals are cited in abbreviated form. Their full titles, and places of publication for those published outside of the United States, are supplied under "Periodicals."

Periodicals

Chrysalis: A Magazine of Women's Culture
Feminist Issues
Feminist Review (London)
Feminist Studies
Gay Information: A Quarterly Journal (Sydney)
Hecate: A Women's Interdisciplinary Journal (Brisbane)
Heresies: A Feminist Publication on Art and Politics
Ms.
Monthly Review
Radical History Review
Refractory Girl: A Feminist Journal (Sydney)
Resources for Feminist Research/Documentation sur la Recherche Féministe (Toronto)
Scarlet Woman: A Socialist Feminist Magazine (Sydney)
Signs: Journal of Women in Culture and Society
Socialist Review
Thesis Eleven: A Journal of Socialist Scholarship (Melbourne)
Quest: A Feminist Quarterly
Women's Studies Quarterly (formerly *Women's Studies Newsletter*)

Books and Articles

Abbott, Sidney, and Love, Barbara. *Sappho Was a Right-on Woman: A Liberated View of Lesbianism.* New York: Stein and Day, 1972.

"Abortion: The Issue That Won't Go Away." *Newsweek,* 31 January 1983, p. 32.

Agel, Jerome, ed. *The Radical Therapist.* New York: Ballantine Books, 1971.

Alderfer, Hannah, Altman, Meryl, Ellis, Kate, Jaker, Beth, Nelson, Marybeth, Newton, Esther, Snitow, Ann, and Vance, Carole S., eds., *Diary of a Conference on Sexuality,* from *The Scholar and The Feminist IX: Toward a Politics of Sexuality,* Barnard College Women's Center, New York, April 1982.

Allen, Pamela. *Free Space: A Perspective on the Small Group in Women's Liberation.* New York: Times Change Press, 1970.

Alpert, Jane. *Growing Up Underground.* New York: William Morrow, 1981.

Altbach, Edith, ed. *From Feminism to Liberation.* Cambridge, Mass.: Schenkman, 1971.

Altman, Dennis. *The Homosexualization of America, The Americanization of the Homosexual.* New York: St. Martin's Press, 1982.

Ardill, Susan, and Neumark, Nora. "Putting Sex Back into Lesbianism: Is the Way to a Woman's Heart through Her Sadomasochism?" *Gay Information* 11 (Spring 1982):4–11.

Association of African Women for Research and Development. "Genital Mutilation: A Statement by the Association of African Women for Research and Development (AAWORD)." *Resources for Feminist Research* 9, no. 1 (March 1980):7–9.

Association of Salvadoran Women, The. "Participation of Latin American Women in Social and Political Organizations: Reflections of Salvadoran Women." *Monthly Review* 34, no. 2 (June 1982):11–23.

Atkinson, Ti-Grace. *Amazon Odyssey.* New York: Links Books, 1974.

Barrett, Michèle. *Women's Oppression Today: Problems in Marxist Feminist Analysis.* London: Verso Editions and NLB, 1980.

Barry, Kathleen. *Female Sexual Slavery.* Englewood Cliffs, N.J.: Prentice-Hall, 1979.

———. "Beyond Pornography: From Defensive Politics to Creating a Vision." In *Take Back the Night,* edited by Lederer, pp. 307–12.

Beechey, Veronica. "Women and Production: A Critical Analysis of Some Sociological Theories of Women's Work." In *Feminism and Materialism,* edited by Kuhn and Wolpe, pp. 155–97.

———. "On Patriarchy." *Feminist Review* 3 (1979):66–82.

Bem, Sandra L. "Probing the Promise of Androgyny." In *Beyond Sex-Role Stereotypes,* edited by Kaplan and Bean, pp. 48–62.

Beneria, Lourdes, and Sen, Gita. "Accumulation, Reproduction, and Women's Role in Economic Development: Boserup Revisited." *Signs* 7, no. 2 (1981):279–98.

Benjamin, Jessica. "The Bonds of Love: Rational Violence and Erotic Domination." In *Future of Difference,* edited by Eisenstein and Jardine, pp. 40–70.

*Bernikow, Louise. *Among Women.* New York: Harmony Books, 1980.

Bick, Barbara, and Hartsock, Nancy C. M. "Parenting and the Human Malaise." *Monthly Review* 31, no. 8 (1980):47ff.

Blaxall, Martha, and Reagan, Barbara. *Women and the Workplace: The Implications of Occupational Segregation.* Chicago: University of Chicago Press, 1976.

Boyd, Blanche McCrary. "Growing Up Racist." *Village Voice,* 5–11 August 1982, pp. 1 ff.

Bridenthal, Renate. "The Dialectics of Production and Reproduction in History." *Radical America* 10, no. 2 (March–April 1976):3–11.

————, **and Koonz, Claudia, eds.** *Becoming Visible: Women in European History.* Boston: Houghton Mifflin, 1977.

Brownmiller, Susan. *Against Our Will: Men, Women and Rape.* New York: Simon and Schuster, 1975.

Bulkin, Elly. "Racism and Writing: Some Implications for White Lesbian Critics." *Sinister Wisdom* 13 (Spring 1980):3–22.

Bunch, Charlotte. "Not for Lesbians Only." In *Building Feminist Theory,* edited by Bunch et al., pp. 67–73.

*————, **Flax, Jane, Freeman, Alexa, Hartsock, Nancy, and Manther, Mary-Helen, eds.,** *Building Feminist Theory: Essays from Quest, A Feminist Quarterly.* New York: Longman, 1981.

Burke, Carolyn G. "Rethinking the Maternal." In "Psychoanalysis and Feminism in France," by Jane Gallop and Carolyn Burke. In *Future of Difference,* edited by Eisenstein and Jardine, pp. 107–14.

Burton, Clare. "From the Family to Social Reproduction: The Development of Feminist Theory." Ph.D. dissertation, Macquarie University, Sydney, 1979.

Cade (Bambara), Toni, ed. *The Black Woman: An Anthology.* New York: New American Library, 1970.

Califia, Pat. "Feminism and Sadomasochism." *Heresies,* no. 12 (1981), pp. 30–34.

*Carden, Maren Lockwood. *The New Feminist Movement.* New York: Russell Sage Foundation, 1974.

Carter, Angela. *The Sadeian Woman and The Ideology of Pornography.* New York: Pantheon Books, 1978.

Cassell, Joan. *A Group Called Women: Sisterhood and Symbolism in the Women's Movement.* New York: David McKay, 1977.

Chesler, Phyllis. *Women and Madness.* Garden City, N.Y.: Doubleday, 1972.

————. *About Men.* New York: Simon and Schuster, 1978.

————, **and Goodman, Emily Jane.** *Women, Money and Power.* New York: William Morrow, 1976.

Chicago, Judy. *Through the Flower: My Struggle as a Woman Artist.* Garden City, N.Y.: Doubleday, 1975.

————. *The Dinner Party: A Symbol of Our Heritage.* Garden City, N.Y.: Doubleday, 1979.

Chodorow, Nancy. "Family Structure and Feminine Personality." In *Women, Culture, and Society,* edited by Rosaldo and Lamphere, pp. 43–66.

————. "Oedipal Assymetries and Heterosexual Knots." *Social Problems* 23 (April 1976): 454–68.

————. *The Reproduction of Mothering: Psychoanalysis and the Sociology of Gender.* Berkeley: University of California Press, 1978.

————. "Mothering, Male Dominance, and Capitalism." In *Capitalist Patriarchy,* edited by Z. Eisenstein, pp. 83–106.

————. "Gender, Relation, and Difference in Psychoanalytic Perspective." In *Future of Difference,* edited by Eisenstein and Jardine, pp. 3–19.

Christ, Carol P. *Diving Deep and Surfacing: Women Writers on Spiritual Quest.* Boston: Beacon Press, 1980.

Clavir, Judith. "Choosing Either/Or: A Critique of Metaphysical Feminism." *Feminist Studies* 5, no. 2 (Summer 1979): 402–10.

Combahee River Collective. "A Black Feminist Statement." In *Capitalist Patriarchy,* edited by Z. Eisenstein, pp. 362–72.

Cook, Blanche Wiesen, ed. *Crystal Eastman on Women and Revolution.* Oxford: Oxford University Press, 1978.

————. "The Historical Denial of Lesbianism." *Radical History Review* 20 (Spring–Summer 1979): 60–65.

————. "'Women Alone Stir My Imagination': Lesbianism and the Cultural Tradition." *Signs* 4, no. 4 (Summer 1979): 718–39.

Cooke, Joanne, Bunch-Weeks, Charlotte, and Morgan, Robin, eds., *The New Women: A MOTIVE Anthology on Women's Liberation.* Greenwich, Conn.: Fawcett Publications, 1970.

Coote, Anna, and Campbell, Beatrix. *Sweet Freedom: The Struggle for Women's Liberation.* London: Picador, 1982.

Daly, Mary. *The Church and The Second Sex.* 1968. Reprint. New York: Harper Colophon, 1975.

————. *Beyond God the Father: Toward a Philosophy of Women's Liberation.* Boston: Beacon Press, 1973.

————. *Gyn/Ecology: The Metaethics of Radical Feminism.* Boston: Beacon Press, 1978.

————. Interview. "The Coming Out Show." Australian Broadcasting Company, 5 September 1981.

Davis, Angela Y. *Women, Race and Class.* New York: Random House, 1981.

D.C. Area Feminist Alliance. "Open Letter to Feminist Organizations." *Feminist Studies* 6, no. 3 (Fall 1980): 584.

de Beauvoir, Simone. *The Second Sex.* Translated by H. M. Parshley. New York: Alfred A. Knopf, 1953, originally published as *Le Deuxième Sexe* (Paris: Gallimard, 1949).

Deckard, Barbara Sinclair. *The Women's Movement: Political, Socioeconomic, and Psychological Issues.* 2d ed. New York: Harper and Row, 1979.

Delphy, Christine. "Women's Liberation in France: The Tenth Year." *Feminist Issues* 1, no. 2 (Winter 1981):103–12.

Diamond, Arlyn, and Edwards, Lee R., eds. *The Authority of Experience: Essays in Feminist Criticism.* Amherst: University of Massachusetts Press, 1977.

Dickstein, Morris. *Gates of Eden: American Culture in the Sixties.* New York: Basic Books, 1977.

Didion, Joan. "The Women's Movement." In *The White Album,* pp. 109–19. New York: Simon and Schuster, 1979.

Dinnerstein, Dorothy. *The Mermaid and the Minotaur: Sexual Arrangements and Human Malaise.* New York: Harper and Row, 1977.

Dreifus, Claudia. *Woman's Fate: Raps from a Feminist Consciousness-raising Group.* New York: Bantam Books, 1973.

Dubois, Ellen Carol. *Feminism and Suffrage: The Emergence of an Independent Women's Movement in America, 1848–1869.* Ithaca, N.Y.: Cornell University Press, 1978.

Dworkin, Andrea. *Woman Hating.* New York: E. P. Dutton, 1974.

———. *Our Blood: Prophecies and Discourses on Sexual Politics.* New York: Harper and Row, 1976.

———. *Pornography: Men Possessing Women.* New York: Perigee/G. P. Putnam's, 1981.

Edholm, Felicity, Harris, Olivia, and Young, Kate. "Conceptualizing Women." *Critique of Anthropology* 3, nos. 9–10 (1977):101–30.

Editors of Questions Féministes. "Variations on Some Common Themes." *Feminist Issues* 1, no. 1 (Summer 1980):3–21.

Edwards, Alison. *Rape, Racism, and the White Women's Movement: An Answer to Susan Brownmiller.* Chicago: Sojourner Truth Organization, n.d.

Ehrenreich, Barbara, and English, Deirdre. *For Her Own Good: 150 Years of the Experts' Advice to Women.* Garden City, N.Y.: Anchor Press/Doubleday, 1978.

Ehrensaft, Diane. "When Women and Men Mother." *Socialist Review,* no. 49 (January–February 1980), pp. 37–72.

Ehrlich, Carol. "The Unhappy Marriage of Marxism and Feminism: Can It Be Saved?" In *Women and Revolution,* edited by Sargent, pp. 109–33.

Eichler, Margrit. *The Double Standard: A Feminist Critique of Feminist Social Science.* New York: St. Martin's Press, 1980.

Eisenstein, Hester, ed. *The Scholar and The Feminist III: The Search for Origins.* New York: Barnard College Women's Center, 1976.

————. "Is 'Objectivity' a Code-Word for Male Domination?" The Second Sex—Thirty Years Later, New York Institute for the Humanities, 28 September 1979. A conference paper.

————. "On the Psychosocial Barriers to Professions for Women: Atalanta's Apples, 'Women's Work,' and the Struggle for Social Change." In *Socialization, Sexism, and Stereotyping: Women's Issues in Nursing,* edited by Janet Muff. St. Louis: C. V. Mosby, 1982, pp. 95–112.

————. "Which Way Out of the Impasse? The Politics of Feminist Theory in the 1980's." *Thesis Eleven* 5/6 (1982):259–270.

————, **and Jardine, Alice, eds.** *The Future of Difference.* Boston: G. K. Hall, 1980.

————, **and Sacks, Susan Riemer.** "Women in Search of Autonomy: An Action Design." *Social Change* 5, no. 2 (1975):4–6.

Eisenstein, Zillah R., ed. *Capitalist Patriarchy and the Case for Socialist Feminism.* New York: Monthly Review Press, 1979.

————. "Developing a Theory of Capitalist Patriarchy." In *Capitalist Patriarchy,* edited by Z. Eisenstein, pp. 5–40.

————. "Some Notes on the Relations of Capitalist Patriarchy." In *Capitalist Patriarchy,* edited by Z. Eisenstein, pp. 41–55.

————. *The Radical Future of Liberal Feminism.* New York: Longman, 1981.

English, Deirdre, Hollibaugh, Amber, and Rubin, Gayle. "Talking Sex: A Conversation on Sexuality and Feminism." *Socialist Review,* no. 58 (July–August 1981), pp. 43–62.

***Evans, Sara.** *Personal Politics: The Roots of Women's Liberation in the Civil Rights Movement and the New Left.* New York: Vintage Books, 1979.

Ferguson, Ann, and Folbre, Nancy. "The Unhappy Marriage of Patriarchy and Capitalism." In *Women and Revolution,* edited by Sargent, pp. 313–38.

————, **Zita, Jacquelyn N., and Addelson, Kathryn Pyne.** "On 'Compulsory Heterosexuality and Lesbian Existence': Defining the Issues." In *Feminist Theory,* edited by Keohane et al., pp. 147–88.

Figes, Eva. *Patriarchal Attitudes.* New York: Stein and Day, 1970.

Firestone, Shulamith. *The Dialectic of Sex: The Case for Feminist Revolution.* New York: Bantam Books, 1970.

————, **ed.** *Notes from the Second Year: Women's Liberation–Major Writings of the Radical Feminists.* New York: Notes (From the Second Year)—Radical Feminism, 1970.

***Fisher, Elizabeth.** *Woman's Creation: Sexual Evolution and the Shaping of Society.* Garden City, N.Y.: Anchor Press/Doubleday, 1979.

Fitzgerald, Frances. "The Triumphs of the New Right." *New York Review of Books,* 19 November 1981, pp. 19 ff.

Flax, Jane. "The Conflict Between Nurturance and Autonomy in Mother-Daughter Relationships and Within Feminism." *Feminist Studies* 4, no. 2 (June 1978):171–89.

————. "Mother-Daughter Relationships: Psychodynamics, Politics, and Philosophy." In *Future of Difference,* edited by Eisenstein and Jardine, pp. 20–40.

Freeman, Derek. *Margaret Mead and Samoa: The Making and Unmaking of an Anthropological Myth.* Cambridge, Mass.: Harvard University Press; Canberra: Australian National University Press, 1983.

Freeman, Jo. *The Politics of Women's Liberation: A Case Study of an Emerging Social Movement and Its Relation to the Policy Process.* New York: David McKay, 1975.

————, ed. *Women: A Feminist Perspective.* Palo Alto, Calif.: Mayfield Publishing, 1975.

Friday, Nancy. *My Mother/Myself.* New York: Delacorte Press, 1977.

Friedan, Betty. *The Feminine Mystique.* New York: Dell Publishing, 1963.

————. *It Changed My Life: Writings on the Women's Movement.* New York: Random House, 1976.

————. *The Second Stage.* New York: Summit Books, 1981.

Fritz, Leah. *Dreamers and Dealers: An Intimate Appraisal of the Women's Movement.* Boston: Beacon Press, 1979.

Gilligan, Carol. "In a Different Voice: Women's Conceptions of Self and of Morality." In Eisenstein and Jardine, eds., *Future of Difference,* pp. 274–317.

————. *In A Different Voice: Psychological Theory and Women's Development.* Cambridge: Harvard University Press, 1982.

Gilman, Charlotte Perkins. *Herland.* Edited, with introduction, by Ann J. Lane. New York: Pantheon Books, 1979.

Gintis, Herbert. "Communication and Politics: Marxism and the 'Problem' of Liberal Democracy." *Socialist Review,* nos. 50–51 (March–June 1980), pp. 189–232.

*Glennon, Lynda M.** *Women and Dualism: A Sociology of Knowledge Analysis.* New York: Longman, 1979.

Gordon, Linda. *Woman's Body, Woman's Right: A Social History of Birth Control in America.* New York: Grossman Publishers, 1976.

————. "The Struggle for Reproductive Freedom: Three Stages of Feminism." In *Capitalist Patriarchy,* edited by Z. Eisenstein, pp. 107–32.

————, and **Dubois, Ellen.** "Seeking Ecstasy on the Battlefield: Danger and Pleasure in Nineteenth Century Feminist Sexual Thought." The Scholar and The Feminist IX, Barnard College Women's Center Conference, New York, 24 April 1982. A conference paper.

Gornick, Vivian. "Consciousness." In *Essays in Feminism,* New York: Harper and Row, 1978, pp. 47–68.

————, and **Moran, Barbara K., eds.** *Woman in Sexist Society: Studies in Power and Powerlessness.* 1971. Reprint. New York: Signet Books, 1972.

Gould, Lois. "X." *Ms.,* May 1980, pp. 61–64. Originally published as "X: A Fabulous Child's Story," *Ms.,* December 1972, pp. 74–77; reprinted, New York:

Daughters Publishing Co, 1978, and rev. ed., New York: Stonesong Press, 1980.

———. "Creating a Women's World." *New York Times Magazine,* 2 January 1977, pp. 10 ff.

Greer, Germaine. *The Female Eunuch.* 1971. Reprint. New York: Bantam Books, 1972.

Griffin, Susan. "Rape: The All-American Crime." In *Rape: Power of Consciousness,* pp. 3–22.

———. *Woman and Nature: The Roaring Inside Her.* New York: Harper and Row, 1978.

———. *Rape: The Power of Consciousness.* San Francisco: Harper and Row, 1979.

———. *Pornography and Silence: Culture's Revenge Against Nature.* New York: Harper and Row, 1981.

———. "The Way of All Ideology." *Signs* 7, no. 3 (Spring 1982):641–60.

Gross, Elizabeth. "On Speaking About Pornography." *Scarlet Woman* 13 (Spring 1981):16–21.

Gross, Harriet Engel, Bernard, Jessie, Dan, Alice J., Glazer, Nona, Lorber, Judith, McClintock, Martha, Newton, Niles, and Rossi, Alice. "Considering 'A Biosocial Perspective on Parenting.'" *Signs* 4, no. 4 (Summer 1979):695–717.

Hamilton, Roberta. *The Liberation of Women: A Study of Patriarchy and Capitalism.* London: George Allen and Unwin, 1978.

Hanisch, Carol. "The Personal is Political." In *Radical Therapist,* edited by Agel, pp. 152–57.

Hartmann, Heidi. "Capitalism, Patriarchy, and Job Segregation by Sex." In *Women and the Workplace,* edited by Blaxall and Reagan, pp. 137–69.

———. "The Unhappy Marriage of Marxism and Feminism: Toward a More Progressive Union." In *Women and Revolution,* edited by Sargent, pp. 1–41.

Hartsock, Nancy. "Feminist Theory and the Development of Revolutionary Strategy." In *Capitalist Patriarchy,* edited by Z. Eisenstein, pp. 56–77.

Heilbrun, Carolyn G. *Toward a Recognition of Androgyny.* New York: Alfred A. Knopf, 1973.

———. *Reinventing Womanhood.* New York: W. W. Norton, 1979.

———. "Androgyny and the Psychology of Sex Differences." In *Future of Difference,* edited by Eisenstein and Jardine, pp. 258–66.

Herschberger, Ruth. *Adam's Rib.* 1948. Reprint. New York: Harper and Row, 1970.

Hole, Judith, and Levine, Ellen. *Rebirth of Feminism.* New York: Quadrangle, 1971.

Hollibaugh, Amber, and Moraga, Cherríe. "What We're Rollin Around in Bed With—Sexual Silences in Feminism: A Conversation Toward Ending Them." *Heresies,* no. 12 (1981), pp. 58–62.

Hooks, Bell (Gloria Watkins). *Ain't I A Woman: Black Women and Feminism.* Boston: South End Press, 1981.

Hosken, Fran P. *The Hosken Report: Genital/Sexual Mutilation of Females.* Lexington, Mass.: WIN News, 1979.

*Hubbard, Ruth, Henifin, Mary Sue, Fried, Barbara, Druss, Vicki, and Starr, Susan Leigh.** *Women Look at Biology Looking at Women: A Collection of Feminist Critiques.* Cambridge, Mass.: Schenkman Publishing Co., 1979.

Jaggar, Alison M., and Struhl, Paula Rothenberg, eds. *Feminist Frameworks: Alternative Theoretical Accounts of the Relations Between Women and Men.* New York: McGraw-Hill, 1978.

Janeway, Elizabeth. *Man's World, Woman's Place: A Study in Social Mythology.* New York: Dell Publishing, 1971.

————. *Between Myth and Morning: Women Awakening.* New York: William Morrow, 1974.

————. *Powers of the Weak.* New York: Alfred A. Knopf, 1980.

————. "Who is Sylvia? On the Loss of Sexual Paradigms." *Signs* 5, no. 4 (Summer 1980):573–89.

————. *Cross-Sections from a Decade of Change.* New York: William Morrow, 1982.

Jay, Nancy. "Gender and Dichotomy." *Feminist Studies* 7, no. 1 (Spring 1981):38–56.

Jehlen, Myra. "Archimedes and the Paradox of Feminist Criticism." *Signs* 6, no. 4 (Summer 1981):575–601.

Johnston, Jill. *Lesbian Nation: The Feminist Solution.* New York: Simon and Schuster, 1974.

Joseph, Gloria I. "The Incompatible Ménage à Trois: Marxism, Feminism, and Racism." In *Women and Revolution,* edited by Sargent, pp. 91–107.

————. **and Lewis, Jill.** *Common Differences: Conflicts in Black and White Perspectives.* Garden City, N.Y.: Anchor Books, 1981.

Kaplan, Alexandra G., and Bean, Joan P., eds. *Beyond Sex-Role Stereotypes: Readings Toward a Psychology of Androgyny.* Boston: Little Brown, 1976.

Kazickas, Jurate, and Sherr, Lynn. *The Woman's Calendar for 1980.* New York: Universe Books, 1979.

Keller, Evelyn Fox. "The Anomaly of a Woman in Physics." In *Working It Out,* edited by Ruddick and Daniels, pp. 77–91.

————. "Gender and Science." *Psychoanalysis and Contemporary Thought* 1 (1978):409–33.

————. "Feminism and Science." *Signs* 7, no. 3 (Spring 1982):589–602.

Kelly(-Gadol), Joan. "The Social Relations of the Sexes: Methodological Implications of Women's History." *Signs* 1, no. 4 (Summer 1976):809–24.

————. "The Doubled Vision of Feminist Theory." *Feminist Studies* 5, no. 1 (Spring 1979):216–27.

————. "Early Feminist Theory and the *Querelle des Femmes,* 1400–1789." *Signs* 8, no. 1 (Autumn 1982):4–28.

Keohane, Nannerl O., Rosaldo, Michelle Z., and Gelpi, Barbara C., eds., *Feminist Theory: A Critique of Ideology.* Chicago: University of Chicago Press, 1982.

*Kessler, Suzanne J., and McKenna, Wendy. *Gender: An Ethnomethodological Approach.* New York: John Wiley, 1978.

Kessler-Harris, Alice. *Out to Work: A History of Wage-Earning Women in the United States.* New York: Oxford University Press, 1982.

Koedt, Anne, ed. *Notes From the Third Year: Women's Liberation.* New York: Notes from the Third Year, 1971.

————. "The Myth of the Vaginal Orgasm." In *Radical Feminism,* edited by Koedt et al., pp. 198–207.

————, Levine, Ellen, and Rapone, Anita, eds. *Radical Feminism.* New York: Quadrangle, 1973.

Komarovsky, Mirra. "Cultural Contradictions and Sex Roles." *American Journal of Sociology* 52 (1946):184–89.

————. "Functional Analysis of Sex Roles." *American Sociological Review* 15, no. 4 (August 1950):508–16.

————. *Women in the Modern World: Their Education and Their Dilemmas.* Boston: Little Brown, 1953.

Kraemer, Ross S. Review of *Gyn/Ecology,* by Mary Daly. *Signs* 5, no. 3 (Winter 1979):354–56.

Kuhn, Annette, and Wolpe, Ann Marie, eds. *Feminism and Materialism: Women and Modes of Production.* London: Routledge and Kegan Paul, 1978.

Lasch, Christopher. *Haven in a Heartless World: The Family Besieged.* New York: Basic Books, 1979.

*Laws, Judith Long. *The Second X: Sex Role and Social Role.* New York: Elsevier, 1979.

Lazarre, Jane. *The Mother Knot.* New York: McGraw-Hill, 1976.

————. *On Loving Men.* New York: Dial Press, 1980.

Leacock, Eleanor. "Women in Egalitarian Societies." In *Becoming Visible,* edited by Bridenthal and Koonz, pp. 11–35.

————. "History, Development, and the Division of Labor by Sex: Implications for Organization." *Signs* 7, no. 2 (1981):474–91.

Lear, Martha Weinman. "The Second Feminist Wave." *New York Times Magazine.* 10 March 1968, pp. 24 ff.

Lederer, Laura. "*Playboy* Isn't Playing: An Interview with Judith Bat-Ada." In *Take Back the Night,* edited by Lederer, pp. 121–33.

————, ed. *Take Back the Night: Women on Pornography.* New York: William Morrow, 1980.

Lerner, Gerda. *The Female Experience: An American Documentary.* Indianapolis, Ind.: Bobbs-Merrill, 1977.

————. *The Majority Finds Its Past: Placing Women in History.* New York: Oxford University Press, 1979.

Levine, Suzanne, Lyons, Harriet, Edgar, Joanne, Sweet, Ellen, and

Thom, Mary. *The Decade of Women: A Ms. History of the Seventies in Words and Pictures.* New York: Paragon Books, 1980.

Lewis, Diane. "A Response to Inequality: Black Women, Racism, and Sexism." *Signs* 3, no. 2 (Winter 1977):339–61.

*Lips, Hilary M., and Colwill, Nina Lee.** *The Psychology of Sex Differences.* Englewood Cliffs, N.J.: Prentice-Hall, 1978.

Longino, Helen E. "Pornography, Oppression, and Freedom: A Closer Look." In *Take Back the Night,* edited by Lederer, pp. 40–54.

Lorber, Judith, Coser, Rose Laub, Rossi, Alice S., and Chodorow, Nancy. "On *The Reproduction of Mothering:* A Methodological Debate." *Signs* 6, no. 3 (Spring 1981):481–514.

Lorde, Audre. "An Open Letter to Mary Daly." In *This Bridge Called My Back,* edited by Moraga and Anzaldúa, pp. 95–96.

MacKinnon, Catharine. "Feminism, Marxism, Method, and the State: An Agenda for Theory." *Signs* 7, no. 3 (Spring 1982):515–44.

Maeroff, Gene. "Female President Settles in Comfortably at University of Chicago." *New York Times,* 16 March 1980.

Makward, Christiane. "To Be or Not to Be . . . A Feminist Speaker." In *Future of Difference,* edited by Eisenstein and Jardine, pp. 95–105.

"Male Dominance Revisited." Review of *The Red Lamp of Incest,* by Robin Fox, *Time Magazine,* 22 September 1980.

Manderson, Lenore. "Self, Couple, and Community: Recent Writings on Lesbian Women." *Hecate* 6, no. 1 (1980):67–79.

Marable, Manning. "Black Nationalism in the 1970s: Through the Prism of Race and Class." *Socialist Review,* nos. 50–51 (March–June 1980), pp. 57–108.

Marks, Elaine, and de Courtivron, Isabelle, eds. *New French Feminisms: An Anthology.* Amherst, Mass.: University of Massachusetts Press, 1980.

McBride, Theresa M. "The Long Road Home: Women's Work and Industrialization." In *Becoming Visible,* edited by Bridenthal and Koonz, pp. 280–95.

Medea, Andra, and Thompson, Kathleen. *Against Rape.* New York: Farrar, Straus, and Giroux, 1974.

Members of Samois, eds. *Coming to Power: Writings and Graphics on Lesbian S/M.* San Francisco: Samois, 1981.

Milkman, Ruth. "Organizing the Sexual Division of Labor: Historical Perspectives on 'Women's Work' and the American Labor Movement." *Socialist Review,* no. 49 (January–February 1980), pp. 95–150.

Miller, Jean Baker, ed. *Psychoanalysis and Women.* Harmondsworth, England: Penguin Books, 1973.

———. *Toward a New Psychology of Women.* Boston: Beacon Press, 1976.

Millett, Kate. *Sexual Politics.* 1970. Reprint. New York: Avon Books, 1971.

———. *Flying.* New York: Alfred A. Knopf, 1974.

———. *The Prostitution Papers.* New York: Ballantine Books, 1976.

———. *Sita.* New York: Farrar Straus and Giroux, 1977.

———. *The Basement: Meditations on a Human Sacrifice.* New York: Simon and Schuster, 1979.

Mitchell, Juliet. *Woman's Estate.* 1971. Reprint. New York: Vintage Books, 1973.

―――. *Psychoanalysis and Feminism.* New York: Pantheon Books, 1974.

Molyneux, Maxine. "Socialist Societies Old and New: Progress Toward Women's Emancipation?" *Monthly Review* 34, no. 3 (July–August 1982):56–100.

*Moraga, Cherríe, and Anzaldúa, Gloria, eds. *This Bridge Called My Back: Writings by Radical Women of Color.* Watertown, Mass.: Persephone Press, 1981.

Morgan, Robin, ed. *Sisterhood is Powerful: An Anthology of Writings from the Women's Liberation Movement.* New York: Vintage Books, 1970.

―――. *Going Too Far: The Personal Chronicle of a Feminist.* New York: Random House, 1977.

―――. "Theory and Practice: Pornography and Rape." In *Take Back the Night,* edited by Lederer, pp. 134–40.

―――. "A Quantum Leap in Feminist Theory." *Ms.,* December 1982, pp. 101 ff.

―――. *The Anatomy of Freedom: Feminism, Physics, and Global Politics.* New York: Doubleday/Anchor, 1982.

Moschkovich, Judit. "'—But I Know You, American Woman.'" In *This Bridge Called My Back,* edited by Moraga and Anzaldúa, pp. 79–84.

Murphy, Robert F., Alland, Alexander, Jr., and Skinner, Elliott P. "An Abortive Attack on 'Coming of Age.'" Letter to the *New York Times,* February 6, 1983.

Myron, Nancy, and Bunch, Charlotte, eds. *Lesbianism and the Women's Movement.* Baltimore: Diana Press, 1975.

National Commission on the Observance of International Women's Year. *The Spirit of Houston: The First National Women's Conference.* Washington, D.C.: National Commission on the Observance of International Women's Year, 1978.

Not a Love Story (film), Canadian Film Board, 1981.

Oakley, Ann. *Women's Work: The Housewife, Past and Present.* New York: Vintage, 1974.

*―――. *Subject Woman.* New York: Pantheon Books, 1981.

Oglesby, Carl. "The Idea of the New Left." In *The New Left Reader,* edited by Oglesby. New York: Grove Press, 1969, pp. 1–20.

Ortner, Sherry. "Is Female to Male as Nature is to Culture?" In *Women, Culture and Society,* edited by Rosaldo and Lamphere, pp. 67–87.

Pagels, Elaine H. "What Became of God the Mother? Conflicting Images of God in Early Christianity." *Signs* 2, no. 2 (Winter 1976):293–303.

Petchesky, Rosalind Pollack. "Reproductive Freedom: Beyond 'A Woman's Right to Choose.'" *Signs* 5, no. 4 (Summer 1980):661–85.

―――. "Antiabortion, Antifeminism, and the Rise of the New Right." *Feminist Studies* 7, no. 2 (Summer 1981):206–46.

―――. *Reproductive Freedom: The Social and Political Dimensions of Birth Control.* New York: Longman, forthcoming.

Piercy, Marge. *Vida.* New York: Summit Books, 1979.

Plotke, David. "Facing the 1980s." *Socialist Review,* no. 49 (January–February 1980), pp. 7–35.

Pringle, Rosemary. "The Dialectics of Porn." *Scarlet Woman* 12 (March 1981):3–10.

Radicalesbians. "The Woman-Identified Woman." In *Radical Feminism,* edited by Koedt et al., pp. 240–45.

Rape Culture (film). Cambridge Documentary Films, Inc., 1975.

Raymond, Janice. *The Transsexual Empire: The Making of the She-Male.* Boston: Beacon Press, 1979.

Réage, Pauline. *Story of O.* Translated by S. D'estree. New York: Grove Press, 1965. Originally published 1954.

Redstockings. *Feminist Revolution.* Edited by Kathie Sarachild. New Paltz, N.Y.: Redstockings, 1975.

*****Reiter, Rayna R[app],** ed. *Toward an Anthropology of Women.* New York: Monthly Review Press, 1975.

Rich, Adrienne. *Of Woman Born: Motherhood as Experience and Institution.* New York: W. W. Norton, 1976.

————. *The Dream of A Common Language: Poems 1974–1977.* New York: W. W. Norton, 1978.

————. "'Disloyal to Civilization': Feminism, Racism, and Gynephobia." *Chrysalis* 7 (1979):9–27. Reprinted *On Lies, Secrets, and Silence,* pp. 275–310.

————. "Foreword: On History, Illiteracy, Passivity, Violence, and Women's Culture." In *On Lies, Secrets, and Silence,* pp. 9–18.

————. *On Lies, Secrets, and Silence: Selected Prose, 1966–1978.* New York: W. W. Norton, 1979.

————. "Compulsory Heterosexuality and Lesbian Existence." *Signs* 5, no. 4 (Summer 1980):631–60.

Rosaldo, Michelle Zimbalist. "Woman, Culture, and Society: a Theoretical Overview." In *Women, Culture, and Society,* edited by Rosaldo and Lamphere, pp. 17–42.

————. "The Use and Abuse of Anthropology: Reflections on Feminism and Cross-Cultural Understanding." *Signs* 5, no. 3 (Spring 1980):389–417.

*————, **and Lamphere, Louise,** eds. *Woman, Culture, and Society.* Stanford: Stanford University Press, 1974.

Rose, Willie Lee. "Reforming Women." *New York Review of Books,* 7 October 1982, pp. 47 ff.

*****Rosenberg, Rosalind.** *Beyond Separate Spheres: Intellectual Roots of Modern Feminism.* New Haven: Yale University Press, 1982.

Rossi, Alice S., ed. *The Feminist Papers: From Adams to de Beauvoir.* New York: Columbia University Press, 1973.

————. "A Biosocial Perspective on Parenting." *Daedalus: Journal of the American Academy of Arts and Sciences* 106, no. 2 (Spring 1977):1–31.

Rossman, Michael. *On Learning and Social Change: Transcending The Totalitarian Classroom.* New York: Vintage Books, 1972.

Roszak, Theodore. *The Making of a Counter Culture.* New York: Doubleday, 1969.

Rothman, Sheila M. *Woman's Proper Place: A History of Changing Ideals and Practices, 1870 to the Present.* New York: Basic Books, 1978.

Rowbotham, Sheila. *Woman's Consciousness, Man's World.* London: Penguin Books, 1973.

*————. *Women, Resistance, and Revolution: A History of Women and Revolution in the Modern World.* 1972. Reprint. New York: Vintage Books, 1974.

————, **Segal, Lynne, and Wainwright, Hilary.** *Beyond the Fragments: Feminism and the Making of Socialism.* London: Merlin Press, Ltd., 1979.

Rubin, Gayle. "'The Traffic in Women': Notes on the 'Political Economy' of Sex." In *Anthropology of Women,* edited by Reiter, pp. 157–210.

Ruddick, Sara. "Maternal Thinking." *Feminist Studies* 6, no. 2 (Summer 1980):342–67.

————, **and Daniels, Pamela, eds.** *Working It Out: 23 Women Writers, Scientists, and Scholars Talk About Their Lives and Work.* New York: Pantheon Books, 1977.

Russell, Diana E. H. "Pornography and the Women's Liberation Movement." In *Take Back the Night,* edited by Lederer, pp. 301–06.

————, **and van de Ven, Nicole, eds.** *Proceedings of the International Tribunal on Crimes Against Women.* Millbare, Calif.: Les Femmes, 1976.

***Ruth, Sheila, ed.** *Issues in Feminism: A First Course in Women's Studies.* Boston: Houghton Mifflin, 1980.

Sacks, Karen. "Engels Revisited: Women, the Organization of Production, and Private Property." In *Women, Culture, and Society,* edited by Rosaldo and Lamphere, pp. 207–22.

Sacks, Susan Riemer, and Eisenstein, Hester. "Feminism and Psychological Autonomy: A Study in Decision-Making." *Personnel and Guidance Journal* 57 (April 1979):419–23.

Sarachild (Amatniek), Kathie. "The Power of History." In *Feminist Revolution,* edited by Redstockings, pp. 7–29.

————. "Consciousness-Raising: A Radical Weapon." In *Feminist Revolution,* edited by Redstockings, pp. 131–36.

Sargent, Lydia. "New Left Women and Men: The Honeymoon is Over." In *Women and Revolution,* edited by Sargent, pp. xi–xxxii.

————, ed. *Women and Revolution: A Discussion of the Unhappy Marriage of Marxism and Feminism.* Boston: South End Press, 1981.

Schafran, Lynn Hecht. "Sandra O'Connor and the Supremes: Will the First Woman Make a Difference?" *Ms.,* October 1981, pp. 71 ff.

Schneir, Miriam, ed. *Feminism: The Essential Historical Writings.* New York: Random House, 1972.

See, Katherine O'Sullivan. "Feminism and Political Philosophy." *Feminist Studies* 8, no. 1 (Spring 1982):179–94.

Sherfey, Mary Jane. "A Theory on Female Sexuality." In *Sisterhood is Powerful,* edited by Morgan, pp. 220–30.

Sherman, Julia A., and Beck, Evelyn Torton. *The Prism of Sex: Essays in the Sociology of Knowledge.* Madison: University of Wisconsin Press, 1979.

Shulman, Alix Kates. "Sex and Power: Sexual Bases of Radical Feminism." *Signs* 5, no. 4 (Summer 1980):590–604.

———. "Dancing in the Revolution: Emma Goldman's Feminism." *Socialist Review,* no. 62 (March–April 1982), pp. 31–44.

Simons, Margaret A. "Racism and Feminism: A Schism in the Sisterhood." *Feminist Studies* 5, no. 2 (Summer 1979):384–401.

Smith, Dorothy E. "A Sociology for Women." In *The Prism of Sex,* edited by Sherman and Beck, pp. 135–87.

Snitow, Ann Barr. "Thinking About the Memaid and the Minotaur." *Feminist Studies* 4, no. 2 (June 1978):190–98.

———. "Mass Market Romance: Pornography for Women is Different." *Radical History Review* 20 (Spring–Summer 1979):141–61.

———. "The Front Line: Notes on Sex in Novels by Women, 1969–79." *Signs* 5, no. 4 (Summer 1980):702–18.

*Sokoloff, Natalie J.** *Between Love and Money: The Dialectics of Women's Home and Market Work.* New York: Praeger, 1980.

Stage, Sarah. "Women's History and 'Woman's Sphere': Major Works of the 1970s." *Socialist Review,* nos. 50–51 (March–June 1980), pp. 245–53.

Stimpson, Catharine R., and Person, Ethel Spector, eds., *Women: Sex and Sexuality.* Chicago: University of Chicago Press, 1980.

Stone, Merlin. *When God Was A Woman.* New York: Harcourt Brace Jovanovich, 1978.·Originally published as *The Paradise Papers* (London: Virago, 1976).

Taylor, Letta. "Abortion Battle Continues Nationwide." *Guardian,* 23 July 1980, p. 4.

Thomas, Marlo, et al. *Free to Be . . . You and Me.* New York: McGraw-Hill, 1974. Presented as a television special, 11 March 1974, ABC-Television.

Thompson, Martha. "Comment on Rich's 'Compulsory Heterosexuality and Lesbian Existence.'" *Signs* 6, no. 4 (Summer 1981):790–94.

Tiger, Lionel, and Fox, Robin. *The Imperial Animal.* New York: Delta, 1971.

Valeska, Lucia. "The Future of Female Separatism." In *Building Feminist Theory,* edited by Bunch et al., pp. 20–31.

Vicinus, Martha. "Sexuality and Power: A Review of Current Work in the History of Sexuality." *Feminist Studies* 8, no. 1 (Spring 1982):134–56.

*Vida, Ginny, ed.** *Our Right to Love: A Lesbian Resource Book.* Englewood Cliffs, N.J.: Prentice-Hall, 1978.

Vogel, Lise. "Marxism and Feminism: Unhappy Marriage, Trial Separation, or Something Else?" In *Women and Revolution,* edited by Sargent, pp. 195–217.

Wallace, Michele. *Black Macho and the Myth of the Super-Woman.* New York: Dial Press, 1979.

Webster, Paula. "Pornography and Pleasure." *Heresies,* no. 12 (1981), pp. 48–51.

Weinbaum, Batya. *The Curious Courtship of Women's Liberation and Socialism.* Boston: South End Press, 1978.

Weisstein, Naomi. "'Kinder, Kuche, Kirche' As Scientific Law: Psychology Constructs the Female." In *Sisterhood is Powerful,* edited by Morgan, pp. 205–20.

Willis, Ellen. *Beginning to See the Light: Pieces of a Decade.* New York: Wideview Books, 1981.

———. "Nature's Revenge." *New York Times Book Review,* 12 July 1981, pp. 9 ff.

———. "Peace in Our Time? Betty Friedan's No-Win Feminism." *Village Voice Literary Supplement* 2 (November 1981):1 ff.

———. "Sisters Under the Skin? Confronting Race and Sex." *Village Voice Literary Supplement* 8 (June 1982):1 ff.

Wittig, Monique. *Les Guérillières.* Translated by David LeVay. New York: Viking, 1971. Originally published 1969.

———. "One is Not Born a Woman." *Feminist Issues* 1, no. 2 (Winter 1981):47–54.

Yates, Gayle Graham. *What Women Want: The Ideas of the Movement.* Cambridge: Harvard University Press, 1975.

Young, Iris. "Socialist Feminism and the Limits of Dual Systems Theory." *Socialist Review,* nos. 50–51 (March–June 1980), pp. 169–88.

———. "Beyond the Unhappy Marriage: A Critique of the Dual Systems Theory." In *Women and Revolution,* edited by Sargent, pp. 43–69.

Index